Taking the Adventure

Taking the Adventure
Faith and Our Kinship with Animals

Gracia Fay Ellwood

Preface by
Carol J. Adams

RESOURCE *Publications* • Eugene, Oregon

TAKING THE ADVENTURE
Faith and Our Kinship with Animals

Copyright © 2014 Gracia Fay Ellwood. All rights reserved. Except for brief quotations in critical publications or reviews, no part of this book may be reproduced in any manner without prior written permission from the publisher. Write: Permissions, Wipf and Stock Publishers, 199 W. 8th Ave., Suite 3, Eugene, OR 97401.

Wipf and Stock
An Imprint of Wipf and Stock Publishers
199 W. 8th Ave., Suite 3
Eugene, OR 97401

www.wipfandstock.com

ISBN 13: 978-1-62564-652-1

Manufactured in the U.S.A.   10/08/2014

Scripture quotations are taken from the following translations:

English Standard Version (ESV) Crossway Bibles Copyright © 2001 Good News Publishers.

God's Word Translation (GW) Scripture is taken from GOD'S WORD® Copyright 1995 God's Word to the Nations. Used by permission of Baker Publishing Group.

International Standard Version (ISV) Copyright © 2011 ISV Foundation.

New American Standard Bible (NASB). Scripture taken from the NEW AMERICAN STANDARD BIBLE® Copyright © 1960, 1962, 1963, 1971, 1972, 1973, 1975, 1995 by The Lockman Foundation. Used by Permission.

New International Version (NIV) THE HOLY BIBLE, NEW INTERNATIONAL VERSION® Copyright © 1973, 1978, 1984, 2011 by Biblica, Inc.® Used by permission. All rights reserved worldwide.

New Living Translation (NLT) Scripture quotations marked (NLT) are taken from the Holy Bible, New Living Translation, Copyright © 1996, 2004, 2007 by Tyndale House Foundation. Used by permission of Tyndale House Publishers, Inc., Carol Stream, Illinois 60188. All rights reserved.

Grateful acknowledgment is made for permission to quote the following:

Material from *Heading Toward Omega* by Kenneth Ring. Copyright © 1984, 1985 Sobel Weber Associates. All Rights Reserved. Used By Permission.

Material from *Living From the Center* by Jay McDaniel. Copyright © 2000 Chalice Press. All rights reserved. Used By Permission.

A portion of "The Story That Never Grows Old" by A. H. Ackley. © 1934 Word Music, LLC. All Rights Reserved. Used By Permission.

A portion of "Wood-Thrush" by John Hall Wheelock. Reprinted with the permission of Scribner Publishing Group, a division of Simon & Schuster, Inc. from *This Blessed Earth* by John Hall Wheelock. Copyright © 1956 by John Hall Wheelock. All rights reserved.

"Kyria Sophia," "Splendor," translation of stanza 1 of Friedrich Schiller's "An die Freude," "God is There," and stanzas 2 and 3 of "Be Known to Us" by Faith L. Bowman. Copyright © 2014 www.faithpoems.net/ by Faith L. Bowman. Used by Permission.

A portion of "Prophets and the Hidden Paradise" by Gracia Fay Bouwman Ellwood in *Call to Compassion: Religious Perspectives on Animal Advocacy*, edited by Lisa Kemmerer and Anthony J. Nocella II, copyright © 2011 by Lisa Kemmerer and Anthony J. Nocella II, is reproduced in chapter 17, "The Hidden Paradise, the Hidden Hells." Used by Permission.

with boundless gratitude
for Fay Elanor Ellwood
because God's gift
put my best dreams to shame

"I will take the adventure that God will send me."

—THOMAS MALORY

Table of Contents

Preface by Carol J. Adams | xi
Acknowledgments | xv
Abbreviations | xvii

1   Taking the Adventure | 1
2   The Great Wall | 7
3   We Were Slaves to Pharaoh | 13
4   The Work of Human Minds | 19
5   Speaking to the Heart | 26
6   Neither Wickedness Nor Sorrow | 29
7   "He Came to Himself" | 34
8   By the Waters of Babylon | 41
9   I Am a True Beast | 45
10   "Like the Foul Stable" | 51
11   Save the Day! | 59
12   The Animals Are Waiting | 66
13   Wound Round With Mercy | 71
14   The Sky is Falling | 77
15   To Seek the Bright Enchanted Gold | 83
16   With an Act of Pity | 90
17   The Hidden Paradise, the Hidden Hells | 96
18   Strength to Love | 107
19   No Second Beer for George | 113

20 The Usefulness of Honor | 118
21 The Prophet From Nazareth | 124
22 Stranger at the Table | 131
23 "All Animals Are Equal . . . " | 137
24 The Animals and the Angels | 141
25 Whatever One Sows | 152
26 Divine and Feline Grace | 156
27 Jonah, the Big Fish, "as Well as Many Animals" | 160
28 Narnian Paradise | 166
29 Return to Eden, Part I: The Garden Feast | 178
30 Return to Eden, Part II: The Emmaus Feast | 183

Appendix A to Chapter 16 | 197
Appendix B to Chapter 24 | 200
Appendix C to Chapter 25 | 204
Appendix D to Chapter 30 | 207

Bibliography | 213

Preface
by Carol J. Adams

ON MY REFRIGERATOR, A magnet holds this quotation in place: World peace starts right here: *I will not raise my child to kill your child.* I have been unable to learn anything about the author of this statement, Barbara Choo. But I find in the writings of Gracia Fay Ellwood a continuation of this thought that extends our understanding of to whom we are making this promise: "World peace starts right here: *I will not raise my* (human) *child to kill* (or benefit from the killing of) *your* (non-human) *child*."

Gracia Fay is concerned with what it means to live peaceably, to work for peace, and to embody that vision in part through veganism. Veganism is one of the ways that we keep this promise. To cows, to pigs, to chickens, and to all other animals whose bodies are used to produce offspring for consumption: I will not raise my children to look at your children as objects.

In July 2004, the first issue of *The Peaceable Table* was published. It is a journal intended for the mutual support, education, and inspiration of people of faith in the practice of compassionate love for our fellow animals and Peaceful dining. Through essays in the pages of the journal, further developed in this book, Gracia Fay explores mythology, novels and poems, biblical stories, theology, and personal experience to provide meditations on compassionate living. From her own deep spiritual practice, she draws on and expands the wisdom tradition. She shows us how to widen our sense of being in the world. With her, we stand at a place that looks outward to what is happening in the world and inward, to ourselves, our spiritual needs. It turns out that healing the world and healing ourselves may be the same act. *World peace starts right here.*

To state to another "I will not raise my child to kill your child" requires imagination. We imagine another to whom we can make such a promise knowing that the loss of a child is one of the worst experiences to endure. Indeed, it is often called unimaginable. Imagination helps us develop compassion and compassion propels imagination. Compassion means learning that a cow laments when her child is removed from her—laments to such a degree that people in one town called the police when they heard strange sounds and learned that the noises were coming from mother cows who were lamenting the separation from their calves. Imagination asks the questions: If a cow laments the loss of her child, how are we not to include her experience in our ethical framework? As Gracia Fay points out in chapter 6, a reflection on the parable of the prodigal son, the cow whose calf was killed for the feast grieved as the human father grieved when his younger son was gone. But she can never say "This my son was dead and is alive again."

The great French mystic Simone Weil suggests that love of our neighbor, in its fullness, means being able to ask, "What are you going through?" and to be able to be attentive to the answer. The question, Weil says, "Is a recognition that the sufferer exists, not only as a unit in a collection," but as an individual. Compassion involves imagination and attention. Attention to suffering makes us ethically responsible. To be able to ask of nonhumans, "What are you going through?" requires a sense of the self that is related and interdependent, a sense of self that can make a promise to others.

What are you going through, cow, pig, goat, rabbit, chicken, deer, fish?

If we are willing to listen, the answer is disruptive and upsetting. Animals experience disabling treatment, imprisonment, torment, and then death. Vegans know the shattering that happens as we learn how animals are treated in our culture. We cannot feel at peace with ourselves or the world if we ingest what required suffering and death.

To those non-vegans who are concerned with peace and who have reached for this book: I pray for your openness to the ideas expressed here. Mary Midgley describes the change in perspective that occurs as one approaches the subject of eating animals: "The symbolism of meat-eating is never neutral. To himself, the meat-eater seems to be eating life. To the vegetarian, he seems to be eating death. There is a kind of gestalt-shift between the two positions which makes it hard to change, and hard to raise questions on the matter at all without becoming embattled." Non-vegans, let the spirit that guided you here help you receive the insights that can create a gestalt shift.

Preface

If you fear separation, a break in one's relationship with friends and family, or a disrupting of one's family or inner circle, take heart. Embark on the hero's journey of knowledge and transformation; take the adventure.

If you fear being different, and being judged for that, or don't wish to give up what is convenient and tasty, take courage. Discover new possibilities, new life, new relationships. You may think change is hard, but not changing is harder. Awareness interrupted, deflected, or denied can lead to guilt and defensiveness. Though it is thought that becoming a vegan requires energy, in fact, not becoming a vegan requires energy too. The difference is that the vegan can follow awareness about animals' suffering, rather than using their energy constantly to derail attention or subdue guilt. The non-vegan must block or redirect awareness of their neighbors. When awareness leads to attention, and attention to engagement, feelings about nonhumans' suffering are not frightening. With the greater openness that enables us to share their suffering also comes a capacity for deeper joy.

If you fear the loss of security and enjoyment and identity of being a meat eater, discover the chance to care and be connected to others, to discover a new kind of abundance from plant foods that nourishes your spirit as well as your body. Eating will not mean scarcity; it will mean feasting.

Simone Weil also said, "The capacity to give one's attention to a sufferer is a very rare and difficult thing; it is almost a miracle; it is a miracle." Gracia Fay Ellwood teaches us how to make that rare and difficult thing a part of our lives. Each time someone embraces this miracle, we make it a little less rare, a little less difficult. And with that, world peace starts right here.

Acknowledgments

MANY PEOPLE HAVE GUIDED, accompanied, and helped me in the making of this book. I can offer my thanks to only a few here:

To Carol J. Adams, for many life-giving insights and supportive friendship.

To Barbara Booth, rescuer of cats in need, for hundreds of encouraging e-letters.

To Marcus Borg, whose writing taught me much about the Prophet from Nazareth who came to proclaim liberty to the captives.

To Kate Carpenter, Chief Cooking Officer, and the other members of Quaker Animal Kinship who have taken the adventure with me, and who kept on keeping on when it has been hard.

To Solange "Angie" Cordeiro, who cooks peaceable food fit for an Emmaus Feast.

To my dear family, Robert, Richard, and Fay-Ellen Ellwood, who have listened to my complaints and my enthusiasms, and gone on loving in word and action.

To Marian Hussenbux, pioneering Friend to animals in need, and friend indeed to me.

To Brother Lancelot, OCG, without whose patience and technical Care none of it could have happened.

To Orange Grove Friends, for much-appreciated financial help.

To Richard Schwartz, president of the Jewish Vegetarians of North America, for helpful counsel regarding the Sabbath Practice of Paradise.

To Benjamin Urrutia, longtime friend and co-worker toward the Peaceable Kingdom.

Abbreviations

DR	Douay-Rheims
ESV	English Standard Version
GW	God's Word translation
ISV	International Standard Version
KJV	King James Version
NASB	New American Standard Bible
NIV	New International Version
NLT	New Living Translation

1

Taking the Adventure

A Paradoxical Feast

FOR OVER TEN YEARS, on the afternoon of every third Sunday of the month, a small group of vegan Quakers have held a gathering. Some refreshment is in order first: it is a potluck luncheon that has evolved into a feast of abundant, colorful, and luscious gifts from Earth's bounty. Looking at this wonderful cornucopia of good things, and the caring and enthusiastic Friends seated around the table, I always feel an immense gratitude for the food that was virtually unknown to me in the days before I came to embrace a "restricted" vegan diet. A feast is more than a meal; it is a refreshing communal celebration of plenty and life and joy and love. We feel this especially when we know that no innocent blood was shed in its preparation.

As with many other people of faith, we are committed to simplicity of lifestyle, to taking no more than our share in a world in which our planet is being devastated and millions do not have enough to sustain life adequately, while rich people take much more than they need. A simple lifestyle is crucial to the survival of the earth. How can it be compatible with the rightness of sitting down to so overwhelmingly abundant a feast?

Knights and Dragons

A complex of images that suggests an answer to this question, and other related questions, can be found in an unlikely place: the stories of King Arthur's knights and the Quest for the Holy Grail. That this source is unlikely hardly needs emphasis. To begin with, the stories appear, confusingly,

Taking the Adventure

in a number of different versions, with varying implications. (In what follows, I draw upon the retelling of the Arthuriad by Roger Lancelyn Green in his book *King Arthur and his Knights of the Round Table*.) Even more problematic is the fact that in most of the tales the exploitation of animals is taken for granted. The knights' chargers are slaves (sometimes valued slaves) controlled by bit and bridle; hunting, especially of deer and wild pigs, may be frequent; virtually every feast is centered in a dead body. The stories show occasional signs of anti-semitism. Furthermore, the whole cycle is heavily male-centered, with female figures tending to be dangerous temptresses and sorceresses, demi-goddess figures, or helpless Damsels in Distress. Problems are usually solved with the sword.

Then what is left? Quite a lot, actually. The Arthuriad took shape in a medieval world where civilization and order still had a shaky hold, where justice and peace were dreams—dreams that coalesced around valiant heroes who cared about the defenseless and could challenge the robber barons, evil knights, and the dragons of greed or chaos that threatened to plunge the world into endless night. In view of the widespread subjection of women, with arranged marriages and frequent rape by marauding knights or invaders, probably many damsels *were* in distress much of the time. The poor of both sexes were subject to the casual violence of the powerful.

Modern Damsels

In Western culture today, concepts of women as frail beings needing protection and control are rightly seen by most as false and harmful. But that there actually are millions of defenseless prisoners in the clutches of agribusiness' robber barons—including furred and feathered damsels in terrible distress in dairy and egg factories—is indisputable. The victims are many, the champions far too few.

Does this mean we cast ourselves in the role of the Knights in Shining Armor who ride out to give battle to the pollution-breathing corporate dragons and blood-splattered human oppressors? Well—no and yes. A minority of animal defenders evidently do, in a semi-literal manner: their sword-thrusts are shouts of abuse and verbally violent phone calls to slaughterhell managers or laboratory directors, harassment of abusers' families, even bombing threats—sometimes carried out. (However, it should be noted that sometimes these abusive actions are "false-flag" attacks staged by agribusiness itself to make opponents look bad.) Unhappily, this violent but conspicuous minority tends to be highlighted by a press eager to present a newsworthy image of animal activists as a destructive lot. With friends like these . . . we need to proceed with Care.

While rejecting the idea of ourselves as sword-wielding warriors, we can still find the knight-in-armor image helpful. It can inspirit an activist not oversupplied with courage who faces, with beating heart, the prospect of civil disobedience—or even just speaking up to her family and associates, or church or temple, on behalf of the animals. In another way, the drama implicit in the images can be helpful in enabling us to get some distance on ourselves and on our mission, perhaps laugh at ourselves a little. Dragons, however terrifying, are mythological beasts!—and our fearsome Evil Knights are not what they seem, either. The victims are very much physical victims, in physical chains and cages, but the wicked oppressors are less tangible. Hidden in the heart of the hardest and greediest agri-baron is the divine image, the divine Light/Love, the seed of transformation. Our war, as the author of Ephesians says, "is not against human opponents, but against rulers, authorities, cosmic powers in the darkness around us, and evil spiritual forces in the heavenly realm.[1]

Behind the Black Visor

Remarkably, one of the narratives of the Arthurian epic already exemplifies this truth in a powerful way. It is the cycle of stories about Balin, who together with his beloved brother Balan (the names suggest they are twins) was a Knight of the Round Table. Sir Balin is a zealous but undisciplined warrior determined to be the Bravest Fighter on behalf of the Worthiest Cause. In the tale in which he first appears, he comes under the spell of an accursed sword; inflamed by a desire for its power, he defies warnings and seizes it. The curse follows him. Later, pursuing an evil knight into and even through the hallways of the Castle of the Grail, he bursts into the holy chapel where the sacred Chalice and Spear are kept. When the guardian of the Grail, the Fisher King, tries to block his intrusion, Balin grabs the Spear and with it wounds the King. The result of this Dolorous Blow is that all the countryside for miles around withers into a perpetual Waste Land. Furthermore, the castle and the chalice disappear from ordinary sight, withdrawn into another plane of being.

---

1. Eph. 6:12, ISV.

Taking the Adventure

In a still later story Balin approaches a strange castle and is challenged to fight its champion, a black-armored knight with no identifying device on his shield. Unable to bear being thought a coward, Balin, who lacks a shield, borrows one (likewise without an insignia) and gives battle. Both opponents fight valiantly, finally giving one another mortal wounds. But before they die, Balin raises the visor covering his enemy's face. What he sees is the face of his brother.

Today's Knights in Shining Armor—the small handful of animal advocates whose hearts burn to save all the billions of innocents from hellish suffering and death at the hands of animal agribusiness—are dwarfed many times over by their giant opponents. Imagine a young person trying to persuade her family or spiritual community (which may contain a small handful or a few hundred people out of the three hundred million in the United States—to show compassion to animals by not eating them. He or she may be repeatedly blocked by a few other members, otherwise good people who refuse to see the monstrous evil they are championing. Another example: a small group of activists doing a midnight open rescue know they can save perhaps twenty hens out of a hellhole containing two hundred thousand—and they know what will happen to all the others. In so grotesquely unequal a situation, with its painful frustrations, how does one who cares about animals bear in mind that the human beings whose callous and violent acts they are opposing are, under their visors, her own sisters and brothers? How does she hold this knowledge in her heart so that she can resist the temptation to hate and attack them even in her thoughts?

The Chalice of Light

The Arthurian stories contain another important theme, the Quest for the Holy Grail, which can help us meet this formidable challenge. The background of the story is the aforementioned Waste Land, which had lain desolate for years. Linked to this scene of nature in the grip of death was a mysterious seat at the Round Table, the *Siege Perilous*. It had long stood empty until finally taken by the High Prince Galahad, young offspring of the tragic affair of Sir Lancelot (in an enchanted state) and the Princess Elaine of the Grail Castle.

The day the young Galahad takes the seat of power, on the Feast of Pentecost at Camelot, the knights all heard a peal of thunder and saw a blaze of celestial light, in the midst of which appeared the Holy Grail. They were awestruck with wonder; when it vanished they each vowed to go on quest to find it. Most of them wandered about, distracted by other adventures, and some never returned. In one version it was only three, whose dedication to the cause was deeper, who were able to find the elusive Grail Castle. Sir Lancelot, whose heart was divided between Queen Guinevere and the Quest, fell into a deep trance outside the castle, and got no further. Sir Bors and Sir Percival entered the castle hall and saw the procession holding the Grail and blood-dripping Spear, but were struck dumb and deprived of initiative. Only Sir Galahad was able to act, asking the crucial question: "Whom does the Grail serve?" He was also able to take the chalice and look into it. The blaze of light from the heart of the Cup permeated and galvanized him, and he was translated from the human plane into the Light. He had "achieved the Grail." The wounded Grail King was healed, and the new life of Spring came at last to the Waste Land.

To Will One Thing

Although medieval readers apparently admired Sir Galahad, modern readers are likely to find him problematic. He is described as a magnificent knight, but he seems scarcely human; totally dedicated to his mission to find and achieve the Grail, he has no friendly warmth, no cravings or weaknesses with which we can identify. His saying "My strength is as the strength of ten because my heart is pure," needs translation if we are not to dismiss him as an ego-bound brat.

Who and what is this High Prince? We may find some help from the title of Søren Kierkegaard's book *Purity of Heart is to Will One Thing*. If we say that Sir Galahad's strength is as the strength of ten because his heart is one, that oneness being intent on the Source of Light, we will begin to understand why he is the only knight who achieves the Grail. Like the child in the biblical Peaceable Kingdom scene who leads the lion and plays over the adder's den, Galahad represents the dimension of every human being, which is linked to the Infinite. Despite his birth out of a tragic and confused love affair, in a sense he has always been gazing into the Divine Light, and thus is able to act with the Divine strength.

If we interpret the High Prince in this way, the image suggests that every action of ours to champion the victims of oppression and violence must also be our inner Galahad's Quest for the Grail. Unless in all our work we are informed by and intent on the Divine Light, the Spirit that lives within all beings, we are in danger of falling to burnout or distraction, like the knights who allowed themselves to be drawn aside from the Grail quest. Worse, we may become like Sir Balin, passionately dedicated and well-intentioned, but also undisciplined, easily blinded, and led astray by self-dramatizing passion. The result is terrible calamity. But if we hold to the more difficult path of following the gleam of the Light within, we may begin to tap into its power to transform even the Waste Land—which our earth is rapidly becoming—back into the Garden of God.

Bread for the Journey

We can now see the outlines of an answer to the question with which this essay began: how can we balance a table laden with more (vegan) good things than we can eat with the adequate-but-modest fare appropriate for those who are very aware of the hunger in the world? The feast does have its cherished place: from time to time, especially on Pentecost, the knights gather at the Round Table to enjoy bounty and good fellowship, to hear of some great deed, and to be available to a call to action. But feasts are relatively infrequent, and when the summons to adventure comes, one must be ready to leave behind things that may be good in themselves, so that we can travel light. We remember that there are no supermarkets available to the adventuring knight, and there may not be time to look for whatever wild berries, roots, or herbs particularly please his palate. Above all, this knight is hardly about to seek out and kill an innocent creature for supper. She carries enough food in her bag for the journey; he dines moderately. Those on Quest do not complain about inconvenience or the absence of sugary treats, because they have bigger concerns in mind.

Let us take the Adventure that God sends us.

2

The Great Wall

The Protective Circle

Picture a medieval walled city or castle, fortified and guarded by armored knights peering warily over the ramparts. The inhabitants live uncomfortable lives, with drafty, smoky or cold rooms, bad smells, an unbalanced diet, frequent disease. But their world is full of dangers; their lives are precious, and despite reliance on the wall and the fighting men, they are chronically anxious.

Most human communities are encircled by a culturally-built wall that marks off those who have value in themselves from the outsiders who don't. According to historian of religion Mircea Eliade's *The Sacred and the Profane,* at early levels of human development, one's tribe or ethnic group is likely to be seen as enclosing all who matter; it is the whole moral community, the center of the world. Outside it is the realm of threatening chaos, to be either shunned, or fought and overcome.

At later stages of cultural development, the wall encloses the privileged race or nation, but there are also usually various inner walls, maintaining degrees of value inside the circle. These cultural walls are created by human beings, though the community is likely to be unaware of this fact. Some of the inner walls, when understood to be human-made and relative, provide necessary structure to society. But when a wall, especially the outer Great Wall, is thought to be beyond question, it makes for a cosy in-group that is also a stifling prison surrounded by an infinite and threatening no-man's-land. As expressed in Faith Bowman's poem "Kyria Sophia,"

Taking the Adventure

> Long years I kept behind my castle wall,
> My ramparts guarded warily withal.
> Those others, who conspired toward my fall
> Would find my moat was deep, my towers tall.
> My walls were stout and arrow-loops were small.
> The air was dim and stifling in my hall,
> No step, no voice, no song or cup at all
> And only echoes echoed to my call,
> But I was my own lord, and not a thrall.[1]

Walls have great power and influence, shaping their human shapers. But, as sociologist of religion Peter Berger points out in *The Sacred Canopy*, they require regular maintenance; more about this in chapter 14, "The Sky is Falling." Individuals sometimes forget them, or seem unable to understand them in the first place. Children question them, and must be taught to fear and despise those whom their elders fear and despise. Philosophers may question them. Prophets loudly challenge them, arousing anxiety and often hostility among their hearers.

The major religions have all taught that we are to "do unto others" as we would be done by, and avoid doing what we would not want done to ourselves. Theoretically, these others include all human beings. The foundation for this principle is expressed in various ways; for many Jews and Christians, the ideation may be that God created and loves all people. Quakers affirm that the Divine Spirit dwells in all persons, and that thus all are in essence equal. Many Buddhists and Hindus hold that our separateness as persons is illusory; we are all one. However the principle is understood, the ideal continues to be held, even though few people of faith live up to it. It entails that no one should be exploited; no one exists merely to benefit others; no one should be subject to the violence that enforces exploitative systems.

But most of these same people of religious and/or moral convictions have assumed that animals are on the other side of the Wall, in the realm of chaos and darkness, sometimes symbolized in ancient times as a dragon or sea monster. Many people believe that if uncontrolled by humans, animals are red in tooth and claw. Kindness to these four-legged outsiders is admirable in some cultures, but justice (and injustice) is limited to the two-legged and many-worded, those who look like us. Keeping animals against their will as property is not slavery; killing them for food or other reasons

---

1. Bowman, "Kyria Sophia," *Faith Poems*.

of human convenience is not murder. Because of the wall, otherwise compassionate people can look at such violence and simply not see it.

The Challenges to the Wall

The central issue of the animal concern is to present to the public the challenges to this wall that prophetic thinkers and activists have been making, especially in the last thirty or forty years. Their message is that as a moral boundary, the wall is as imaginary as those previously believed to demarcate tribes, classes, genders, nations, or races. The reality is not a neat, clear situation of who may own or eat whom—humans vs. animals—but an untidy scene of gradation. We humans are much closer to cows in consciousness and behavior than cows are to clams.

What, after all, is it that makes us human beings think ourselves to be the sole bearers of intrinsic value, distinguished as the only proper inhabitants of the charmed circle? One traditional answer is rationality; "we" think and talk, whereas "they" can't; we not only know, we know that we know. An answer frequently heard in Judaism and Christianity is that we humans are made in the image of God, or possess a soul: " . . . God formed man *of* the dust of the ground, and breathed into his nostrils the breath of life; and man became a living soul (*nephesh*)."[2] Our aliveness is derived from the Divine Breath/Spirit; thus we have the capacity to be united with God our Source.

These terms are variously defined, or left vague, but an element common to most conceptions of the terms is consciousness, awareness, that which differentiates a living body from a dead one. God is the living God; we are alive with life from God. The words certainly refer to something real. Most contemporary religious Westerners hold that we humans have souls while animals do not. But unfortunately for those who depend on the authority of translated biblical texts to support this assumption, the same Hebrew word for soul is also applied to animals. (Uncomfortable translators usually select for animals a different term, such as "creature," to mask the identity.) Since animals, according to the text, have souls, it follows that they too are alive with the breath of the Divine.

Scientists as well as lay persons increasingly acknowledge that animals have consciousness, and some animals show definite signs of being not only conscious but self-conscious, of "knowing that they know." Still

2. Kaufman & Braun, *Good News*, 5.

Taking the Adventure

another trait thought to set humans apart from animals is the conviction that "we" have a capacity for love and empathy, whereas "they" operate out of instinct. But the term "instinct" is so vague that often it is little more than a term meant to put down animal consciousness, with its urges, feelings, and skills. All too often, the exaltation of human beings at the expense of animals arises out of ignorance of "them," those "others."

However the identifying characteristic of the "insiders" is understood, probably the main reason animal protectors have challenged the wall, claiming it to be full of holes, is what philosophers dealing with animal issues call "borderline cases." The boundary is not as clear-cut as is usually assumed. Some human beings are born so defective mentally that they will never speak. Some are so defective morally that they show no sign of love, and even commit appalling crimes without any detectable twinge of conscience. (Yet people of faith are right to affirm that they still live from the divine Breath, bear the Divine Spirit.) Some animals do better; close attention, both informal and scientific, to animals has shown that many bond together in deep attachments, sometimes for life; some are capable of altruistic actions toward other animals, even those of different species, and toward humans. In humans this would be called compassion or love; it is only the human-built wall that authorizes us to demean these actions as "instinctive." Studies of bonobos, chimpanzees and gorillas by scientists such as Frans de Waal, Francine Patterson, and Jane Goodall show that they can acquire vocabularies in the hundreds or thousands of words in sign language. Animals have central nervous systems; they show signs that they dream; they communicate by sounds and gestures; they suffer; they enjoy. When we perceive that the wall was not created by God or Natural Law, but by human beings, it follows that to confine, harm, or destroy the bodies of creatures that have these capacities—that have their own point of view—is real violence against them. From their point of view, it is slavery and murder. They have opinions which deserve to be heard and weighed.

One Response to the Challenge

In many cases, people (including people of faith) who resist the challenge presented by animal protectors insist that whether one eats "meat" or not is a personal decision; some further claim that their liberties ought not to be infringed by the tyranny of vegetarians. (The latter is hardly a new point; John Calvin made it in regard to fast-days more than 400 years ago.)

This argument, which seems convincing to many who have given the issue little thought, still takes the wall for granted rather than defending it against the challenge.

Of course the issue is much more than a matter of logical argument; strong feelings on both sides are involved. Imagine that the members of a supper club or religious congregation should suddenly learn that the "meat" they had been eating came not from animals but from mentally defective human beings. Although the victims may in fact have had a more restricted consciousness than normal cows or pigs, the diners would all feel sick and horrified to find they had eaten "one of us" who live inside the Wall. No one would think that whether or not human beings eat human flesh should be a matter of individual choice. Such a scenario might help some meat-eaters to understand the feelings of vegetarians who have long come to regard the Wall as imaginary.

In dealing with the painful divisions that this issue opens within our families, circles of friends, and spiritual communities, it is important that we bear in mind that we all breathe by the one Divine Spirit; we must make strong efforts when we speak to be knowledgeable, accurate, and loving. It is possible, though not easy, to condemn cultural constructs like the Great Wall without condemning persons, and this we must continually strive to do.

The Walls Came Tumbling Down

In the fall of 2013, when a three-year anti-bullfighting campaign by the mayor and other residents of the city of Concepcion in Peru ended successfully, the decision was taken to demolish the city's fifty-year-old bullring. One can find online photos and video clips of the wall being attacked by heavy equipment, see a hole appear, and watch it enlarge as the structure begins to crumble into rubble. It is a vivid symbol of the dismantling of the Great Wall toward which we are working. The image is not a perfect fit; the bullfighting arena walled *in* the cruelty, rather than walling it and its victims *out*. But perhaps the hopeful feelings the scene arouses in those who seek compassion and freedom for animals are a little like those felt by enslaved African-Americans who sang "Joshua fought the battle of Jericho ... And the walls came a-tumbling down."

In the last two stanzas of "Kyria Sophia" the narrator describes a similar scenario, then takes it a step further as he tells what happens to

Taking the Adventure

his fortress, and to him, when he meets and falls in love with the divine Creator, Sophia:

> And then She came!
> Fair as the moon, ablaze like the noonday sun,
> Terrifying, a many-bannered host.
> By tender violence I was unmade.
> My crossbow clattered down from nerveless hands;
> Rafts swarmed my moat, my tall portcullis split;
> With roars and billowing dust my walls were breached.
> A mightier than I became my Liege.
>
> She ground my fort to dust and digged anew.
> My fetid moat, back in its ancient bed,
> Streams sparkling life; spring flowers of every hue
> Begem its soft-grassed banks; and in the stead
> Of my stout keep, a Tree, whose windy breadth
> Of worldspread branches shelters bird and beast;
> Whose apple blossoms promise death to death,
> And in whose light we neighbors lay a feast.[3]

---

3. Bowman, ibid.

3

We Were Slaves to Pharaoh

IN 2007, THE 200TH anniversary of the passage of a law in Great Britain abolishing the slave trade drew much attention to "the peculiar institution," as human slavery was once called. The film *Amazing Grace*, released at the same time, depicted the decades-long efforts of William Wilberforce, supported by his mentor John Newton and other colleagues, to abolish the vile trade. They encountered determined resistance from moneyed interests and the latter's representatives in Parliament; not only that, wartime paranoia blocked action for years before success was finally attained.

The hellish and profitable trafficking in human bodies was curbed but did not actually stop with the passing of the 1807 law. England was heavily invested in its war with Napoleon, and at first enforcement was limited to two elderly ships patrolling 3,000 miles of African coastline. Violations were numerous enough that in 1811, a further bill was passed by Parliament making slave-trading punishable by up to fourteen years of transportation to prison colonies. Human slavery itself was not to be abolished in the British empire until July of 1833, three days before the death of Wilberforce, and thirty years before Abraham Lincoln signed the proclamation abolishing it in the Confederate states of the US. In some countries, it remained legal into the twentieth century.

Present-Day Human Slavery

Slavery—holding others as property, exploiting their bodies or their labor without meaningful recompense, under threat of psychological or physical violence—is illegal in all countries today. Unfortunately, it is nevertheless also thriving in scores of them. In Mauritania, West Africa, for example, it is widespread (and has been for 800 years) in its traditional form, chattel slavery: persons are openly bought, sold, given away, willed to the next generation. It is based on darker skin color and supported by a perverted form of Islam, in which slaves are taught that to serve their masters diligently is to serve God. (Mainstream Islam in fact has a better record than most major religions regarding race.) Laws in Mauritania prohibiting slavery are scarcely more than paper ordinances, and authorities look the other way.

The other three forms of slavery take a sociologically different form, feeding upon poverty and involving major trafficking. Ivory Coast is an example of forced-labor slavery. Desperate poverty in nearby states such as Mali results in children, especially boys about eleven to sixteen, being abducted or lured away by slavers with promises of jobs, and sold to farmers to work long hours with dangerous machetes cutting cocoa pods from trees, and dragging the heavy sacks of pods. They are locked up at night. Many are half starved and severely beaten if they are unable to perform as demanded, or if they try to run away. Others make no attempt to escape because they have no idea how to find their homes again. Since many of the cocoa farms are small and off the beaten track, it is relatively easy for the hellish situation to go uncorrected. Thanks to documentaries and other exposés in recent years, various authorities and organizations have worked to rescue individual children and abolish the evil practice, but results have fallen short of promises made by major chocolate companies.

Ivory Coast produces nearly half of the world's cocoa. Some farms do not have slaves, but when cocoa prices fall, use of slave labor increases. Cocoa beans from slave-worked farms and from farms staffed by free labor are mixed together, so that one can expect that nearly any bar of major-brand chocolate purchased in the US and Europe will be flavored with the blood of enslaved children and teens.

(However, chocolate-lovers of conscience need not swear it off; organic chocolate is much less likely to be slave-harvested, and fair-trade chocolate is by definition slave-free. Consumers must be prepared to pay more.)

Bonded or debt slavery, including sex slavery, takes place when people from impoverished countries are promised good jobs, smuggled into wealthier countries, then faced with a hugely inflated fee for the smuggler's service. They are confined, isolated physically and/or psychologically, and kept down by threats of violence. Some are given wages, but charged high "rent" and allowed to spend their money only at the "company store," where grossly inflated prices guarantee that they will never be able to pay off the debt. In southeast Asia, debt slavery traps millions and may involve whole families, with children born in slavery and parents passing on the unpayable debt to them. In the United States debt slaves in many cases come from desperately impoverished peoples in Central America and/or Mexico, and end up harvesting fruit and vegetables, particularly in Florida. (Of course not all smuggled aliens are enslaved, though most are exploited.) Girls and women lured with promises of jobs and then enslaved as prostitutes in brothels can be sold over and over again, acquiring a new debt as soon as the previous one is paid off. If they become pregnant they may be forcibly aborted, or after birth their babies may be torn from their arms and sold.

Many people are still ignorant of the facts of human trafficking and enslavement, but with gradually increasing awareness and outrage, in some places efforts are being made to enforce the laws prohibiting them. For example, a boycott of Taco Bell from 2001-2003 on behalf of exploited or enslaved tomato pickers ended with some improvement in their still-deplorable status. But for the most part, secrecy, fear, and language barriers make change difficult, and progress slow.

Nonhuman Slavery

One form of slavery is still legal virtually everywhere: that of nonhuman animals. These living, sentient beings are held in such low regard that their status as chattel, to be bought and sold, is taken for granted; correspondingly, an animal is most often referred to as "it" rather than "she" or "he." That this is slavery is hard for most people to see, partly because most nonhuman animals held as property in the "first world" are kept not for their labor, but for the exploitation of their bodies.

The status of animals kept as "pets" is ambiguous. Most are either chattel or "strays." Those whom people adopt chiefly to benefit themselves, e.g. to guard their property, and whom they may callously abandon when their presence becomes inconvenient, are indeed slaves. Those kept for breeding in puppy-mills, or captured in the wild (especially goldfish and tropical fish, dolphins, and parrots) and trafficked out for sale, are slaves for at least part of their lives. But many adopted animals are warmly loved, and some are taken in by compassionate persons purely for the animal's sake. Thus calling them slaves is very inappropriate. In order to raise consciousness on the subject, the organization In Defense of Animals (IDA) has for years led

Taking the Adventure

a campaign to phase out the objectionable terms "owners," "pets," and "it," substituting "caretaker," "animal companion" (I find this a mouthful—how about "cat friend," "dog friend," etc.?) and "she" or "he." Some cities have agreed to put this new language into their ordinances, either as replacements for the old, or as alternatives. The matter may seem trivial at first glance, but it is an important part of awakening our culture from its moral coma regarding animals.

That in most cases keeping animals is indeed slavery is evident from the many disturbing similarities between animal enslavement and that of human beings. Marjorie Spiegel's powerful little book *The Dreaded Comparison* describes some of these parallels in regard to the historic enslavement of Africans: capturing/kidnapping, branding, hellish transportation conditions, auctions and other sales leading to the destruction of family ties and friendships, whips and prods, fetters, muzzles, and collars, the secrecy of many abuses and tortures, claims that the enslaved are better off than when free in nature, denial that they have much or any feeling, use of either demeaning or euphemistic language regarding them. The deepest motivation in both cases is of course the powerful drive for Profit. There are real differences too, of course. (Some persons may resent comparing animal-keeping to human slavery, says Spiegel, but in many cases that is because they have an up-down worldview in which for an oppressed party to gain value, the formerly oppressing group necessarily loses value.)

Two forms of slavery, that of "dairy" cows and of "layer" hens, bear a particular resemblance to human sexual slavery. Like humans kept as sex slaves, these female animals are kept for the exploitation of their sex and secondary-sex organs, and their offspring are stolen/kidnapped from them. Will Tuttle has pointed out in *The World Peace Diet* a broader link between the exploitation of cows and the objectification of women; for example, "just as cows are forced by hormone injections to have unnaturally large and swollen mammary glands to over-produce milk for the dairy industry, the resulting foods produce unnaturally large mammary glands in the women who consume them—a feature that is prized in our herding culture and further reinforces women's status as mere objects for the eyes of men." The patriarchal herding mentality, says Tuttle, "sees both animals and women as 'meat,' to be milked and eaten in one case and used sexually in the other."[1] He also points up that just as the unsanitary, crowded, stressful conditions in which these and other animals are kept make them sick, consuming their

---

1. Tuttle, *World Peace Diet*, 122.

products and their bodies tends to makes human beings sick. We become the victims of our victims.

Exodus

Every spring brings Passover, the Jewish festival celebrating God's freeing of their Israelite ancestors from slavery in Egypt. Exodus is arguably the founding story of all three of the Abrahamic faiths (Judaism, Christianity, and Islam), because it shows that the heart of God is compassionate love. Unlike many pagan deities of the time, the God of the Exodus identifies not with the royalty and the powerful in society but with the despised and exploited ones, and delivers them "with a mighty hand and an outstretched arm." In the liturgy of the Passover Seder, those present are reminded that Exodus is not merely something that happened thousands of years ago; rather, all who celebrate the festival must acknowledge that what happened to these distant ancestors happens to those keeping the feast today. The implication is that all in the Abrahamic faiths are called to take "the view from below," to empathize with the slave, and rejoice that our God is a God who wills to free those unjustly held in bondage.

With the passage of time, as political and social changes bring new forms of enslavement and exploitation, even sanctioned by religious authorities, the biblical God calls prophets to intervene and to renew Exodus. Like Moses they are charged to speak truth to corrupt power, even though it is the powerful of God's people; speak comfort and release to the slaves and the afflicted; and announce God's will for a commonwealth of compassion, justice, and peace on earth. *Exodus cannot remain locked in the past: it is for all time.*

Most Christians give little thought to the fact that Jesus saw himself as a prophet in this tradition. In Luke's story of the onset of his ministry, Jesus cites Isaiah chapter 61:

> The spirit of the Lord is upon me,
> because he has anointed me to proclaim good news to the poor.
> He has sent me to proclaim liberty to the captives
> and recovering of sight to the blind,
> to set at liberty those who are oppressed . . . [2]

---

2. Luke 4:18, ESV

Taking the Adventure

His execution at the time of Passover, at the hands of the Roman overlords in collusion with their creatures the Temple authorities, (*not* the Jewish people as a whole), was the answer of the Pharaoh of his day to Jesus' prophetic proclamation of the Kingdom/Commonwealth of God. His resurrection was God's response, "with a mighty hand and an outstretched arm," to the hideous violence that enforced the rule of the Roman Pharaoh. Easter proclaims God's will that we be liberated both from human slavelords, and from bondage to the fear of death: Life and Love transcend death.

New Occasions, New Duties

Every Exodus message comes through human minds, with human limitations. While a prophet's message condemns one form of exploitation, it may take another form for granted, or even reinforce it with its imagery. Examples: in the Exodus narrative the Israelites' lambs and the horses of the Egyptians remain enslaved, and are killed either by God's command or as a result of God's deliverance of Israel. A number of the writing prophets use the image of an adulterous wife to denounce Israel's sins, reinforcing men's dominance and women's oppression. Yet, as Rosemary Radford Ruether points out, the core of the prophetic critique goes on, a divine gift out of which later prophets are called to develop, correct, and widen the message of earlier ones.

Thus Exodus indeed contains good news for animals too. Throughout the centuries, occasional Spirit-inspired voices crying in the wilderness have protested the cruel treatment and killing of animals, holding that they are included in God's all-encompassing love. Most have barely been heard, and seemed forgotten. But in the last several decades, prophets proclaiming release for these captives are growing both more audible and more radical. We are becoming harder to ignore.

Whatever the discouragements, we who are called to be daughters and sons of the great prophets must remember that the proclamation of liberation from the latest Pharaoh is not finally ours, but God's.

4

The Work of Human Minds

> The idols of the nations are silver and gold,
> the work of human hands . . .
> Those who make them become like them,
> so do all who trust in them.[1]

WE ALL KNOW PERSONS who have been alienated by the religious context in which they grew up, whether the focus of the trouble was tyrannical or toxic parents mouthing God-talk, abusive teachers in parochial schools, ministers propounding a God ready to throw into hell everybody who is not converted according to their formula, or some other form of abusive religion. Such religious refugees may flee to a liberal church, to a completely different religion, become "spiritual but not religious," or conclude, with immense relief, that there is no God/god at all. Some of the last-named may become hostile to the very idea of a Deity. But a case can be made that what they are reacting against is not religion or God per se, but against one or another form of idolatry hiding in plain sight within it. And the harm done by idolatry is vast, extending far beyond the damage done to certain individuals born within the scope of the religion.

What exactly is idolatry? What might it have to do with the oppression and the liberation of animals? We usually think of the concept as arising from a worldview in which other people's (small "g") gods are false, merely lifeless statues, over against worship of the one true, living God, namely, ours. The passage from Psalm 135 quoted above expresses this idea; however, it also suggests a wider meaning to idolatry, and offers a potential critique of many commonly-used metaphors of the Divine.

---

1. Ps. 135:15, 18, ESV

Taking the Adventure

The Golden Calf

One place to start exploring the concept of idolatry is an important event in the saga of Israel's journey from Egypt to Canaan, narrated in Exodus 32. This chapter tells of a crisis that developed while Moses was closeted with God on Mt. Sinai for several weeks. The people, evidently feeling uncertain and rudderless, asked Moses' brother Aaron to make an image (*eidolon*, idol) of of their God to focus on while they worship. Aaron complied, producing a calf of gold, and the people held a festival, feasting and dancing. But Moses, warned by God up on the mountain as to what was going on, returned in wrath. He vented his rage first by shattering the stone tablets containing the Ten Commandments against the rocks.

What is this scene all about? Why are the figures of God and Moses in this story enraged to the point of killing some of the people who chose to have an a visible image to represent their God, which for some of them was meant to be of YHWH, the selfsame Deity who brought them out of Egyptian slavery? And why is it a calf? Does this image suggest a sense of oneness with animals, or a feeling that there is something divine in them?

It is hard to say how much if any historical truth there is in this incident, so there is some uncertainty regarding questions such as: would the choice of the calf image in this story have been influenced by Egyptian worship of Apis the bull God and Hathor the cow Goddess, or is it more likely to be a backwards projection of the later worship of the Canaanite fertility God Ba'al? ("Ba'al" meant "Lord," "Husband," and was actually a title of various local Deities.) I believe it is most likely that the calf-image points to the fertility religion of Canaan. It is certainly true that such fertility Gods were important in ancient cultures based on the yearly agricultural cycle dependent on rain, and that once agriculture became Israel's primary source of sustenance. the worship of Ba'al and Ashtoreth his consort appeared again and again in its history over centuries. The Ba'als were sometimes linked to the image of the bull, bulls being thought particularly potent. Orgies meant to "prime the pump" both for rain and for human and animal reproduction might be involved.

"Your God is Too Small"

There are apparently two issues here: for some of the Israelites in this story, worshipping a God other than YHWH, and for others, representing YHWH

The Work of Human Minds

with a visible image. Both are prohibited by the Ten Commandments. Passing over the first issue, let us focus on and probe the latter. One explanation as to why visible images for worship are objectionable is that they localize and thus limit the Divine. The calf in this story is probably a symbol of the renewal of the energy of life for humans, animals, and food-bearing plants; our society will survive despite the yearly death of vegetation during the hot summer. Anxieties are quieted; new life will come out of the death of seeds and sacrificed animals. Thus despite a society's imagining the Divine in animal or part-human-part-animal shape, their religion may not hold actual animals in any particular regard, and may victimize some individual animals even more than a religion employing no animal images.

There is no doubt that this assurance of the continuation of a human society is very important to everyone in it, but this symbolically-presented conception of the Divine is still too limited. Not only is it limited to an agricultural society, it does not affirm each individual human and animal; it does not say that God values and cherishes every living being. This we need to know to live a fully moral life; or perhaps I should say that most people need assurance that living justly and compassionately with others is in keeping with the nature of the Ultimate, the Source of all. (There is a minority who can live morally without this assurance; see chapter 13, "Wound Round With Mercy."

Your God Looks Like You

So the fact that visible images such as this one are objectionable because they are limited is valid. An even more important limitation bound up in idolatry is that specific mental images involve projecting onto God specific human characteristics. People who see themselves as made in the image of God are at the same time usually making God in their own image. (This truth doesn't mean, however, that they are *not* made in the image of God; things aren't simple.)

In one way this process of projection can hardly be helped, unless we are willing to settle for thinking of God in purely abstract terms, which usually satisfies only very cerebral persons. Over time Judaism (and later its daughter religion Islam) learned well to reject visible images or symbols of God or of any competing Power, such as Caesar in Jesus' time, that demanded ultimate loyalty. But the use of verbal images does not come under this ban, and here idolatry may creep in. The Bible employs many verbal pictures: God is a liberator of the enslaved, a "man of war," a husband, a father, a food-giver, a woman in labor, a nursing mother, a shepherd, a lawgiver, a king, a potter, a bird caring for her nestlings, a shade-giving rock in a desert, a tower of refuge. Verbal images are limiting just as visible ones are; this, as Sallie McFague points out in *Metaphorical Theology*, is the reason we need different ones to help balance out one another. But one image may become so central and dominant that others stand in its shadow. This is a model, and models have particular dangers; they tend to be taken as literal, and balance is lost.

From the various figures of speech listed above (there are others) one can see that, of the human-shaped images, some are compassionate and nurturing, some tend to power-over, control, and violence, and some tend both ways. For instance, God the legislator gives many extraordinary laws that protect the poor (including widowed women, orphans, and domestic animals) from the powerful, but also assumes the centrality of males, and lays down certain laws that favor them over females, fostering power-imbalance and oppression. As a man of war God protects defenceless Israel from aggressors, but at other times leads Israel in aggressive warfare against other peoples. God the husband is devoted and tenderly loving, but when roused to jealousy becomes violent. Male images of God predominate, and it is these that are dangerously ambivalent. The few female images of the Divine are mostly maternal and nurturing; the impersonal images also tend to be protective and supportive. But neither rises to the status of a model.

Which God is God?

In general, one can see which of these metaphors are life-giving and which have a destructive side, but the distinction is not always neat. Furthermore, since we can't help projecting, and since both evil and good abound in humanity, how can we test the validity of an image, especially of a model, and determine that God is inherently loving rather than violent or indifferent? Following the process theologians Charles Hartshorne, Daniel Dombrowski and others, I suggest that the basic touchstone for judging images is whether they are compatible with the infinity of Divine consciousness. A God who shares the awareness and feelings of *all* finite beings, and thus suffers with all who suffer and rejoices with all who rejoice, is bound to love all beings and want the best for them for God's own sake as well as for theirs: "whatever you did for one of the least of these brothers and sisters of mine, you did for me." God cannot be on one side and against the other in the sense of inherent partiality to this or that group, gender, class, or species. God cannot favor humans over other species and justify them in enslaving and eating animals, because all the kinds of fear, suffering, and pain that cows and pigs and chickens and sheep undergo, whether on small sustainable farms or in factory farms and slaughterhells, God's consciousness experiences with them. It is true that in certain situations God might seem to take sides, in that God wants the oppressed to be protected and liberated, and the exploiters and killers to be stopped in their tracks. But they need to be stopped for their own sakes as well as for the sake of God and of their victims. "As I live, declares the LORD God, I have no pleasure in the death of the wicked, but that the wicked turn from his way and live."[2] The wicked are out of sync with the empathetic nature of God and the ultimate nature of the universe; they are not thriving spiritually, but fatally sick in soul unless touched, through creaturely means, by the Divine Healer.

(This chapter will not attempt to deal with the obvious problem that the will of an all-loving God is obviously not done on earth as in heaven. The issue is touched on in chapter 13, "Wound Round with Mercy.")

Dangers

It is obviously extremely important which human qualities we project in our verbal images of God, especially in our chief models, because when we do so, we legitimize and reinforce them in ourselves. If Zeus neglects his wife Hera and goes about raping any young woman he takes a fancy to, Greek males who honor him can ignore marital responsibilities and give free rein to their own sexual urges. If Kali wants goats or roosters killed in sacrifice, her Hindu devotees who like meat can feel free to kill and eat goats or roosters. If the Trinitarian God is an all-powerful king-emperor demanding submission from all people, Christians can feel justified in conquering other peoples and building empires. Or the idol authorizing empire-building may be not a human-shaped image representing the Deity, but the nation itself. In these idols, the work of human minds, the worst aspects of human nature are sacralized, and claim our ultimate loyalty. Insofar as Zeus is a macho rapist, he is an idol; so far as Kali drinks animal blood, she is an idol; so far as God is a king-emperor demanding submission and punishing disobedience with death or hell, God is an idol. When

2. Ezek. 33:11, ESV.

heads of state and their retainers can engage in evil actions (such as launching wars of aggression based on lies) and never face accountability, the state has become an idol. It is easy for us to see this process in past empires, from the Romans to the National Socialists, but hard for most citizens to recognize while it is going on. "Those who make them become like them; so do all who trust in them."

Our authorities for the nature of our idols partake of their idolic (to coin a word) status. The Greek myths that describe the sexual exploits of Zeus are quasi-idols; so are the long-established rituals of sacrifice to the Indian Goddess Kali; so are the biblical passages that describe God as a conqueror or as hating and demonizing certain groups of people or justifying the enslavement of animals or certain people. (Obviously this last-mentioned is incompatible with the foundational Exodus theme.) Parts of a modern state's constitution, pivotal laws, or major court decisions can be quasi-idols. Clearly, idolatry and the authorities that support it have terribly destructive tendencies.

Sorting Out God

But when we view a religion or other way of life as a whole, we find that idolatry is seldom an either-or business; a given religion's God can be an idol in some ways and life-giving in others, and the harm such a mixed God does *is* a matter of tendencies, not of necessary result. For one thing, in a religion or state there will be a few brave prophets committed to truth and justice, who, because they are grasped by the divine Love that is central, will see the evil being done and speak up. But in a context of rampant idolatry the truth feels threatening to many, and so long as the prophets are few, they are more likely to be ignored, rejected, or silenced than heard and heeded. For another, there are many good people who can be nourished by the lifegiving and love-giving images of their God and seem quite unharmed by the idolic ones. For example, the nineteenth-century Indian mystic Ramakrishna loved the Goddess Kali passionately and felt her presence in his wife, in animals, in people at the bottom of society; he embarrassed his friends by dancing with drunks in the street, and letting a dog share his plate of food; he gave some of the sacred food-offerings, intended for a worship ceremony in Kali's temple, to a cat, saying "Eat it, Mother." He claimed that those who described his beloved Goddess as bloodthirsty were simply wrong: "Mother is everything! . . . Do you dare call her wrathful?

No! . . . she's nothing but pure love!"³ Thus he was aware of the idolatry in conventional worship and rejected it, but there are even good, loving people who not only seem unharmed by idolic images of their God, they do not even notice that there are serious problems. Such people can read the Bible or the Qur'an daily, draw upon its many life-giving themes to grow spiritually, and quickly forget any passages that attribute death-dealing traits to God. Many of them do great good in the world. But the vast majority still pay out money every week that keeps the slaughterhells running, and they close their eyes in prayer before every meal to thank an idolic God for the blood-laced bounty on their plates. Quasi-innocence isn't good enough.

Thy Will Be Done on Earth

LIke the innocent blood shed in the temples of Kali for her well-meaning but benumbed devotees, the unseen blood on the plates of good and devout Jews, Christians, and Muslims makes for an unmitigated tragedy mirrored and magnified many times over, as horrors wreaked on the innocent go on and on behind concrete walls, and human consumers become the victims of their victims. These agonizing scenes underline the vital importance of our prophetic calling today on behalf of our helpless animal cousins and unawakened human sisters and brothers. With a courage like that of Moses, but without the violence ascribed to him in this story, we must denounce idols and their death-dealing work; we must show and exemplify the way to the Love at the divine center.

---

3. Isherwood, *Ramakrishna*, 78.

5

Speaking to the Heart

A BIBLICAL IMAGE THAT may be helpful to animal activists in distress, especially those who no longer feel at home in their spiritual communities, is that of the desert journey. It is linked to the themes of Exodus and Exile.

The Original Story

The ancient narrative of Israel's Exodus from slavery in Egypt, the encounter with God at Mt. Sinai, and entry into the Promised Land includes a long period of journeying through wilderness or desert. The somewhat archaic term "wilderness," though harder for us to visualize than "desert," is appropriate because "wild-" suggests a place inhospitable to human life, and the opposite of home, comfort, and security. According to the saga, in this trackless waste land the people are lost, dependent on God's daily provision of food, and of guidance via a pillar of cloud leading them by day, becoming a stationary pillar of fire by night. They wander for forty years, the number forty coming in later writings to represent such a period of distress and dependency.

Water, essential to human life, is scarce. Occasionally they are led to oases, but at one point, when they feel thirst is about to claim their lives, Moses at God's command opens a miraculous fountain from a great rock. Food is likewise hard to find. The people are dependent on manna, the "bread from heaven," that appears on the ground in the early mornings. Unvarying manna finally gets tedious, and the people crave flesh. God reluctantly responds to their complaints by sending a great flock of quails, but as the people are eating the bodies of the birds, God is angered by their greed (and perhaps their violence). and destroys many of them.

The wilderness journey is a period of necessary closeness to God, with signs and wonders, but also of need, frustration, uncertainty, anxiety, boredom, of forced dependence on an inscrutable Providence. Often that Providence acts on their behalf, but at other times lashes out violently at them. Finally, after long wanderings, the next generation reaches the Promised Land of plenty; but most of those who left Egypt fell in the wilderness.

Wilderness as Symbol

Biblical writers speaking to later times draw on this theme of the wilderness journey, promising a renewal of Exodus to a new generation mired in idolatry and suffering under oppression. Examples from the Hebrew scriptures are the prophet Elijah's flight into the wilderness to escape Jezebel and Ahab, the promised return of the people from exile in Babylon in the fortieth chapter of Isaiah, and the passage in Hosea in which God, symbolized as abandoned, grieving, and angry husband, expresses a desire for reconciliation with and closeness to his unfaithful wife: "I will lead her into the wilderness, and there I will speak to her heart."[1] In the Gospels, Jesus is moved by the Spirit to go into the wilderness for forty days, where he fasts, lives with wild animals, and interacts with angels. The forty-day liturgical season of Lent, during which a Christian may forego a favorite food or other pleasure, also draws on this image. The familiar line from the Lord's Prayer, "Give us this day our daily bread," alludes to Israel's total dependence on God for the day's manna.

Christian mystics have made use of the wilderness theme to represent an arduous phase in the relationship of the soul seeking union with God. At some point, after an awakening, or blissful initial experience of union, the soul finds "herself" (rarely, "himself") painfully separated from her Beloved, often from human friends as well, and desperate with longing. She feels lost in a waterless wasteland where nothing grows: "Ah, how long in anguish / Shall my spirit languish, / Yearning, Lord for thee . . . ,"[2] says seventeenth-century poet Johann Franck. The period of loneliness may go on for a very long time. Eventually, however, the mystic comes to perceive a transformative Presence in the Nothingness: God tenderly "speaks to her heart" without words, conveying a life-giving Something that the mind cannot comprehend. This divine fullness is not received in the midst of

---

1. Hos 2:14, DR
2. Franck, "Jesu meine Freude, *Cyber Hymnal*

the comfortable, the familiar, the safe. It is offered only when all that upon which we ordinarily depend is withdrawn: in the wilderness.

There is no way to show someone going through the wilderness how to receive this Gift, for it is, in its essence, found in total dependence on God. It can help, however, simply to know that it exists, that it has been experienced by those undergoing the wilderness. Another thing that can help is that we address God, either during prayer/meditation, or during the day's activities, in the form of a one-word question, as though we were groping in the darkness for him/her. The interrogative can help us get beyond the tendency of words repeatedly used in contemplative prayer to lose their meaning, and can help us keep attuned to the Source from moment to moment. Or we can visualize or imagine a Someone present with us, always looking at us, silently listening and offering nurturance. One can be active and life-giving even during years of spiritual hunger and thirst in the wilderness, as the world learned about Teresa of Calcutta after her passing.

Heart Speaking to Heart

As we learn to keep our heart turned seekingly to God, we can increasingly receive grace to speak to the hearts of others. When those we care about resist the message of compassion and insist on their right to (kill and) eat animals, especially when their words are subtly or conspicuously abusive, our immediate temptation is to withdraw in pain, or respond in kind to the other's hostility. Either response is almost always counterproductive. Instead, out of the divine Presence-in-Nothingness in our own hearts, we can learn to speak to their troubled hearts, where the divine Light which is Love lies hidden. Light reflects Light, Love kindles Love. Sometimes the process will result in the awakening of Love in the other in this area of life where it was dormant, and the other will have, in mystic George Fox's phrase, a "great opening."

Sometimes there seems to be no response. We may or may not continue to relate or work actively with such persons, but consigning them to the realm of Outsiders is not an option; they remain flesh of our flesh and bone of our bone. Most of us can recall past times when we closed our ears to an unwelcome divine call to "Follow me," and the potentially bright coal of Love in our hearts, instead of blazing up, remained banked over. We can be grateful that God did not give up on us then.

6

Neither Wickedness Nor Sorrow

Fanny and the Stars

IT IS A SUMMER evening (in about 1808), as described in Jane Austen's *Mansfield Park*; the scene is the music room in the great country house of a wealthy English baronet. While their companions gather at the candlelit pianoforte to sing, two young people, Frances "Fanny" Price and the cousin she adores, Edmund Bertram, stand at a window looking out at a scene

> ... where all that was solemn and soothing, and lovely, appeared in the brilliancy of an unclouded night, and the contrast of the deep shade of the woods. Fanny spoke her feelings. "Here's harmony!" said she, "Here's repose! Here's what may leave all painting and all music behind, and what poetry only can attempt to describe. Here's what may tranquilise every care, and lift the heart to rapture! When I look out on such a night as this, I feel as if there could be neither wickedness nor sorrow in the world; and there certainly would be less of both if the sublimity of Nature were more attended to, and people were carried more out of themselves by contemplating such a scene."[1]

Given the setting, one might think that the speaker is a naive and sheltered heiress, ignorant of the cruelties of the powerful and the suffering of the defenseless in the world of two hundred years ago. But that is not the case. Fanny is not a spoiled daughter of the house but a penniless relative, adopted unofficially at age ten from the squalid household of immature, uncaring parents. In this huge mansion her bedroom is a small unheated

---

1. Austen, Mansfield Park, 113.

attic. She is ordered about by her two aunts, sometimes worked beyond her strength, and made to feel her inferior status at almost every turn. The chief abuser is her Aunt Norris (the name is derived from a notorious defender of slavery), whose unpredictable verbal attacks relentlessly work on her nervousness and insecurity. And far from being ignorant about wars and social evils, Fanny is well-read on current events, including the struggle at that time against human slavery.

What we have here then is a most extraordinary situation: a wounded soul, victim of long-term and ongoing child abuse and neglect, who when she looks at the stars feels as if there could be "neither wickedness nor sorrow in the world"! Knowing and feeling, mind and heart seem hopelessly at odds. She asserts her sense that human evil and sorrow do not exist in the face of her painful daily experience of both; and she remains convinced that they would be lessened if people would spend more time contemplating the night sky, and thus be "carried out of themselves" into rapture, as she now is.

Significantly, Fanny's rapture is brief: her beloved, who had just agreed to go outdoors with her for better stargazing, drifts away from the starlit scene toward the candlelit one; he forgets the celestial harmony in favor of what is probably a popular choral song (in which Mary Crawford, a neighbor with whom he is falling in love, is participating). Fanny sighs alone at the window until Mrs. Norris attacks her with an order to get away from there, pretending concern for her health. (The reader knows it is pretended, because on other occasions she deliberately exposes Fanny to cold, heat, and expected rain.)

Nature Mystic

There has been little critical comment about the paradox this scene represents, but it is worth a second look. I believe it contains a strain of hope for those of us who, if not ourselves much victimized by human wickedness, do share deeply in the sorrow and anguish of our kin who are victims, and are tempted to feel bitter that we are helpless to do much of anything about the powerful institutional evil causing it. But the scene is dark in more ways than one. I see one explanatory hint in the heroine's name. Though she is always referred to as Fanny (then a common and acceptable diminutive), there is no question but that her real name is Frances, after her mother; during this period of history, many first daughters were named after their mothers. Furthermore, there are a number of suggestions in the novel that she is a nature mystic, a spiritual daughter of the beloved saint of Assisi who was the first in the Christian West to give voice to the conviction that all things and beings in nature, stemming from the same loving Source as ourselves, are our brothers and sisters. In nature this sensitive Frances finds the only tender, nurturant parent she has ever known. Contemplating nature's scenes gives her peace, arouses her sense of wonder and gratitude, renews her hope. She finds guidance in the nature poetry of William Cowper, who in his long poem *The Task* speaks of perceiving in nature "the unambiguous footsteps of the God / Who gives [the] lustre to an insect's wing, / And wheels his throne upon the rolling worlds."[2] And there is a suggestion, from two translucent pictures in the windows of her shabby sitting room, that she also cherishes Wordsworth's poetry, which describes feeling the presence of the same life-giving spirit pervading nature and humanity.

If we see Fanny as a nature mystic, it is not surprising that the sorrow she experiences daily is lessened when she contemplates the stars. Jay McDaniel, philosopher, teacher, and friend to all creation, casts further light on how this can happen in his book *Living From the Center:*

> Sometimes, if something terrible has happened . . . it can help to follow the advice of Walt Whitman . . . to go outside on a clear night and gaze into the dark and starlit sky . . . The sky and its stars can be a holy icon, an enfolding womb in which we feel small but included in a greater wholeness. The greater wholeness is God, the Open Space. The moist night air, which gives freedom and freshness to our souls, is God's Breathing.
>
> We experience this Breathing in two ways. First, . . . through the healing grace of the sky itself, which reminds us that there is something more to the universe, much more, than is contained in our suffering, no matter how intense it might be. Here, the sky functions as a stained glass window through which divine light shines: a dark light, to be sure, but a holy light as well.
>
> Second, we experience the Breathing through our own internal . . . wonder at the spectacle of the sky, through our delight in the beauty of its thousand points of light. In our amazement God breathes as deeply as in the sky itself. Complementing this amazement, there can also emerge an additional and more subtle feeling: a sense of opening out into the night sky and trusting the mysterious [P]resence, the dark mystery, that shines through it . . . This opening out into trust is what I mean by "faith" . . .[3]

2. Cowper, *The Task,* 100
3. McDaniel, *Living from the Center,* 121-22

Taking the Adventure

Of course, not everyone who has the opportunity to see a clear sky full of stars consciously experiences this Presence, but most who do have the opportunity feel something of that awakened awe, a hint of its power to lighten sorrow, even if not as intensely as a mystic such as Fanny might. Jay McDaniel affirms this lessening of pain when he goes on to say, "Faith has a healing effect in our lives . . . But it does not do so by changing the objective situation. Rather, it does so by giving us the inner resources to deal with a bad situation, no matter how horrible it might be."[4]

This lessening of sorrow is a blessing to be cherished. But how could attending to the stars possibly lessen wickedness? An even greater mystery: how could there be any reality behind Fanny's feeling that *neither wickedness nor sorrow can exist*? As we noticed from the close of Austen's scene, the evil embodied in Mrs. Norris is definitely still there, not at all diminished by the numinous Presence in the starry night, and there is no sign in the story that she would behave with less cruelty even if she attended to the stars.

Melted Into Unity

But we can perhaps gain some understanding of a reality behind Fanny's extraordinary claim by looking briefly at the concept of the mysticism of union. The union in question refers not only to the experience of the mystic that in her rapture she is united with God or the Ultimate, but affirms an intuition that all things, all concepts and categories, including opposites, are finally One. Speaking both experientially and as a philosopher of religion, William James (who in his personal life dealt both with prolonged, deep depressions and the death of his little son) says in his classic text *The Varieties of Religious Experience*,

> Looking back on my own experiences, they all converge towards a kind of insight . . . The keynote of it is invariably a reconciliation. It is as if the opposites of the world, whose contradictoriness and conflict make all our difficulties and troubles, were melted into unity. Not only do they, as contrasted species, belong to one and the same genus, but one of the species, the nobler and better one, *is itself the genus and so soaks up and absorbs its opposite into itself.*[5] (emphasis in original)

---

4. Ibid.
5. James, *Varieties*, 379.

Neither Wickedness Nor Sorrow

To some readers, statements such as this will ring true, however little sense they make literally; for others, they will remain meaningless, unless perhaps they are cast into the future tense, as in the well-known line of another mystic, Julian of Norwich: "All shall be well, and all shall be well, and all manner of thing shall be well."[6]

Either way, the value of such claims, as of the feelings of union underlying them, is in their workability: their ability to enable us to be "carried out of ourselves," out of our self-preoccupation, encapsulation, separateness, to a realization that we are one. The cultural wickedness that leads to the vast suffering and sorrow of human and animal slavery is based on the illusion of encapsulation; it regards the slave as a separate thing, an object that serves the benefit of the separate master. An experience and a conviction that we are not confined to individual capsules but are all One can empower us to take liberating action on behalf of both our human and our animal kin, and to keep on keeping on, even when the stars are invisible in the light of common day.

---

6. Julian, *Revelations*, 57.

7

"He Came to Himself"

WHAT DOES IT MEAN to "come to oneself?" Those who become vegetarian to improve their health or for ecological reasons may not experience their choice as a major life change, but to many who do so primarily for compassionate reasons, it is a reshaping of the self so profound as to amount to a conversion. The Hebrew word for the inner action at the center of this transformative process is *t'shuvah*, literally "return." A particularly rich image of *t'shuvah* is that favorite among Jesus' parables, the story of the Prodigal Son in the gospel of Luke chapter 15, in which the principal character rejects a wasteful and empty way of life and "[comes] to himself." In Quaker terms, it is finding the Divine Light within, that Light which has been covered over and forgotten; or one could use other Christian or Jewish language of turning back from evil and returning to one's true self, to the image of God within. On the deepest level, coming to oneself is returning to God, to our Divine Source.

The Tale of the Prodigal

Jesus' parable tells of a younger son who demands that his father give him his inheritance, evidently caring little that by this request he is in effect saying "I wish you were dead now." Shortly thereafter the son goes abroad to squander his money in wild living. When it is all gone, the country is struck with famine, and the only job the erstwhile high-living youth can find is feeding pigs—the lowest of the low, according to the sensibilities of ancient Hebrews and some other cultures of that area. He becomes so hungry he wants to eat some of the pods he feeds the pigs. Finally, he "comes to himself" and realizes he would be better off going home, eating humble pie, and asking his father to take him back as a hired servant. But the father, who sees him coming at a great distance—he must have spent a lot of time gazing longingly down the road—cuts short his apology, has him dressed in expensive clothes and jewelry, and orders a slave to "kill the best calf" for a celebratory feast, for "this my son was dead and is alive again."

The older son, coming home from the fields and hearing the sounds of music and dancing, asks what is going on. But when he is told that this is his father's way of celebrating his brother's return, he angrily refuses to go in. So his father comes out to beg him to join the party. "Look," says the older son, "I've slaved away for you all these years, but you never even gave me a kid to kill for a party with my friends. But when this son of yours comes back after wasting your money with whores, you kill the best calf for him."

"My son," the father said, "you are always with me, and everything I have is yours. But we had to celebrate and be glad, for this brother of yours was dead and is alive again."

The Meanings of the Parable

The deep appeal of the story of course centers around this change of heart of the thoughtless, extravagant younger son, and the father's forgiving love. It is not hard to see the spiritual implications: however foolishly and recklessly we have lived, however much we have wounded the divine Heart, if we "come to ourselves," *return*, we will be welcomed back into the embrace of boundless love and festal joy.

But around the edges of this story's luminous center remain some disturbing problems. Christian readers are so used to equating the father with God (an example of a model) that they almost cease to see the story as an extended metaphor, which means that the father is a human being who is like God in some ways and unlike God in others. Most do not notice that for this father's passionate love and capacity for joy to be completely unknown to *both* his sons despite all the years they have lived together means that there is something profoundly wrong with his parenting. Apparently he found it terribly hard to put his arms around his boys or say "I love you"—and there seems to be no mother in the picture to offer nourishing tenderness in this psychological famine. Judging from his sons' actions and attitudes, they have no idea what love is. The father also seems never to have put himself in his sons' place and appreciated the need of youth for joy and fun. In order for the climax of this story to unfold, as the younger son was "coming to himself," the father had to come to himself as well. All that time he spent gazing down the road, and especially the ecstatic moment when he saw his ragged son in the distance trudging toward him, he was realizing how much he had loved his boy, and how intensely he now wanted to show it.

Major cultural evils are also evident in the story. It is told in a society under Roman rule in which, according to Dominic Crossan, Marcus Borg and other scholars of the historical Jesus, perhaps 90 or 95 per cent of the people lived on or over the edge of subsistence, a society in which the powerful elites were confiscating peasant families' land as a result of tax indebtedness, causing more and more of them to become day laborers, beggars, or slaves. But this parable's family is among the tiny wealthy minority; it has both hired servants, *mistheoi*, and slaves, *douloi*. To be both wealthy and innocent in this oppressive culture was nearly impossible; as one of Jesus' sayings has it, "it is easier for a camel to go through the eye of a needle than for a rich man to enter into the Kingdom of God."[1]

And, of course, the violence against animals is not only an element in the tale, it is emphasized; the characters even use the killing of a baby or juvenile animal as a synonym for feasting! But what about the terror and pain of the calf? What about the helpless grief of the mother cow? Alas, it never occurs to the happy father, who orders a slave to kill a calf, or to the bitter older son who wanted to have a kid killed for a party, that the grieving—and silenced—mother cow or goat could never say "This my son was dead and is alive again."[2] There are Christians ready to use this story as evidence that God approves killing animals for food. But if the fact that this story's father owns slaves does not give divine sanction to human slavery, neither can it be used to sanction eating animals.

A Modern Tale of the Prodigal

Like all parables, Jesus' tale is brief, symbolic, richly suggestive; but a parable is too short to be a deep character study. A psychologically insightful retelling of the plot can be found in *Mansfield Park*, perhaps the darkest and richest of Jane Austen's comedies, discussed in the previous chapter.

Mansfield is the great estate of a wealthy English baronet, Sir Thomas Bertram, who owns additional property, no doubt a slave-worked sugar

1. Matt 19:24, KJV
2. Luke 15:24, KJV

plantation, in Antigua in the West Indies. He was among the "haves" in another period, probably around 1808, in which the gap between rich and poor was widening, with confiscation and enclosure of peasant lands, and much suffering and hunger among the "have-not's." Sir Thomas' mansion is "modern-built," which clues us in that his wealth is not primarily inherited from a long line of forebears who ruled the estate, but came within the present or previous generation, primarily from the plantation in Antigua. He also has some political power, being a member of Parliament. Furthermore, Sir Thomas seems fortunate in his family; he has a harmonious marriage to a still-beautiful wife, and four handsome grown children highly regarded in their social circles. He also has a sister-in-law, the reprehensible Mrs. Norris, and an adopted niece, Fanny Price, the story's main character, both of whom are deeply involved with the Bertram family and working devotedly for them.

But like the father in the parable, Sir Thomas cannot express his love to his children. Neither does their mother; Lady Bertram is so passive as to be almost as non-existent as a mother in Jesus' story. The active mothering the two Bertram daughters do receive is from their Aunt Norris, who flatters and spoils them, while she relentlessly bullies the insecure Fanny. Sir Thomas is pleased with his daughters' high social achievements and marital expectations, but he is unaware that they have developed little or no moral fiber, and that his formidable presence makes home a dull and suffocating place to them. For years he is undisturbed by Mrs. Norris' cruel abuse of Fanny.

The older son, Tom, who is to inherit the estate, becomes the prodigal son, spending much of his time away from home: drinking, betting at horse races, and fettering the family with huge gambling debts. In order to pay them, Sir Thomas has to make a major financial sacrifice, which will almost surely deprive the younger son, the serious, conscientious Edmund, of much of his expected future income as a clergyman. Furthermore, the sugar plantation in Antigua is failing, perhaps in part due to the recent abolition of the slave trade, and Sir Thomas has to sail there despite wartime dangers, and take over in order to make it profitable again. He is absent from home for two years, and during this time things at Mansfield begin to fall apart.

Exploitation of and violence against animals is a marginal part of the total picture, including the killing of wild animals for "sport" by the young men in the story. While the father himself is not depicted as hunting, one passage suggests that he too is a hunter. In any case, his general emotional numbness, reproduced in his sons and their friends in regard to wild creatures, is clearly a prerequisite to finding it fun to terrify and kill harmless innocents.

Shortly after Sir Thomas returns, he puts an end to a questionable play the young people had been happily absorbed in rehearsing, during which they were perilously losing hold of the boundary between fictional drama and real life. The older daughter, Maria, engaged to a wealthy dolt whom she holds in contempt, was playing a role opposite that of their neighbor Henry Crawford; she is in love with Henry, but he is only trifling with her. She is crushed when he suddenly drops her and decamps at the abrupt ending of the theatricals. Feeling humiliated, and desperate to escape from her father's suffocating presence, she marries her embarrassing fiancé. After only six months the farcical union ends when she leaves him for an adulterous affair with Henry, creating a huge, reeking scandal.

Maria, then, becomes the prodigal daughter. This affair leads to the wreckage of Edmund's hopes to marry Henry's sister, and so alarms the younger Bertram daughter Julia, who fears her father's increased repression, that she elopes and marries a frivolous and debt-laden socialite she doesn't love. The scandal of Maria's adultery seriously damages—perhaps destroys—the social standing of the Bertram family. Furthermore, it takes place shortly after Tom, injured, seriously ill, and abandoned by his worldly friends, is brought home hovering between life and death.

During his long illness, Tom is nursed devotedly by the compassionate Edmund, the very brother whose financial future Tom's gambling had undermined, and who would have inherited the estate had Tom died. As a result of his suffering and this undeserved brotherly love, the prodigal son comes to himself, recovers, and becomes a new and responsible person.

The family's catastrophes also cause Sir Thomas to come to himself. He realizes how egregiously he has failed his daughters, and, apparently, how he has neglected and wronged his niece Fanny. He is comforted by the change of heart in Tom, and by Edmund's continued reliability. Perhaps the chief means of grace to Sir Thomas is Fanny herself, who suffered so greatly as a result of his oppressiveness, negligence, and failure to protect her from her Aunt Norris: she accepts him as her father, and becomes the daughter of his heart. Fanny and Edmund also become means of healing and fulfilment to one another.

"He Came to Himself"

Reflections on the Theme of the Prodigal

Like the father and the prodigal son in the parable, the family in *Mansfield Park* is embedded in the appalling cultural evils of class oppression, gender oppression, race-based slavery, and abuse of animals. The novel, even more than the parable, shows that these evils are intertwined. Sir Thomas, the powerful lord of all he surveys, has been taught an outlook of emotional distance and unyielding control over his property, his human subjects, and his own feelings. As a result his older son runs wild, and he remains ignorant of what is going on in his daughters' hearts until inner pressures build to an explosion.

Just as the prodigals and other characters in the parable and the novel reach bottom and have to face themselves, so people in our society are faced with the urgent prophetic word about the cultural evil of violence against animals and the threats the animal agribusiness system poses to human health and the very life of our planet. Both characters and present-day persons have to make crucial decisions. Either they will deliberately continue down the destructive paths of their inherited lifestyle, or take the frightening alternative—coming to themselves, acknowledging complicity in these evils, and venturing into an unfamiliar path not sanctioned by the mainstream. In the parable, the novel, and our own world, divine compassion and forgiveness flow out through human hearts to those who come to themselves.

Jane Austen's characters are too genuinely human for her story to manifest anything like a perfect resolution. Sir Thomas awakens to his responsibility for his family's social disaster, but never comes to terms with his guilty involvement in human slavery. Neither Tom nor Edmund face up to the evil of their violence against animals, nor does Fanny condemn it, even though both Edmund and Fanny would almost surely have encountered impassioned prophetic critiques of "sport" hunting in William Cowper's *The Task*, which is one of their favorite poems. The prodigal daughter Maria had hoped to regain her place in society by marrying Henry, but when he betrays her by refusing her this ticket back to respectability, she finally leaves him in bitter frustration. Unhappily, we see no sign that she comes to herself, and her father never accepts her back. (Considering how a patriarchal society usually regards sexual violations by a woman, would the father in Jesus' parable have welcomed a prodigal daughter?) Neither is Jesus' parable completely resolved; we never learn how the now penniless younger son will support himself in the future, nor do we know the spiritual outcome for the embittered older son.

God is with us—*Immanuel*—reaching out loving arms to welcome those of us who gather the courage to come to themselves and change their destructive ways, particularly their share in the culture's horrifying treatment of animals and the spiritual and physical dangers it creates for humans as well. But perfect fulfillment on this earth we are unlikely to see; alongside wonderful expressions of love and renewal, there will probably always be unanswered questions and unfulfilled hopes.

We must live in the in-between place, the place of waiting. We must work in faith and hope as we offer ourselves as a means to the enactment of God's compassionate, forgiving love.

8

By the Waters of Babylon

The Theme of Exile

Exile is a major theme in Western religion. It resonates through Jewish writing: repeated expulsions, mass captivity, or geographic exile over thousands of years have stimulated reflections on all of human life as exile. "By the waters of Babylon we sat down and wept . . . How can we sing the Lord's song in a strange land?"[1] mourns the psalmist. Christian mystics and hymn writers have pondered their individual life's journey as that of an exile or pilgrim far from home: "I am a stranger here, within a foreign land . . . "[2]

It appears frequently in literature as well. Several of Jane Austen's novels are based on the theme of young women forced out of their homes by male heirs (or under threat of same), and thrown on the world with small or nonexistent resources, thanks to heartless patriarchal inheritance laws and practices. J. R. R. Tolkien's epic fantasy *The Lord of the Rings* has a background theme of the age-long exile of the High Elves from their native country, expressed particularly in the Lady Galadriel's song that voices her longing and mourns the great breadth of the Sundering Seas between Lorien in Middle Earth and her original home in Eldamar.

In George Eliot's classic tale *Silas Marner*, the theme has an ecclesiastical dimension that is likely to resonate with those in a strained relationship with their spiritual communities. Silas, a devout young man in a small

---

1. Ps. 137:1, 4 KJV.
2. Cassel, *Psalter Hymnal*, 446.

Taking the Adventure

Dissenting church (probably Baptist), is framed for the theft of the church's money by his closest friend, and as a result is thrown out of his church. He falls into the black hole of loss of faith and meaning. Silas takes up a reclusive life among strangers, seeking consolation in a soul-shriveling idol, his growing hoard of gold coins. But thanks to an unexpected event one winter night during Christmastide, to his surprise he begins to find God's hand at work in his life once more. I will have more to say about this novel in later chapters.

Prophets in Exile

Those of us who, finding ourselves called to the role of prophet, have presented the animal concern to our religious communities or circles of friends and family, and have encountered repeated, sometimes harsh resistance may, like Silas, feel exiled from our souls' homes. The pain can be acute and long-lasting. We may not have been literally pushed out; some of us, though feeling unwelcome, may continue living in our homes, attending our familiar religious or social events. But we shared Silas' experience of anguished astonishment: our fellows—whom we assumed had given their first loyalty to Love, to the Good News of peace on earth and compassion for victims of oppression and violence—seemed after all more intent on their own security or gratification. They appear oblivious to the anguish and death of innocent creatures, to animal products' threats to their own health, and to the great harm being done by animal agribusiness to our home the earth. Many tend to shut out the whole moral issue. Some find support for their lifestyle in harsh and impersonal biological patterns such as "life feeds on life" (I once did myself), which they would never use to justify the killing of their own companion animals. Some accuse us of being, in effect, the Food Police.

In all honesty, we may find that we are not be quite so guiltless as Silas Marner. Feeling that we have been maligned and the Good News of God's love for all betrayed, we may have responded uncharitably; replying angrily to our (perceived) opponents, expressing our bitterness to colleagues and supporters, or letting our rage simmer within our own minds. The self-righteousness we were sometimes unfairly accused of may, after all, make its appearance. And we may be discomfited by seeing signs that our friends or fellow worshippers we felt had done the betraying may still have good qualities, may not be such villains after all. Of this, too, more later.

By the Waters of Babylon

The Choices of Exile

Where does this state of affairs leave us? To begin with, if we leave our circles of friends or spiritual communities, we cannot count on going home again. It is not impossible that widespread transformation will after all come soon, but as with the movements in England and the US to end human slavery, the change we seek may well take decades. We do well to learn to live in exile, and we may even find some unexpected blessings there. Our experience and our sympathies are likely to enlarge, as we find new friends and wise teachers among prophetic individuals from both our own and other spiritual traditions.

How are we to conduct ourselves in exile? The question is a vitally important one. However frustrated and few and marginalized we may often feel in the face of the mighty mainstream, the spiritual alternatives we face are as crucial as those we have been presenting to our friends and fellow worshippers. Dwelling on our frustrations and anger on behalf of the animals and ourselves will increase a bitterness that can do enormously more harm than we realize. All things, all beings are connected, and we do not know what toxic fruit our resentment might bear; we cannot afford to cultivate it. We must live as though our thoughts, words, and actions will fan out and shape the future to an extent beyond our imagining: in short, we must love both friends and those we experience as foes.

The Block

Knowing that our resentment is very harmful can help us curb it, but doesn't give us much relief from pain and anger. An approach which has been a great blessing to me is Carol J. Adams' central idea, in *Living Among Meat Eaters*, that the person who resists the message is a *blocked vegetarian*. The discourteous, sabotaging, unkind, or even cruel response seemingly aimed at us as vegans or vegetarians does not come from the resisting person's real self, nor are vegetarians the real targets. The vast majority of people are not monsters; in their inner being they are decent folk who want to be and do good, and often succeed. But they let their anxieties, or cravings, or stress, or busy schedule, or inertia get in the way of changing their eating practices. Here they identify with the habits they have inherited rather than with their innermost being where Divine Love for animals as well as all other beings is found. They let the block stop them from taking the adventure of more fully becoming their true selves. They don't like the discomfort of this inner conflict, so they project it outward, blaming the vegetarian whose presence or message reminds them of it. Becoming aware of this duality in the other enables the vegetarian to get out of the way of the attack, and respond in an intelligent and compassionate manner that will help the blocked person to stop projecting and deal with his or her own problem. Carol Adams' book analyses various attitudes and situations that arise and offers many sensitive, common-sense suggestions for implementing these insights.

The Inner Home

The core of the issue is spiritual. Our ultimate refuge from spiritual homelessness, the indispensable source of life and of the universal compassion we are called to incarnate, must be within our hearts. A psalm attributed to Moses, who, the story tells us, was born in exile and never set foot in the promised land, begins with the line "Lord, through all the generations you have been our home!"[3] Still another psalm, perhaps by an exile who had once thought Israel's God dwelt only in one locality, now celebrates an unbounded God who is found wherever she or he may set foot: "If I go up to heaven, you are there; if I go down to the grave, you are there."[4] We can live with grace in exile and faithfully fulfill our prophetic calling by returning daily, even hourly if possible, to this inner Home, to our Beloved. It is after all this Source of Love who has called and inspired us in the first place to speak and enact Her/His love and liberation for all: for the animal victims, who might be called the least of all our brothers and sisters—and also for the blocked human beings who still insist on killing (vicariously) and eating them.

As Augustine is reputed to have said, "There is no saint without a past, no sinner without a future."

---

3. Ps. 90:1, NLT.
4. Ps. 139:8, NLT.

9

I Am a True Beast

The Myth of the Birth of the Hero

The Horse and his Boy (originally entitled *Narnia and the North*) by C.S. Lewis is a story in the mould of the ancient Myth of the Birth of the Hero. Here is a sketch of the myth as studied by psychoanalyst Otto Rank and comparative mythologist Joseph Campbell: a prediction is made that a forthcoming child, of noble, royal, or divine birth (in some cases with one human and one divine parent) is a threat to the king. As a result, he is separated from his home and parents in infancy, and abandoned: perhaps exposed on a mountainside, or like Moses, set adrift in a small boat. He is rescued, often by impoverished peasants who raise him in their hovel in the midst of an oppressed and blighted world. But already in childhood he shows signs of being special. He may have unexplained traits or unusual powers. He may have a twin; he may have a birthmark or other sign that will eventually prove his identity as a person of destiny. In his teens or early adulthood he undergoes an adventure or ordeal, struggling with the evil powers that threatened his life and are sucking the life out of society. He has help from a supernatural source: a potent talisman, an all-knowing guide, a remarkable animal. Ultimately he overcomes the evil powers, thus freeing his world from tyranny and blight, and returns to his true home and family, where he is acclaimed, perhaps enthroned.

The recurrence of the story in many places and times shows that it meets a deep need in human nature. It is a myth, not in the more usual sense of a false account, but rather as a tale embodying a profound psycho-spiritual truth. Some instances of it may be historically true in part; for example, the beloved story of Abraham Lincoln, the gifted boy born in poverty in a log cabin who was destined to become president and guide his country through the worst crisis in its history—and in fact Lincoln in fact had a strong sense of being propelled by destiny—has a few elements of the Birth of the Hero story. The story of Jesus is a powerful instance of the pattern, with at least some of its elements historical; Jesus almost certainly had healing powers, related to God as his divine father, and after his terrible death, apparitions of him were seen by a number of his followers. (Of this more in later chapters.) Or the tale may be wholly fictional, like the adventures of Luke Skywalker and his twin in the *Star Wars* saga.

The story of Shasta, the child-hero of C. S. Lewis' Narnian novel The *Horse and His Boy*, is shaped from beginning to end by the birth-of-the-hero myth. In what follows I will look at the plot with this pattern in mind, focusing primarily on the element of of the help he receives from an extraordinary animal. Shasta differs from most heroes in that he is guided—sometimes forcibly—by more than one such animal.

He grows to youth in the hut of an impoverished and abusive fisherman named Arsheesh at the seashore in Calormen, "the land of tyrants and slaves." But he has always longed to know what lies to the north. Shasta one night overhears Arsheesh tell an aristocratic visitor that the boy is not his son. Then Shasta makes the astounding discovery that the visitor's horse, Bree, can talk. Bree tells him how, as a foal, he was kidnapped out of Narnia far to the north and has always longed to return to home and freedom. So the two decide to escape together. Bree uses his strength and geographical knowledge to guide their journey and avoid certain dangers.

Other Animal Guides

Shasta's first encounter with another animal guide is less happy. As the refugees travel along the seashore one moonlit night, they detect a rider going in the same direction, evidently a Tarkaan on a fine blood mare. Anxiously they try to stay clear of the unknown figure. But a lion's dreaded roar from ahead on the right, then on the left, forces them and the other rider closer until they are neck and neck. They escape the lion, but Shasta and Bree soon learn that the other rider is an aristocrat, a rather arrogant girl his own age named Aravis, and the mare another talking horse. The four escapees learn that they are all fleeing to Narnia, and join forces.

I Am a True Beast

Shasta's next encounter with an unknown animal guide is more reassuring. He is separated from his companions outside the north gate of Tashbaan, Calormen's capitol city, spending the night alone in a reputedly haunted cemetery there, on the edge of the desert that divides Calormen from Archenland and Narnia beyond that. Here the anxious boy encounters a very large domestic cat that suddenly touches his leg from behind. Looking into the cat's eyes, Shasta feels the creatures knows secrets he won't tell. Greatly comforted, Shasta goes to sleep with the cat at his back. He is awakened by the cries of approaching jackals, but protected by a huge shaggy-headed animal who bounds toward them with roars that disperse them. Then the great beast approaches the terrified Shasta. But instead of teeth and claws, the boy feels the comforting cat, who again settles at his back and keeps him warm.

His third cat encounter is frightening like the first. During the companions' separation in Tashbaan, Aravis has learned that the hotheaded crown prince of Calormen plans to take two hundred horsemen across the desert to raid Anvard, the castle of Archenland, an act which will enable Calormen to take over the country. The children and horses have enough of a lead to warn Anvard in time, but, exhausted, they fall asleep and lose many precious hours. Shortly after they reach the green hills of Archenland they look back to see a distant line of horsemen coming up rapidly. The two horses break into a gallop; a lion's snarling roar in pursuit gives them the even greater speed of terror for one more mile. The spent horses and their riders reach the refuge of a hermit's enclosure; Aravis and the horses can rest, but the hermit sends Shasta running on northward.

Shasta's climactic encounter with a mysterious animal guide takes place that same night. He has encountered King Lune of Archenland and his courtiers, whom he meets out hunting (!), and has delivered his warning. They lend him a horse and he joins them riding eastward toward Anvard, but Shasta falls behind in a fog and takes the wrong road, going north up the mountains. At length, in darkness, hungry, cold, and lost, he is frightened out of his tears by the sound of someone *breathing* loudly beside him. The being tells him that the several cats that he met, large and small, were only one: himself. And he tells the boy that he and Shasta also met long ago, when he pushed a ship's boat containing his infant self to the shore near Arsheesh's hovel. As the dawn approaches, Shasta sees a golden radiance on his left, and in it a Lion larger than his horse; then the great beast disappears into the light. The scene is one of the most moving in all the Narnian chronicles.

Shasta finds he is in Narnia. He sends a message to its King, Edmund, about the threat to Anvard, to which Edmund quickly responds by gathering a small army to defeat the besieging raiders. Shasta accompanies them, together with young Prince Corin of Archenland, whom he already met briefly in Tashbaan, and who looks exactly like himself. Anvard is saved, and Shasta, by his exact resemblance to Prince Corin (who is of course his twin), is recognized as Crown Prince Cor, the king's long-missing son and heir.

The Strange Work of Aslan

Many readers will know that the giant lion is Aslan, the creator and lord of Narnia. As Shasta/Prince Cor later remarks, Aslan is somehow behind all the stories about himself. Aslan's guidance, as we can see, shows itself in two forms, which we can encapsulate in Martin Luther's terms "the Strange Work of God" and "the Proper Work of God." There is no question about the Lion's true nature and his proper work, which are glimpsed most clearly in the heart-stoppingly beautiful scene of his mystical-type encounter with Shasta/Cor on the mountain pass. It is seen in a smaller way when he protects Shasta from the jackals, and, as a cat, comforts and warms the anxious, lonely boy. And it is seen most of all in the outcome, the deliverance of Archenland.

But some of the Strange Work of Aslan is difficult. At the beginning of Shasta/Cor's life, a centaur foretells that eventually the boy will save Archenland from its most dreadful peril. It is this prediction that motivates a traitorous courtier to abduct the child and sail for Calormen. One gets the impression that Aslan must be behind this prediction too, and thus the child's abduction, for that act is the foundation of Archenland's rescue. Aslan does not *cause* the traitor to do his evil deed, but in a sense he is responsible for it as well as for a never-resolved consequence: the anguish of his mother, who dies without seeing her child again. Similarly, Bree and Hwin, also kidnapped in early youth, are crucial to the adventure; we are not told whether they are ever reunited with their mothers, who must have grieved as much as the queen. Likewise, Aslan must be responsible for the dreaded event that sparks Aravis' flight, her forced betrothal to a sycophantic older man she detests. Obviously this evil ultimately turns to good, for her presence is crucial to the success of the mission. But to escape she had drugged her stepmother's slave, who overslept, was beaten painfully for it, and never finds justice.

There are not many such loose ends in the tale; the victims are offstage and easily forgotten in the joy of the outcome. In the "real" world, of course, it is quite different. We need committed faith to live as though the Strange Work and the Proper Work of God are ultimately one. And, in fact, stories such as this can warm the heart and strengthen that commitment.

A True Beast

In a scene in the Hermit's enclosure after the deliverance of Anvard, we find Bree, a good creature but sometimes a tiresome know-it-all, holding forth to Hwin and Aravis that people who think of Aslan as a real animal are naive. If he really *were* an animal, says Bree scornfully, "he'd have four paws, and a tail, and *Whiskers!* " At this point Bree gives a squeal of shock and fear as he feels Aslan's very real whiskers tickling his ear; he bolts. Aslan summons him back: "Touch me. Smell me. Here are my paws, here is my tail, these are my whiskers. I am a true Beast."[1]

Why does it matter that Aslan, who is the divine Presence in Narnia, is a genuine animal—visible, audible, and tangible? He has often been called a Christ-figure, but that interpretation does not apply to several of the stories. Lewis, who was in many ways a traditional Christian, has claimed that in Aslan he was imagining a unique animal Incarnation of God in Narnia parallel to the one human Incarnation in our own world. The huge and enduring popularity of the Chronicles certainly owes much to the way the divine Lion has kindled and enriched the faith of many Christians, whatever their age.

But I believe this image of an animal as God-With-Us also has much to offer others whose worldview does not include a unique divine Incarnation. There are people of faith who hold that the pervasive presence of the Divine Spirit throughout the world, and in particular in the soul, means that God is incarnate in all beings, in greater or lesser measure depending on a being's degree of consciousness and love. As Faith Bowman's poem "Splendor" expresses it,

> Earth is charged with splendor,
> Glowing, flaming with the Light supernal,

---

1. Lewis, *Horse and His Boy*, 171

Taking the Adventure

> From the Still Point streaming,
> Swelling, full, and ever vernal.
> Every bush is burning;
> Eden shines in every sunlit river;
> Every lamb is holy;
> Every moment holds forever.
> Though our eyes are heavy
> And our hearts like winter earth are cold,
> Though illusions lure us
> In a dim and stony wasteland,
> Still the Light is shining,
> Quenchless, deep in every soul . . .
> From a Heart we journey,
> Ever to a Heart return.[2]

For centuries there have been a few with eyes to see the divine Light all around them, who have resonated to the divine Love in all the living, whether human or nonhuman, even in the depraved. But many more of us have only in recent years been opening our hearts to the reality of love in animals—shall we say Divine love?—because God is there in the flesh, in the lamb and in the lion. Most of us still have a very long, adventurous journey back to the Divine Heart, but we rejoice whenever we see a glimpse of that Heart now: God-With-Us "plays in ten thousand places," in Gerard Manley Hopkins' phrase. We can see God playing in animals, ranging from Scoli, a serene, ordinary-looking house cat who loved his feline enemies and responded to their hisses and growls by licking their faces and turning them into friends—to the one-time adopted lion cub Christian who, a long time after growing up and being released in Africa, did not cease to love his two humans. *God-with-us can have "four paws, and a tail, and whiskers."*

---

2. Bowman, "Splendor," *Faith Poems*.

10

"Like the Foul Stable"

The Birth of the Hero Jesus

MANY CHRISTIANS CONCERNED ABOUT animals rightly find the Nativity narrative in the gospel of Luke to be particularly affirming of farmed animals. This is the familiar story of the angel's appearance to Mary, of her and Joseph's journey to Bethlehem, the birth of Jesus in some kind of animal shed—"she . . . laid him in a manger,"[1] implying the presence of animals—and the angel army's message of "Peace on Earth" delivered to the shepherds in the fields.

Together with the narrative of Moses' birth in Exodus, the Nativity is probably the best-known example of the Myth of the Birth of the Hero in Western culture; in fact the version in the gospel of Matthew, with its tyrant who orders the massacre of babies and the journey of Jesus' family to Egypt, deliberately alludes to the story of Moses' birth. There are a number of such myths both in ancient religions and in biographical accounts of revered political or religious figures. In the previous chapter, "I Am a True Beast," we examined C.S. Lewis' skillful use of the myth in his children's novel *The Horse and His Boy*.

To reprise some of the elements frequently found in the myth: portents precede or accompany the birth; the child is of royal or divine parentage; he (seldom she) may have a twin; at birth or soon afterwards the child's life is threatened. He is rescued and reared by a peasant mother or couple, living close to animals, in a society oppressed by a cruel tyrant. The peasants' animals may stay in the background of the story, or an extraordinarily wise

---

1. Luke 2:7, KJV

Taking the Adventure

animal may be prominent as the hero's guide. In youth or adulthood the hero manifests supernatural powers, with which he engages the tyrannical powers that are crushing out the life of his society. He defeats the tyrant[s], and ultimately takes his true place as the royal or divine being he is.

The nativity story in Luke is unusual in that it has a double reference to animals: the flocks of sheep in the fields, and the implied beasts in the stable. In paintings a few of the sheep often show up with the shepherds who have come to the stable; art that includes figures from the story of the Magi or Wise Men (from Matthew chapter 2) may introduce a third set, the camels.

The presence of these beasts is significant in more than one way; to begin with, it underlines the lowliness of the birth. Whereas stable-hands and sheep-tenders are ranked in the bottom rungs of a traditional society, the animals have even lower status, usually being considered mere property. My brother recently pointed out to me that, according to archaeological evidence he had studied, cellars under human dwellings sometimes served as animal sheds. Such an arrangement would make sense, especially in towns and cities, where space was limited. If it is intended in Luke's Nativity story, it would mean that the image we have used before, of peasants and day-laborers at the bottom of society and animals beneath the bottom, has some literal truth. The beasts' presence also underlines the physicality of the birth. No one denies animals' physicality—in fact many people still think they are nothing but bodies—and in their midst, the story tells us, we find God-With-Us, the Holy present in flesh.

The Nose Knows

There is one aspect of this animal-shed or -cellar hiding the Holy that is seldom mentioned in poetic retellings of the Christmas story: smells. One of the inevitable functions of fleshly existence, both animal and human, is excretion; and if cleanup is delayed or nonexistent, lung-searing nasty smells there will be. For years the only exception I knew of to this understandable artistic blackout was an obscure carol entitled "The Story That Never Grows Old" which I learned in childhood and sang with my schoolmates one long-ago Christmas. The third stanza began thus:

> The world is so dull and the world is so dead
> With ribaldry, pomp, and gain

> And like the foul stable where cattle are fed,
> So life has become profane.²

In History of Religions terminology, a profane world is one from which the Holy is gone. I take the deepest meaning of these lines to be that due to spiritual numbness, the numinous Presence, the Splendor and Wonderfulness at the heart of reality which holds all things together, has been lost to view in the endless scramble for wealth and status. "Ribaldry" suggests that any tender expressions of erotic love are lost in contemptuous, pornographic joking; human sexuality is nothing but dirt. Comparing such a cultural situation to a stinking animal shed is very suggestive. Both spiritual and physical senses can give us unpleasant sensations as well as delights, and when we are faced with foul smells that seem impossible to get rid of, we are tempted to deaden our physical or spiritual senses. The unhappy result is that at the same time, we dull our capacity to experience the joys that may be closely linked to them.

Much later I encountered the same phrase in a Nativity poem by G. K. Chesterton entitled "The House of Christmas," which makes a similar point:

> ... A Child in a foul stable
> Where the beasts feed and foam,
> Only where He was homeless
> Are you and I at home;
> We have hands that fashion and heads that know,
> But our hearts we lost—how long ago!³

Manor Farm

When we look at (for-profit) animal sheds not as symbols but simply as a physical reality, their obnoxious odors have further impact. I have some peripheral experience of this reality. My siblings and I grew up on a traditional family farm that raised both animals and cash-crops, from early 1945 until 1957; I owe part of what follows to my brother Gareth, who kindly shared his memories with me. Our family ordinarily had seven or eight cows, who grazed in a field by day (except in winter) and were kept in a barn at night, to be milked by hand by my father and brother evenings and

---

2. Ackley, "Story That Never Grows Old," *Triumphant Service Songs*, 171
3. Chesterton, "House of Christmas", *Poems*, 63.

mornings. They would pour the milk into large milk-cans to be shipped to market and made into butter and cheese. Behind the open space where the cows stood, their necks held in stancheons, ran a gutter for their urine and feces, which had to be shoveled out twice daily. For a time we also raised six to eight calves, who were kept separately and whose mess my father and brother cleaned out less often. It would become tightly compacted and took herculean labor to loosen and remove.

We also had about four hundred chickens, nearly all hens, kept about a hundred to a large room in our long chicken coop. My father and brother fed them twice a day. Along one wall of each room were tiers of nesting boxes, to which the hens flew up to lay their eggs. Both floor and nests were lined with straw, which of course became foul over time. Approximately once a month or so my father and Gareth faced the job of getting rid of the Augean mess. They threw it, shovelful by shovelful, out the window, after which it all had to be moved *again*, into the manure spreader, to fertilize the fields. Then clean straw would be forked in to replace it. A month or two later the whole job had to be done over. It always seemed to take up every holiday, something that gave my brother particular delight.

They also gathered the eggs, a job at which I occasionally helped. Most of the time the hens evidently didn't mind, but periodically they would become "broody," that is, have a mind to sit on their eggs and hatch them. A broody hen would resent our stealing her babies-in-the-making, and would peck vigorously and angrily at the thieving hand reaching under her. (I devised a way to protect my hand with an unused shingle when taking her eggs.) Every afternoon my sister and I went down to our basement to face buckets full of eggs to be cased, many with caked-on feces which we had to sand off: our very own much-cherished job.

The Trap

We thought of these animals as *our* cows and *our* chickens. It never occurred to any of us that we were running a slave operation, but when one ventures to take "the view from below," i.e. from beneath the bottom, one begins to see that that is very much what it was. Our blindness to the obvious is perhaps understandable since the animals we took for granted as our property were not draft beasts, whose enforced work does look like human slave labor. But comparing the human and animal systems shows several ways that it was indeed slavery. As was the case with plantation owners in the antebellum South, "everybody"—i.e., our peers and various authorities we respected—supported us in believing that these beings were meant to be property. Another feature of our situation common to human-slave owning was that we controlled the animals' sexuality in order to appropriate what they produced. If they had reproduced and raised their offspring according to their own wills, the whole thing would soon have become even less profitable than it was, and would have spun out of our control. It was perhaps somewhat like human sexual slavery, in that most of "our" chickens were females, and all of "our" cows, but different from that system in that, to achieve such an unbalanced state of affairs, the unwanted male baby chicks and calves were killed (as is still the case in agribusiness operations today). The anger of the broody hens and the grief of the cows bereaved of their little sons (being in the barn only seldom, I was not even aware of the latter till years later) could be disregarded—or scarcely noticed—because the intentions of the owners were the only ones that mattered.

Another similarity is that like us, the keepers of human slaves were supported by pronouncements from the science of the day, and by certain biblical passages (though they had to ignore other passages). A factor even worse than most human-slave operations was that almost none of our slaves died remotely natural deaths. We killed and ate a few of the chickens and sold the rest, when their egg-producing profitability had diminished, to be killed and eaten by other humans. What else were they there for?

Green Growing Things

There were other things that were genuinely good about our farm too, which must not be ignored: a beautiful setting amid meadows, trees, and snow-topped mountains, where I sometimes felt intimations of Eden; beautiful flowering trees in springtime; my mother's flower garden and a burgeoning vegetable garden; a small orchard producing luscious apples, cherries, and plums; a big Concord grape arbor. The wind was fresh and fragrant; on cloudless nights we could see thousands of stars. We never once locked the doors of our house.

Our cash crops, strawberries, raspberries and boysenberies, were not open to the moral objections of our slave-animal operations. They too took enormous work, especially the raspberries, pruning and tying the canes in the cold air of early spring, and picking the fruit during the heat of summer "vacation." Our berries were tastier and more nutritious than the chemically-boosted ones produced by some other farms, but seldom brought us any more profit than did the animals. My father's fondness for experimenting, and his organic farming methods, were too far ahead of their time.

Taken all together, the work of the farm was so hard and overwhelming that sometimes we felt like slaves ourselves, though of course we were not—we children had access to education, and eventually all of us chose to get off the farm. Despite ten- or twelve-hour workdays by my parents, and fewer hours by us four children during the school year, our family could never climb out of debt. When we seemed close to solvency, there would be a crisis such as a drought or too much rain, a slump in the prices of eggs or berries, an increase in the prices we had to pay for feed or supplies, and we would be trapped as tightly as ever. At times my father had to take a second job, but even that didn't bring in enough. Chronic financial anxiety can take much of the joy out of life for a responsible, well-meaning person, can spark frequent verbal violence that blights lives and takes years to heal.

We became the victims of our victims in another way as well. When two family members later struggled with cancer and chemotherapy and survived, when two others suffered and died of the disease, they knew little or nothing about its roots in, among other things, the animal bodies and products we had labored so hard over, and had taken to be an essential part of the fabric of human life.

New and Improved!

Many readers will already be aware of how much worse the situation is in present-day animal-slave operations: crowded, reeking mega-sheds virtually never cleaned out, imprisoning thousands or hundreds of thousands of wretched, immobilized chickens and pigs and calves and cows with ammonia-burned lungs, never free of pain and never seeing sunshine until they are dragged out to be killed. These places dangerously pollute the air and earth and water for miles, breeding diseases that sicken and kill thousands of the animal inmates and their consumers, and may eventually mutate to kill billions of us in a deadly, global influenza pandemic. Both morally and physically, the stench of such houses of horror rises to high Heaven. Little wonder that those who consume the (often-tainted) flesh and eggs and milk coming out of this hell-world unknowingly make themselves "so dull and so dead" to it, lest they might actually awaken and smell what is going on.

It is also little wonder that to many people who care about the planet, our family's kind of small-time, ecologically responsible way of raising animals (if it can be made profitable) looks golden, the kind to which our culture should return. *It was not, and it is not.* If our farm had supported us adequately, we probably would not have suffered in the same way, but we would still have been making our hearts callous. An example of this effect can be seen in the fact that for years my father and brother engaged in hunting mostly for fun, and we females scarcely protested. Further, we would still have been closing down our awareness of the presence of the Holy in our stable; still slowly making our bodies dangerously sick; still dulling and deadening our souls in order to avoid empathizing with the animals, and to keep up the make-believe that only our human feelings and intentions existed. Whatever its size, whether or not it has laudable areas of decent treatment, *every* slave operation has the stench of death.

Still Travails the Heart

This Foul Stable, either traditional or "new and improved," is not the last word. The next line in the carol from my childhood goes "Still travails the heart in the birth of the King . . . "[4] It suggests that despite the numbness so many of us have unconsciously cultivated to evade the physical and moral stench, we are not, after all, dead: at its deepest level, the human heart is not only still living, but pregnant. Indeed, it is in labor with the Holy. Similarly, Chesterton's poem tells us that this lowliest place—of a homeless mother and newborn, of farm[ed] animals in all their fleshliness—is both the Way to the eternal home of all, to "an older place than Eden," and *is* that Home itself, if we have eyes to see.

Affirming this spiritual/artistic insight may be a pure act of faith, a Pascalian wager of sorts, but it may be more than that. Some of us have experienced the Holy for ourselves—as a Presence, as Power, as Light, as Love—either faintly or overwhelmingly, so that we *know* and can never again forget, however great the stench we smell in the Stable. Others may have heard or read stories of such encounters with the Divine, and seen their transforming power, so that faith has some basis in vicarious experience. Both may coexist.

A related possibility (or factor) is that repeated affirmation and action taken together can strengthen an uncertain faith. Telling and retelling

4. Ackley, ibid.

life-giving stories such as a Myth of the Birth of the Hero, singing or chanting songs or liturgies, creating or experiencing poetry or art depicting such traces of the Holy—by any or all of these means, we may keep in our sight a guiding star of hope that enables us to keep going. True, there is always the possibility that what we are thus envisioning is distorted, is partly or wholly illusory; that is the risk that faith takes. It is a better choice than deadening our spiritual senses and giving way to the stench of death.

Let us awaken our hearts, choose hope, and take the Adventure.

11

Save the Day!

IT MAY COME AS a surprise to some that there was a period in the nineteenth century in which the survival of Christmas in urban life was doubtful. For centuries in Europe, Christmastide had been a village celebration extending over twelve days, featuring a combination of Christian and pagan religious images, ideas, and practices, varying from place to place; relatively stable, though with slow changes. But as a result of the mass migrations to cities caused by the industrial revolution and other developments in the late eighteenth and early nineteenth centuries, many people became rootless, losing much of the extended-family and village culture that had given meaning to their lives. And Christmas observance seemed among the many elements of their past life about to erode away. In Charles Dickens' 1843 novella *A Christmas Carol*, set in such an industrial city, we see that both Bob Cratchit's notorious employer Scrooge and the milliner for whom his daughter Martha works are reluctant to give them even one full day off to celebrate—forget about twelve days. It's not good business.

Dickens' Christmas

The portrayal of Christmas in the *Carol* by those unbusinesslike people who still keep it differs significantly from the main emphases today. Gift-giving to individuals is a minor theme in the story: we see it in only one scene, in which the husband of Scrooge's former fiancée Belle comes home with toys for their children. Christmas giving centers rather on sharing one's bounty in the form of donations of food and money to help the poor; it is part and parcel of the major theme of warmth, fun, and abundance for all. Dickens' Christmas in the city means families and friends and perhaps abused apprentices from down the street gathering to play children's games, dance, feast, and sing around blazing fires that defy the darkness and the cold. Little is said explicitly about the Bethlehem stories, but the theme of the Child—vulnerable yet life-giving and joy-giving—permeates the story, whose plot climaxes with Scrooge's transformation on Christmas morning, as he turns somersaults and compares himself to a newborn baby.

Unhappily, the themes of new life, conviviality, and joy do not extend to our animal cousins, who have cameo roles as draught-slaves or unseen providers of fur trim on clothing, and "starring" roles as corpses to be devoured. The big to-do about Scrooge's anonymous gift of a giant turkey-carcass to the Cratchits—happily given and ecstatically received—is of a piece with the charnel-house array at the feet of the Ghost of Christmas Present: "[T]urkeys, geese, game, poultry, brawn, great joints of meat, sucking-pigs, long wreaths of sausages, . . . "[1] together with the festal and harmless apples, oranges, nuts, cakes, and steaming punch, are all expected to whet readers' appetites for the feast. They are more likely to create confused responses in awakened readers, who, in the midst of their applause for celebration and abundance, will shudder at these reminders of merciless violence against the defenseless. Dickens' Christmas is indeed "a good time, a kind, forgiving, charitable, pleasant time,"[2] as Scrooge's nephew says. But the bereaved goose in the movie *Babe* knows that it has another side—"Christmas means carnage!"

Death, New Life, and Animals

As familiar as the story is, its overshadowing themes of death and ghosts are not what we today tend to associate with Christmas. But the fact is that traditionally Christmastide, and Yule in the centuries before it, were seen as one of the in-between periods of the year, the boundary times (like midnight during each twenty-four hours) when the borders between worlds grew thin and porous. Both unquiet ghosts and powerful angels (and perhaps pixies, brownies, elves, elementals et al.) were close at hand, and likely to be involved in human affairs. Most humans might not see the spirits, and a few believed they didn't exist. Yet ghost stories told around

---

1. Dickens, *Christmas Carol*, 106
2. Op. Cit., 20

the fire, with accompanying shivers of fear, delight, or both, were long one of the staples of the season.

A quick survey of Christian customs of Advent and Christmastide from former centuries, and their pagan forbears, suggests not only that animal themes are persistent, but that this duality—violence and/or death on the one hand, awe and joy in the presence of Something life-giving on the other—appears in the animal theme itself. On the grim side: according to Brendan Lehane's *The Book of Christmas*, St. Martin's Day on the eleventh of November was once a time not only of bonfires, feasting, and celebrating a visit from the saint, but of killing enslaved cattle, pigs, and geese, and sometimes sprinkling their blood on the threshold of the house. In Scotland, St. Andrew's day on November thirtieth was celebrated by hunting, killing, and feasting on squirrels. One medieval Christmas practice in southern England involved a pack of young men, their faces blackened, going out with cudgels to find and kill a wren, whose feathers would be shared out among the villagers, and his or her body ceremonially buried. Ordinarily the wren was considered to be sacred, so the event, intended to bring good luck for the coming year, clearly partook of the nature of sacrifice. A distant ancestor of our benign Santa Claus with his reindeer-drawn sleigh and elves (via his equally generous grandfather, St. Nicholas on his white horse) seems to have been the Norse God Odin (to whom horses were sacrificed) on his powerful eight-legged steed. Accompanied by his hound, he led the feared Wild Hunt across the sky, drawing into itself the ghosts of the dying and dead.

But other Christmas themes presented animals as participating in an Edenic harmony that touched earth at this sacred time. A medieval legend tells of ordinary stabled animals gaining the ability to speak on Christmas Eve midnight, as they participate in the power of history's pivotal Event in the Bethlehem stable. A variant of this idea appears in scenes of forest animals, on that same night, all lying harmoniously together in a Peaceable Kingdom scene. A passage in Shakespeare's *Hamlet* gives another such picture of supernatural Christmastide wonder and power, manifesting in unusual birdsong and in ghosts and other harmful forms of magic being kept away from the living:

> Some say that ever, 'gainst that season comes
> Wherein our Saviour's birth is celebrated,
> The bird of dawning singeth all night long;
> And then, they say, no spirit dare stir abroad,

> The nights are wholesome, then no planets strike,
> No fairy takes, nor witch hath power to charm,
> So hallow'd and so gracious is the time.³

A further echo of the themes of animals, death, and spirits at Christmastide appears in Thomas Hardy's "The Darkling Thrush." The setting is a wintry landscape described in metaphors of funerals, crypts, and haunting; the narrator leans on a coppice gate at dusk on the last day of the nineteenth century (and the seventh day of Christmas).

> The ancient pulse of germ and birth
> Was shrunken hard and dry,
> And every spirit upon earth
> Seemed fervourless as I.⁴

Into this cheerless scene, apparently the opposite of the life-renewing themes of Christmastide, breaks the ecstatic song of the bird:

> At once a voice arose among
> The bleak twigs overhead
> In a full-hearted evensong
> Of joy illimited;
> An aged thrush, frail, gaunt, and small,
> In blast-beruffled plume,
> Had chosen thus to fling his soul
> Upon the growing gloom.⁵

The image of the service of Evensong calls up the Song of Mary which is part of its liturgy, a poem in Luke chapter 2 that expresses gratitude for the imminent fulfilment of God's promises through the birth of the child she is carrying. Hardy's narrator can see no reality or meaning to this ancient religious theme in the dying world around him; yet he admits that the frail bird may be singing of "Some blessed Hope whereof he knew, / And I was unaware."⁶

Thus in the Christmastide tradition we humans are simultaneously telling animals "You are beings spiritually attuned, perhaps even more deeply than we, to God's life-giving work among us," but at the same time,

---

3. Shakespeare, *Hamlet*, Act I, Scene 1
4. Hardy, in Williams, *Immortal Poems*, 452.
5. Ibid.
6. Ibid.

"You are mere things, to be crushed and devoured, in order to heighten the pleasures and the energy of the festival." Something here doesn't quite fit! In the distant past, the sacrificial element made a connection that at least had meaning, since violent sacrifice has long been thought to bring about renewal. But it is very hard to establish that this concept does indeed work—and there is much evidence that violence more often leads to psychic numbing and more violence than to new life. However, the killing of animals today is not even sacrificial, but is done out of greed and for the sake of perceived human pleasure.

To Purify Christmas

Those of us who care about animals have been trying to be heard on this issue for a considerable time, but unfortunately, our message tends to be classed with that of Christmas critics of yesteryear, specifically, Puritans, Quakers, and other seventeenth-century dissenters. They saw serious problems, such as pagan roots, carousing excesses, and immoral behavior, with Christmas celebrations; but, sadly, the bloodshed involved in the festival wasn't among their complaints. Their solution to the problems they saw was to wipe the day off their calendars altogether. Early Quakers' objections to Christmas are largely forgotten, but Puritanism is, rather unfairly, still equated with a joy-killing asceticism that defenders of flesh-eating are ready to find in the motivations of animal protectors, whether it is really there or not.

It helps if we acknowledge that their objections to our critique of Christmas probably have a deeper basis than their taste buds. Anything that sounds like an attempt to undermine a holiday, especially a religious one, is likely to awaken profound anxieties that one's roots are being cut, that the meaningfulness of one's way of life, of one's whole spiritual/cultural world, is under threat. (More about this in chapter 14, "The Sky is Falling.")

What we seek to end is, of course, not Christmas, Thanksgiving, or any other celebration, but the institution of animal slavery and killing that stains them with innocent blood. That change is even more radical, but we know that, far from destroying our way of life in the world, it would in fact help to save both our cultural world from its numbness to a vast evil, and the physical world from the ecological menace that hangs over us. Perhaps it will hasten the planet's spiritual evolution toward Peace on Earth among all the living as well. But if we are to make headway in our attempts to bring about such genuine, compassionate, life-giving change, it is important that we work to defuse people's resulting anxieties about losing holidays like Christmas and all that such celebrations mean to them. Those of us of who are Christian do well to accompany our message of a cruelty-free Christmas feast by actively affirming everything that is positive in our tradition, (while implicitly supporting, not putting down, other faiths). Unlike the many painful aspects of abolitionist work, this affirming work is a joy.

Reclaiming Christmas Treasures

The *Christmas Carol* itself offers us concrete suggestions here. The feast will always be important: vegetarianism does not mean scarcity, as many fear, but greater abundance both now and in the future, with greater aliveness and joy, at no one's expense. Furthermore, by proclaiming in action the end of its violence, abolitionists who have Christian roots are affirming the life-giving side of the Christmas animal-theme, in particular, the founding story with its beasts in the stable standing in awe around the holy Child. We are also finding unsuspected depths inherent in the angelic blessing "Peace on Earth." Our commercialized culture's unbalanced emphasis on individual gift-giving, often to people who already have all they need, can be limited by a firm spending cap. Instead we can find greater fulfilment in charitable giving—what might better be called justice-giving—which is as desperately needed now as when the *Carol* was written. Greed, callousness, exploitation, neediness, and suffering have not gone away since 1843.

But we also need to have fun, as the Cratchit family, Fred and his wife and friends, and Fezziwig and his family and protégés all did at their parties. And fun need not cost a fortune. We can try going back to playing intergenerational games, whether they be the blind-man's-buff that Fred and his friends played, musical chairs, charades, or whatever memory calls up. (At my Quaker Meeting we play such games each fall to kick off the First-Day (Sunday) school year; it's energizing and enjoyable for all ages.) If a large room is available, group dancing is a wonderful way to celebrate, and many circle dances can be quickly taught by a visiting folk dance teacher. "Sir Roger de Coverley," the line dance happily if clumsily performed at Fezziwig's ball, is easy to learn even from online instructions. Singing carols around the fire as the Cratchits did is another joyous activity—and if the party site has no fireplace, one can probably find an online fire!

Save the Day!

We have seen that the tradition of telling ghost stories is represented in the whole plot of Dickens' novella, but the *Carol* is really more an angel story. It involves Marley and other unhappy ghosts, to be sure, but focuses on the three powerful, angel-like Ghosts of Christmas Past, Present, and Yet to Come, who all (even the fearsome third one) appear with the compassionate purpose of offering a life-transformation to Scrooge. This story-telling element can be be revived by having some of those in the party tell present-day angel stories, of which many have become available, both in print and online, in recent years. Those present may be pleasantly surprised to find that one or another of the guests have their own personal angel story to share.

Bringing new life to these old forms of merrymaking is important not only for the sake of an effective message on behalf of the animals, but for our own sakes as well. To celebrate the gifts of light and warmth and plenty in the (northern hemisphere's) darkest and coldest time of the year can awaken the Joy that is greater than any happiness in this life: "Joy beyond the walls of the world, poignant as grief."[7] It denies final defeat and death, rejoicing that new life from Elsewhere is brought into the here and now.

---

7. Tolkien, "On Fairy-Stories" in *Monsters and Critics*, 153.

12

The Animals Are Waiting

THE IMAGE OF THE "Peaceable Kingdom" scene in chapter 11 of Isaiah is loved by many. For readers who are not very familiar with the Biblical passage, it may be helpful to quote it:

> The wolf will live with the lamb;
> the leopard will lie down with the young goat.
> The calf and the lion will graze together,
> and a little child will lead them.
> The cow and the bear will graze,
> and their young will lie down together,
> and the lion will eat straw [hay] like the ox.
> The nursing child will play
> over the hole of the cobra,
> and the weaned child will put his hand on vipers' dens.
> They will neither harm nor destroy
> on my holy mountain;
> for the earth will be full
> of the knowledge of the LORD,
> as the waters cover the sea.[1]

The scene has often been portrayed by artists, not least Fritz Eichenberg, the German-American refugee from Nazism; other favorite renditions are those of William Strutt, 1896, and the many versions of Edward Hicks early in the nineteenth century.

---

1. Isa.11: 6–9, ISV

Peace Beyond the Walls of the World?

The Peaceable Kingdom image is a moving one. Its appeal has not diminished in the twenty-five hundred years since the prophet Isaiah formulated it, suggesting that it expresses a deep truth about ultimate reality, a state of peace beyond our space-and-time world that has been cursed by predation and violence for thousands of years even before humans appeared. There have long been intimations that it describes something real. Mystics and Near-Death experiencers (NDErs) have spoken of entering a transcendent peace and unity in which they knew all reality as one, and that one, good. An NDEr, actor Jayne Smith, felt this unity from the inside when she approached death during childbirth in 1952:

> This enormously bright light seemed almost to cradle me. I just seemed to . . . be part of it and be nurtured by it and the feeling just became more and more and more ecstatic and glorious and perfect . . . I knew that everything, everywhere in the universe was OK, that the plan was perfect. That . . . the wars, famine, whatever . . . it was all a part of the perfection . . . nothing could happen to you and you're home forever. That you're safe forever. And that everybody else was.[2]

In his *Varieties of Religious Experience*, William James summarizes this state: "It is as if the opposites of the world, whose contradictoriness and conflict make all our difficulties and troubles, were melted into unity" as we saw in chapter 6, "Neither Wickedness Nor Sorrow."

But what good does this deep truth encountered by mystics and visionaries do for the animals who are suffering and dying, both in the course of nature and as a result of human callousness and cruelty? They cannot count on having transcendent experiences which will lessen their anguish, their sense of something terribly unjust inflicted on them now; they want desperately to live, to be free and free of pain, and to be with their own families in this world. Thus, however profoundly true the message of such mystical experiences is, our knowing of them cannot release us from the prophetic imperative to denounce violence and work toward peace and healing for all. (In fact mystics and those who have Near-Death experiences themselves tend to become active workers toward the healing of the world.)

---

2. Ring, *Omega*, 62

Taking the Adventure

Thy Kingdom Come

Actually, the Isaiah text does not present the scene as eternal, but as something that is going to happen; its verbs are in the future tense. "The wolf *will* live with the lamb ... the lion *will* eat straw [hay] like the ox ... a little child *will* lead them." (Emphasis added) In Romans chapter 8, Paul of Tarsus also envisions such a cosmic transformation as a coming event: "the creation looks forward to the day when it will join God's children in glorious freedom from death and decay."[3] In both passages, human beings lead the way, making it possible for animals to attain this divine peace and fulfillment.

Unhappily, there are no clear signs that the great day is approaching. The natural evil of predator attacking prey has not diminished; the moral evil of human attacking animal, especially for the table, has increased hugely in numbers and, in the last fifty years, descended ever lower in mass depravity. There is no need to repeat the all-too-familiar statistics of victims running into billions. Why then do we continue to hope for and expect the Peaceable Kingdom? For it is not only evangelical Christians and literally-inclined Jews who look to see it realized. Occasionally other people of faith, some influenced by the concept of spiritual evolution, have included animals in their hope that, as Edmund Sears expressed it in his 1849 carol,

> ... the days are hastening on
> By prophet bards foretold,
> When with the ever-circling years
> Comes round the age of gold;
> When peace shall over all the earth
> Its ancient splendors fling ... [4]

In her travel book *Look a Lion in the Eye*, Kathryn Hulme tells how while observing African rhinos on her photographic safari, she suddenly remembered a saying of G. I. Gurdjieff, and understood how it helped explain what she had been seeing throughout the safari:

> "*The animals are waiting for us to move up so they can follow*" ...
> This was the answer I had been unconsciously groping for ever since my first confrontation with Africa's wildlife. This surely was why the animals' long, slow stares had been so deeply affecting to me ... With their great, bifocal eyes they took us in, unaware that

---

3. Rom. 8:21 NLT
4. Sears, "It Came Upon the Midnight Clear," *The Cyber Hymnal*.

they were waiting for us to 'move up' that ladder that Jacob saw in his dream, thronged with angels moving up and down . . . "[5]

If such a process of spiritual evolution is indeed taking place, what might its nature be? Hulme speaks of it as occurring by the "immutable laws of evolution and involution," which suggests that the change will come about inevitably, whatever we do as individuals, groups, or humanity as a whole. Or might its nature perhaps be at least partly conditional, hastened by positive moral and spiritual developments in humanity, or slowed by massive evils? It is of course very difficult to speak with certainty about such a little-known matter, which if real is so much vaster than the scope of our view, whether we think in terms of decades, centuries, or millenia.

Hastening the Day?

Of the various positive human actions that might in fact hasten the process, one that has been put forward is meditation and contemplative prayer, especially when many persons unite in these practices. Reclusive mystics from the major religious traditions who engage extensively in meditation or contemplation have sometimes claimed that despite their generally retired manner of living, they are influencing the world for the better. As with the issue of the effectiveness of prayer overall, certainty on this issue has been elusive. But the social sciences may come to our aid. Since the mid-1970s there has been a long series of experiments in Transcendental Meditation (TM) groups, which strongly indicate that violence does in fact decrease, and movement in the direction of peace and understanding increase (among humans) during the weeks in which large numbers of experienced meditators meet together daily to practice in specific cities. For example: many meditators gathered in Washington, D.C. during June and July 1993, increasing in number over four weeks until they reached 4,000. Over the same period, violent crime against persons decreased as the number of meditators increased, until it was 23 percent less than the average for June and July during the preceding five years. (Other variables were controlled.) Afterwards the level of crime returned to its usual rates.

An earlier experiment with fewer meditators was carried out in Providence, Rhode Island, in June of 1978. According to figures cited in *The Maharishi Effect*, statistics for a number of social ills, including

---

5. Hulme, *Look a Lion in the Eye*, 197–98, emphasis in original.

suicide, homicide, robbery, and traffic deaths, changed markedly for the better (other variables being controlled), though they went back to their usual rates after the meditators decamped. These are only two instances of a considerable number of such experiments. It certainly does look as though during the time that many people gather and jointly cultivate unity with the Ultimate, whether understood as God, the Ground of Being, or the All, some other people in the area become more peaceful. It should also be noted that many people who practice Transcendental Meditation are vegetarians.

But does it reduce violence among animals? I admit that I know of no studies of the effects of these group meditation experiments on the levels of predation among animals, say wild omnivores such as bears. But because there are signs that all the living are linked in many ways, it seems quite possible. It would be promising if omnivores in fact do less killing during periods when many meditators are practicing nearby, as might be determined, e.g., by testing the feces of bears in a given area when both plant and animal food are abundant. If such tests show that the bears are eating measurably more plants and fewer animals when increasing numbers of people nearby take up meditation or contemplative prayer, the idea that such spiritual practices promote overall spiritual evolution would be strengthened. And, since the TM experiments were all short-term, longer studies would be needed as well.

Anything like proof that the Peaceable Kingdom is coming nearer, or that we can hasten it by nonviolent living and the practice of meditation or contemplative prayer as well as political and social action, is still elusive. The TM experiments cited above strongly suggest that such meditation (and probably contemplation) has real power at the time to reduce crime and other social evils. But for now we remain dependent on the visions of mystics, the intuitive gleams of poets, the promises of ancient prophets.

And the animals are still waiting.

13

Wound Round With Mercy

> ... I say that we are wound
> With mercy round and round
> As if with air ... [1]

Intimations of Divine Love

EVERY NURSING MOTHER KNOWS what it is like to be dragged out of desperately-needed sleep, night after night, by insistent crying. Poet Faith Bowman was no exception. The received wisdom of the time made matters harder by forbidding the comforting, common-sense practice of having the baby sleep in the mother's bed, so there was nothing for it but to half-fall out of bed and stumble in the general direction of the nursery. One particular night seemed to be only more of the usual; she remembered being so exhausted that she grazed the doorway on her way in. Picking up the baby, she had no more than seated herself and settled into the familiar nursing routine when the heavens opened: exhaustion was swept away by a flood of unutterable joy and power and love. She became aware of an everywhere-present Divine Mother nurturing all beings in the world, cradling them with infinite tenderness; furthermore, she knew that she was in the midst of this vast process, as though she herself were enthroned on the lap of the Goddess, both receiving abundant Divine Life and giving it to her baby. She found herself murmuring ecstatically "I feel like a goddess! I feel like a goddess!"

The person who undergoes such an experience does not doubt its truth to reality as it is happening, and for some time afterwards. Unless

---

1. Hopkins, "Blessed Virgin Compared to the Air," *Poems of Hopkins*, 55,

she or he has experiences of this sort repeatedly (and Ms. Bowman had several), however, its powerful impact on her consciousness may diminish over time. On the other hand, if she reflects upon it often, reaffirming her first conviction of its truth, exploring its meaning, and acting upon its implications, it may come to shape the entire course of her life.

Darkness and Cold

But what of those who never have such a life-giving experience, or have numinous experiences that seem to give quite a different message? As William James remarks, a mystical experience is "absolutely authoritative" for the one who has it, but not necessarily for others.[2] One can point out that there are all too many facts that seem utterly incompatible with Bowman's sense of the presence of an all-nurturing Divine Mother. To give just one example: it is estimated that in eighteenth-century London, a thousand newborn infants were abandoned on the streets every year by desperate unwed lower-class mothers unable to support them, mothers who were either prostitutes or "fallen" gentry women abandoned by lovers whom society excused from taking responsibility. A parallel situation can be found in the ancient Roman world; according to law, the paterfamilias had the right to decree that any newborn (usually a girl) he chose not to accept must be thrown out, exposed. (The abandoned babies were sometimes "rescued" by slave traders.) How can one say that these innocents, dying of cold, starvation, and fear, were nurtured by an all-loving and all-giving Divine Mother? The idea seems utter nonsense.

Readers who care about animals as well will think of the millions of terrified baby animals, especially newborn male calves, torn from their anguished, screaming mothers and shipped to miserable confinement and violent death, in order to include dairy on the overloaded tables at which sit unthinking and (often) unhealthy human beings. The human mind cannot comprehend how an all-nurturing Deity can be any part of this dreadful picture. The honest mind faces contradiction; Mystical insight is stopped by Mystery.

This conflict between faith in the embrace of the divine Mother and the suffering of little victims of callous institutions is, of course, only one strand of the problem of evil that has bedeviled people who take seriously both religious/mystical intuitions and painful facts. Since the reality of the

2. James, *Varieties*, 414.

intuitions is so much harder to establish publicly than the historical facts that evidently contradict it, why should those who do not have the intuitions trouble themselves with what they imply?

"Is the Universe Friendly?"

One answer has to do with the way our worldview tends to influence us in our efforts to heal the world, especially when we work for years and seem to make little progress. Before unpacking this statement, I must acknowledge that there are some people who would answer William James' question "Is the universe friendly?" with a firm *"No"*—they believe there is no unseen Love that cares for us all—but who nonetheless devote their energies to awakening that world and making it a kinder and friendlier place. Such a one was philosopher Bertrand Russell, who in his essay "A Free Man's Worship" describes the universe as being, according to the testimony of Science, a pitiless place in which every person, with his hopes, ideals, and dreams, is ultimately extinguished by Death. Nonetheless, he exhorts readers to transcend despair and choose to bring what light and warmth they can into the world. "Be it ours to shed sunshine on [our comrades'] path, to lighten their sorrows by the balm of sympathy, to give them the pure joy of a never-tiring affection, to strengthen failing courage, to instil faith in hours of despair. Let us not weigh in grudging scales their merits and demerits, but let us think only of their need. . ."[3] Russell, though a far from perfect person, took his own advice, and gave his support to causes of justice and peace, both by word and deed, sometimes at considerable cost to himself.

I suspect that such admirable folk are exceptions, however—that most of those who work in some way to help repair and heal the world are motivated by a conviction that by doing so *they are attuning their lives and their surroundings to ultimate Reality*. Depending on their worldview, typically Eastern or typically Western, they may feel they are helping to realize a Oneness that underlies all things despite multiple conflicts and contradictions; or that they are heeding the mandate to be compassionate as their all-mothering and all-fathering God is compassionate. In Quaker language, which has something of both Eastern and Western outlooks, they are opening their hearts and hands to the divine Light that is Love which is present in every person, or even every being.

3. Russell, "Free Man's Worship," Bertrand Russell Society.

Taking the Adventure

I suspect that it is when their efforts to bring about transformation and healing are repeatedly blocked that the importance of this faith in the deep "Friendliness" of the universe, of ultimate Reality, comes into fullest play. I think it is a rare activist who can sustain the doggedness necessary for a long struggle without a sense that we humans are ourselves being sustained in the work of transformation—that Love transcends our individual efforts to realize love.

The Lost and the Foundlings

To return to the abandoned babies of London: according to Gillian Pugh's book *London's Forgotten Children*, in 1719 one Thomas Coram, an Englishman who had had a successful career in the American colonies and at sea, came back to England to retire. His expectations of enjoying the good life were brought up short by the horrifying scenes of dead and dying babies that he saw as he walked filthy London streets on a frigid winter morning. A man of action as well as compassion, Coram set about establishing an organization to rescue such victims. There was much accumulated wealth in the hands of the middle and upper classes, and he hoped to reach their hearts for his project.

To us today, this seems the sort of plan everyone would approve. But Coram ran into resistance, ugly, deep-seated, and tenacious, from men who found the project threatening to their privileges and to social ideology. The gist of it was: these babies were, were, after all, only *bastards*! To make provision for them would be to break down the safeguards of female purity; it would encourage young women to a life of vice. There was no equivalent anxiety about male purity, needless to say. Some critics dismissed the whole thing with cynical and amused speculations about Coram's motivations. No doubt he had himself taken many a tumble in the hay, said one wag, and now wanted to salve his tender conscience about the results.

Coram must have been hurt and outraged by such callous reactions, but he did not let it defeat him. He worked with an adamantine persistence, year after year, helped by artist William Hogarth and others. One of the strategies they developed was to appeal directly to wealthy women, including the Queen Caroline, consort of George II, who became concerned and wrote a pamphlet on the subject. Another was to garner the support of painters and musicians. In 1739, after about twenty thousand more such deaths of innocents, a milestone was passed: the seventy-one-year-old

Coram and his colleagues were granted a royal charter to build an orphanage, or "Foundling Hospital." Years of fundraising, building, and other work still lay ahead, but the doors of the Hospital's first structure opened in March, 1741. The directors of the Hospital were themselves not free of class prejudice, and its scope was limited; it could take in fewer than half of the infants abandoned in London each year. But it was a beginning, a presence, an influence on the mind and heart of English society. (The Hospital closed its doors early in the twentieth century, but in its present form, called the Coram Family, it still supports families with children at risk.)

"Blessed Are They . . ."

I have not been able to learn whether Thomas Coram was sustained in his years of heroic labor by faith in Divine compassion, or whether, like Russell, he perceived himself as kindling light and warmth in an ultimately dark and cold universe. But there is no doubt that some of his supporters had such faith. One was the composer George Frideric Handel, not a saint, but a large-hearted, compassionate man who donated an organ to the Hospital's chapel and wrote a suite of inspired anthems based on psalms for the chapel's dedication. The texts situated the Hospital's work firmly in the context of the Jewish and Christian vision of God's love for the lowest and least. An example is the anthem "Blessed are They" based on Psalm 41, "Blessed is he that considereth the poor: the LORD will deliver him in time of trouble,"[4] with the ones delivered in time of trouble perhaps referring, in listeners' minds, both to the Hospital's founders and donors, and the rescued babies. Handel also gave a benefit performance of *Messiah* every year, garnering, over nearly a decade, about a million dollars in today's money for the Hospital (and assuring immortality for his oratorio). No doubt a good number of those who attended were worldlings whose conscious interest was only in enjoying Mr. Handel's delicious music. But there were probably some listeners, genuinely devout, who connected its central section on the birth of the poverty-stricken Divine Child with the foundling babies. Perhaps some of them also linked the aria "He Was Despised" with the contempt that had so long surrounded "bastards."

The problem of how all-embracing Divine Love can coexist with a situation in which thousands and millions of innocent humans and animals continue to be victimized by ignorance or callous resistance to compassion

---

4. Ps. 41:1, KJV.

Taking the Adventure

is, of course, still unresolved. But a willingness to live with the Mystery, and continue to affirm the ultimate reality of unseen Love, can empower us to persist in the face of inertia and blind opposition. In the bleak midwinter, it can help us bring that love to earth.

Peace on Earth, good will to all.

14

The Sky is Falling

East Meets West

PEARL S. BUCK'S 1930 novel *East Wind: West Wind* tells the story of a wealthy, aristocratic Chinese family which is being profoundly shaken by Western influences. Proud of its ancient lineage, the family is a rigidly hierarchical community, with separate men's and women's quarters: the head wife or First Lady presides over the women's sphere of concubines and female servants and slaves, together with the small children and older girls of each; the husband and lord rules the men's sphere of older sons and male servants and slaves.

Kwei-lan, the story's narrator and a daughter of the First Lady and her lord, is married at age seventeen to the man to whom she has been betrothed all her life, leaving her family and home to join his. She is confused and distressed when her new husband, who has returned from several years in the United States with a degree in medicine, asks her to unbind her painfully-achieved tiny feet in which she took such pride. However, trained to please and obey him, she decides to comply, undergoing the original pain all over again. Other disorienting changes take place, such as his insistence that they move out of his parents' house into their own home because of his mother's contemptuous treatment of Kwei-lan, something the girl was trained never to complain about and thus had accepted. These events make her anxious, for she feels they must displease the gods.

But over time, Kwei-lan finds herself liking her stronger feet and increased liberty, and begins to take an interest in the Western science that so absorbs her physician husband. She learns that China, the Middle

Taking the Adventure

Kingdom, is not as she was taught, the center of the world, but one country among many. As she learns, she begins to experience a greater closeness with her spouse than her parents ever knew. Before long they have a son, their pride and joy. Her husband refuses to hand the child over to his parents as expected—another boon of Kwei-lan's new liberty.

But much more seismic changes come when Kwei-lan's elder brother, the family's idolized heir, comes back from his studies in the United States refusing to marry his betrothed, who is a stranger to him, and bringing a Western woman named Mary whom he insists is already his wife, and dearly loved. His mother is enraged and refuses to accept the "barbarian." His father, an irresponsible hedonist, seems to find Mary interesting and amusing. But when pressed, he finally tells his son to send his toy back to her country and do his duty to the family. A dreadful scene takes place between mother and son, with the son disowning his family. Because Kwei-lan loves her mother she is deeply distressed and tries to give comfort, but the First Lady disregards her completely. Not long afterwards the mother dies, apparently from grief and trauma. Kwei-lan is the only one who really mourns her. But in time, as Kwei-lan builds a friendship with her brother and Mary as well as her own husband, she is increasingly consoled and fulfilled.

Readers will find it difficult to understand Kwei-lan's filial love or to sympathize with the First Lady, who is proud, dictatorial, rigid, and contemptuously xenophobic, caring little for her daughter, seemingly caring only for her cherished son. But it turns out that she has no interest in whether he is happy and fulfilled, wanting only that he should submit, carry out his duty, and produce a legally recognized grandson.

At one point, however, we get a glimpse into her soul: we see the deep wound her husband's neglect of her and sexual self-indulgence elsewhere, sanctioned by the culture, have caused. Because she rejects the affection of the one person who cares for her, her inner life is loveless, held together only by empty rewards: the commanding status of First Lady, the long-awaited return of the idolized son, and the deeply rooted hope for a proper grandson from him. But when her son rejects her keystone value, and she loses both son and longed-for grandson at once, she lacks the courage and breadth of soul to look beyond the unbalanced values she has always lived by. Her sky falls, and she lets it crush her.

The Sacred Canopy

This story of events in an alien time and culture has resonance to changes in our world today, and particularly to our movement on behalf of animals. Sociologists of religion have pointed out that religion presides over two conflicting cultural processes: the shaping and support of conventional structures of meaning (the Establishment), and the critique of oppressive structures of meaning, accompanied by a call for their transformation. Its function of supporting the status quo is highly visible, but the critique of oppression, unfortunately, is not often seen.

Peter Berger, whose book *The Sacred Canopy* emphasizes the structure-supporting aspect of religion, points out that meaningfulness is vital to humanness. We need to live in a world that makes sense, that has convincing values, a world where some actions are good and others are bad. Examples: most people hold that cherishing one's children is good, abusing and killing them is bad. In the Confucian culture of the novel's family, obeying one's parents and honoring one's family are good; disregarding both for personal benefits is bad. Similarly, in every culture some things are of greater value and other things of lesser or negative value: diamonds are beautiful and valuable, while equally beautiful soap bubbles are worthless; humans (at least some of them) are valuable, most animals are disposable. In the world of traditional China, males are of vastly greater value than females, with the female infants of slaves even being disposable. Traditional religion undergirds such worldviews. The king rules by the grace of God; the emperor rules by the mandate of Heaven; the priests control access to the divine.

We human beings acting together create our worlds of values, however obviously external they may seem. The term "canopy" in the title of Berger's book is used in the metaphorical sense of the overarching sky, and beyond that, the conception of Heaven/Deity who authorizes the whole cultural setup. Because it is a human creation, the world of values is subject to change and disintegration, and must be continually renewed by our conversations, namely, our reaffirming language and actions. And, in turn, that which we shape shapes us, our values, our intentions, and our actions.

Taking the Adventure

Collapse of the Canopy

Humans can deal with the limited modification of these values that are occurring most of the time; in fact some adventurous personalities welcome change, whereas others resist most changes. The young tend to be more open than the old. But very few can deal with the permanent disintegration of the central structures of their world, even if it is an oppressive world; the soul sickens and withers. This usually happens to a whole culture when it is overridden by a very different culture, as, for example, Native American cultures when crushed by the European/American invasion. Of those who survive the massive physical violence, some individuals will quickly take refuge in the new worldview ("If you can't lick 'em, join 'em"); but many sink into *anomie*, loss of meaning, which manifests in depression, poor health, and widespread alcoholism or other addictions.

But this kind of whole-culture catastrophe is not the only way in which the sacred canopy falls; there is also a kind of internal anomie that can result from less drastic but still substantial changes. When a growing minority (especially if it involves someone important to us) systematically overturns only one or two of our culture's major values by word and deed—even if their new view is lifegiving—deep shudders of anxiety rippling outward may be felt, harder to deal with for being poorly understood.

Some examples: the Darwinian theory of evolution and new forms of biblical scholarship had this effect on thousands of Protestant Christians in the nineteenth and early twentieth centuries. The changes in liturgy and practice in the Roman Catholic church sparked by the second Vatican Council of the 1960s had a similar effect on many Catholics. In both cases some persons benefited, finding the changes liberating; some maintained their old faith-world by refusing to listen to any questioning or critique of it, and taking refuge in a fundamentalist type of rigidity. But others had to endure the sickening fall of their sky.

One cannot always predict which values will be the crucial ones triggering internal anomie for a given person. Confusingly, even some who worked for and welcomed a liberating change may later experience the collapse. For example, there are Catholic clergy and nuns who rejoiced in the "opening of the windows" in their church in the 1960s, affirmed their value as individuals open to the divine Spirit, and joyfully expanded their compassionate work on behalf of humanity—but who later lost their faith. Clearly, there is much about human nature that still makes no sense by our present understanding.

In light of all this, it is helpful for us who are animal advocates or supporters to realize the extent of the threat that our message may represent to many in the audience we seek to reach. If we see resistance only as stemming from people's selfish clinging to favorite foods, we will be tempted to judgmentalism: how can they be caring or even decent people if for so trivial a reason they continue to support such a horrifyingly evil system? But it may well be that they are sensing the approach of the worldquake that might result for them if they unstopped their ears. Of course that does not excuse them from choosing continued numbness and violence over awakening and compassion. But it helps us to know what they are up against; and it may help us reassure them from our own experience.

A Sky Beyond

There is good news for those who courageously let go of their sky, climb out from under the broken pieces, and welcome a new world, yet later find that the change leads to psycho-spiritual catastrophe: anomie is not necessarily fatal to the soul. One can recover. *Those who lose their faith can regain it, finding a far wider sky stretched beyond and above the fallen canopy.* (Peter Berger affirms such a sky in his later book *A Rumor of Angels*.) To pursue two of the previous examples: some Native Americans have re-appropriated themes from their tradition, such as deep human interdependence with the earth and Nature, and combined them with concepts from Western spirituality and ecology, thus gaining the blessing of a renewed worldview richer than either world was before. Some literalist Protestants of the nineteenth and twentieth centuries who found themselves derelict on a desert of meaninglessness after losing a God who dictated the Bible word-for-word have gained a vastly larger (if also more elusive) God in a immensely larger world.

One particularly wise example can be find in the work of Victorian novelist George Eliot, who, as Mary Ann Evans, herself underwent the disaster of loss of faith, and dealt with many aspects of the issue in her writings. *Silas Marner*, cited above, tells of the eponymous hero's loss of faith thanks to a personal catastrophe that befalls him after his best friend frames him for a crime. His narrow, simple religious faith had led him to believe that God would immediately clear him through the church authorities' casting of lots. But the lots declare him guilty; his faith in a God of truth and love disintegrates. Interestingly, he does not conclude that there is no God, but rather that God is a liar and betrayer of the innocent.

Taking the Adventure

Silas endures fifteen years of anomie, of spiritual darkness and drought, clinging to an idol, his growing hoard of gold guineas. His despair grows even deeper when he loses even his idol in another theft. But he regains his faith in a loving Providence as a result of an apparently chance happening and a decision. One snowy night during Christmastide a motherless child toddles into his hut. The other villagers assume that the little girl will be taken to the poorhouse, but Silas, who finds himself believing that she was Sent to him out of the mysterious Somewhere into which his gold coins had disappeared, responds by impulsively deciding to keep her. He becomes her father and mother; as a result, his benumbed soul comes back to life and to love.

Those of us upon whom a once-trusted canopy has fallen can choose to heed "rumors of angels," can choose to reinterpret our lives with faith in Unseen Love as Silas Marner did, and to act with corresponding love to others, both humans and animals. These choices will help us to become whole persons once again in a human-friendly world, under a sacred canopy made by human minds, but also made by That which is beyond human minds.

15

To Seek the Bright Enchanted Gold

Enchantment

WHAT IS ENCHANTMENT, AND why does it draw so many people? What are its effects on those who are caught up in it?

We can find profound insights in J. R. R. Tolkien's children's novel *The Hobbit*. The enchantment that pervades Tolkien's Middle Earth is concentrated in particular places and objects, especially the One Ring and the other Great Rings. Such magical objects often have as their ground metal and stone, especially gold and rough gems, that are formed into things of beauty and power by metalsmiths and gemcutters skillful of hand and learned in the lore of magic. Of the various races, or rather rational species, of Middle Earth, dwarves are particularly involved in the crafts of creating beautiful objects of metal and gems. They have a deep love for their golden treasures, a love that is at once sensitive appreciation of beauty, and a susceptibility to greed, that deadly virus which leads to discord and destruction. Greed has been called the root of all evil; it is certainly a profound root of systemic evils done to vulnerable animals, human or otherwise. But the enchantment closely linked to greed can also lead to refreshment for the soul, refreshment which can sustain us in our quest for justice and freedom for our animal cousins.

The Antipodes

What is it about gold and worked gems—singularly useless things from a practical point of view—which gives them so magnetic a power in Middle

Earth, and in our own world as well? Aldous Huxley suggests, in his essay "Heaven and Hell," that gems give us some access to a region of consciousness he calls the "antipodes of the mind." This realm is far from the familiar everyday mindset in which we jockey to get ahead, rush about, worry, or suffer defeat or boredom. In the visionary world of the antipodes, *being* matters more than *doing*. Things exist for their own sakes, beautiful and wonderful and precious. They may glow with an inner light; they arouse awe. These qualities apply not only to exquisite crafted objects but to living things: flowers, fruit, animals, human beings, nature spirits, angels. To see or sense them is to be rapt, to be in love while one is gazing.

Churches and temples may seek to awaken worshippers to this dimension of Reality by employing stained-glass, gold, gems, burnished chalices, flames atop gleaming candlesticks in a vast and dim interior. Verbal pictures of heaven or the afterlife in different religions may be similar: a gardenlike Western Paradise in one strand of Buddhism, complete with trees bearing gems and marvelous bird music, or a New Jerusalem with gates of pearl, foundations of gems, and streets of gold in the last book of the Christian scriptures. Story, art, and life shape one another; many Near-Death Experiencers (NDErs) tell of having been in a city with gleaming streets, or of strolling through paradisal gardens with flowers, trees, and grass of luminous beauty, inhabited by happy animals, marvelous human or angelic figures radiating love.

These returnees also tell us that the region of the antipodes is not limited to another world; it is also right here, in our familiar world. Mystics and Near-Death experiencers often are enchanted by ordinary things. They now stop to smell the flowers and rejoice in the grass and the sky and the birdsong, rather than rushing through the world as they did when they were unawakened to its splendor. Now they care about ordinary people, including strangers, rather than being oblivious to them or wanting to make use of them. To their opened eyes, the world is full of wonders.

The Treasure and the Dragon

The golden and begemmed treasures that Tolkien's dwarves created and love with such passion symbolize this supernal splendor that fills the world; it is invisible to most of us, yet we seem to hunger for it. In crafted gold objects or even just raw gold, in the gleam of jewels, in flames, and in other luminous things, the Splendor is closer to the surface of our world, and more accessible to ordinary vision. We can almost touch this Glory; we think we can own it. Some wealthy people are willing to pay huge sums to be able to call a piece of jewelry such as a multi-diamond and gold necklace or a ruby tiara their own property. Ironically, such costly jewelry may lie unseen in a bank vault most of the time, and the owner may even have a cheaper copy of it made which she wears to important events. The reason, of course, is that its astronomical price-tag attracts thieves and robbers willing to put their greed into violent action.

Not only in *The Hobbit,* but in many tales and legends of European origin, this hunger for the Divine Splendor which attaches itself to a particular treasured item—*and* arouses the consuming fire of greed—is represented by a dragon. In Tolkien's story, long ago the dragon Smaug had heard stories about the vast treasures the dwarves had mined, created and amassed in their cavern-city under the Lonely Mountain. He flew down breathing fire, killing many people in the nearby town of Dale, as well as many of the dwarves in their underground halls, and claimed the treasure as his own. He could not use it, nor really enjoy it, and certainly could not have the happiness of giving or sharing any part of it; he simply heaped it up and lay on it, reveling in Ownership, ready to blast and set afire any rival claimants.

At the extended climax of *The Hobbit,* as the dwarves and Bilbo work to outwit the dragon and regain the treasure, we see the power of consuming greed appearing not only as the huge, fire-breathing reptile on his hoard, but in the hearts of some of the dwarves themselves. The people of Lake-Town not far away, who had helped the dwarves when they first came and later suffered crippling damage by the dragon, ask for a share of the treasure to rebuild burned houses and public facilities, a reasonable and urgent request because winter was already settling in. But the leading Dwarf Thorin and his loyalists let their intense love for their golden treasure turn into the ferocious possessiveness that will fight and kill rather than share, even with those to whom they owe a debt.

Determined to Find El Dorado

In our own world, countries that conquer other peoples are often motivated in a major way by dragon-greed. Sometimes this has been a literal lust for gold: Smaug swept down on Central and South America in the sixteenth century and beyond, his flaming breath destroying millions of human beings, both deliberately and with casual half-awareness, as he amassed his

Taking the Adventure

hoard of gold and emeralds. In other instances, empire builders have sought to acquire wealth in other products: fine fabrics, bananas, oil, land, or what have you, usually with similar costs to the expendable human beings born in the wrong place at the wrong time.

In such cases the link to actual gold and gems may seem quite tenuous, but, interestingly, the image of gold continues to be applied to such objects of greed, both for individuals and for groups. In Dickens' *Christmas Carol*, when the young Scrooge's fiancée ends their relationship, she says sadly, "Another idol has replaced me . . . A golden one," although the restless, ambitious Scrooge was probably not literally heaping up golden guineas, but boosting the figures in his bank book. Similarly, we speak of plutocrats as following their own "Golden Rule"—"Those with the gold make the rules"—although much of the time the wealth of the "1 percent" is in even more abstract form, blips on computer screens, winging electronically around the world. Nonetheless, it is still transformable into luxury objects: yachts and cruises, beautiful homes (one political figure couldn't recall how many he had!), extravagantly-priced cars and clothes, as well as lustrous golden and begemmed jewelry.

Another crucial common factor is the psychological state of mind of those driven to amass gold, real or virtual. It is often imaged by a thirst or hunger that cannot be satisfied, however great the heap, however astronomical the computer figures. In accordance with this observation, it is rare for obscenely wealthy people to give in proportion to their worth; their seemingly lavish donations to charitable causes are in most cases miniscule when compared to their total worth. It has been claimed that a major reason for this disparity is that wealth also means power; and those hungry for power cannot get enough, either. The villain in *The Hobbit* is akin to that of the power-mad Sauron in *The Lord of the Rings*: Smaug and Sauron are siblings.

Does not a never-satisfied craving for gold, or "gold," suggest that the true object of such desire is also infinite? Might it not be the enchanting Splendor of the divine Presence throughout the universe?

There's Gold In Them There Factory Farms

Not only are most super-wealthy people reluctant to give in proportion to what they possess, most whose enterprises are based on exploitation ferociously resist any reforms, however modest, that might diminish their ill-gotten gains by easing the suffering of their victims. This is hardly news to those of us who find ourselves pitted against animal agriculture's various campaigns: campaigns to silence those pointing out dangers in their products such as state "food libel" laws; campaigns to defeat state referendums intended to end caging; campaigns to criminalize undercover investigations of cruelty; and, perhaps even more horribly, a campaign against a state law requiring the euthanizing of "downer" animals. (The last-named campaign ended in tragic success when the US Supreme Court unanimously voted in favor of the National Meat Association, and against a California law that had been enacted as a result of the airing of a Humane Society video documenting slaughterhell horrors.) The profits from slaughtering downed animals are a relatively small part of the meat moguls' total, but they are very unwilling to lose that small part; they are determined to continue to torture those of their victims in the very worst anguish in order to wring out every cent of profit.

Readers of *The Hobbit* will remember that Smaug behaved similarly when he realized that an intruder had removed one cup from his mountainous heap of treasure:

> "Thieves! Fire! Murder!" Such a thing had not happened since first he came to the Mountain! His rage passed description—the sort of rage that is only seen when rich folk that have more than they can enjoy suddenly lose something that they have long had but have never before used or wanted. His fire belched forth, the hall smoked, he shook the mountain-roots . . ."[1]

Unable to find and incinerate the actual "thief," namely, Bilbo acting on behalf of the dwarves reclaiming their own, he turns his rage on the people of Lake-Town who had helped the dwarves; he intends to set the town afire and burn alive everyone in it. The reason behind this reaction of sadistic violence is not only infinite greed; it is that those burning with dragon-fever fear a slippery slope. One reform may lead to another, until they are left with an income that is no longer gargantuan and ever-growing, but diminishing until it is merely large. To their mind, such a situation would mean powerlessness, defeat, beggary: infinite loss.

But the dragon-fevered really do not know themselves; nor do they always think clearly. When Smaug swept down to vent his rage on the Lake-people, he did not know about a certain vulnerable spot on his underside. He also reckoned without the valor and skill of a resident of Lake-Town

---

1. Tolkien, *Annotated Hobbit*, 272–73,

named Bard, who, during the dragon's flaming rampage, shot an arrow into that spot and killed him. Had he simply accepted the loss of the cup and stayed on his horde, he probably would have remained in possession of all the rest. He over-reached; he lost everything.

We have reason to hope that the actions of the animal-agribusiness plutocrats intent on smashing anyone who threatens even a minor inroad on their treasures will prove similarly self-defeating. Upon occasion, as with the lawsuit of Texas cattlemen against Oprah Winfrey and Howard Lyman for supposed violation of "food libel" laws, the outcome of a long, sensational trial is that their opponents not only gain media airing of their views, but victory. We may hope that other power-politicking actions such as the noxious ag-gag laws—which so obviously show that the agribusiness lords have a lot of stench to hide and care nothing for either human or animal wellbeing—may finally end similarly. But standing in the midst of the conflict as we do, it is hard to put the victories of our cause in a balance with our defeats. It will be a long, demanding struggle, and facile expectations of victory are as unwise as is defeatism. "It does not do to leave a live dragon out of your calculations, if you live near him."[2]

"Full of Thy Glory"

A major theme in *The Hobbit* (and *The Lord of the Rings*) is the surprising power of the small and apparently powerless. The pint-sized hobbit is held in contempt by the mighty Smaug, but in fact the little hero is resourceful, unselfish, dedicated, and "as tough as old tree-roots." Perhaps the central reason for Bilbo's ultimate victory over evil, evil both without and within his heart, is that he knows when he has enough. At one point he feels the magnetic lure of the treasure, when he sees the marvelous Arkenstone on the pile and takes it as his commission, but he curbs that ensnaring desire; rather than keeping the marvelous stone for himself, he gives it away when he sees a chance that the act may bring peace. Being wealthy by hobbit standards from the beginning, he asks for only a small portion of the treasure as his promised commission. In keeping with this refusal to become addicted to gold or center his life around it, he takes pleasure in small, ordinary things in daily life: socializing with visitors, breakfast, blowing smoke-rings from his pipe, basking in the sunshine in his

2. Ibid.

garden, storytelling, song, writing his memoirs—not to mention relishing Gandalf's rare fireworks.

For some persons, such attention to small pleasures may be merely a sign of complacency and limited horizons, but it may also mean that one senses, dimly or clearly, that the divine Splendor, the golden glory that arouses human craving, is here and everywhere we turn. Heaven, as William Blake said, is in a wild flower; one can no more own the Splendor that one can own the sun or the stars. As the narrator in Quaker Harvey Gillman's fine poem "Meeting at Glenthorne" says, angels are treading lightly on the unploughed earth of the hill we just climbed; the cows in the field before us are ministers with messages from the Spirit; "their eyes are heavy with eternity and rain."[3] They are not hard gold on the hoof; they are bearers of living Light.

We must often turn to the true source of joy for refreshment in our arduous Adventure.

---

3. Gillman, "Meeting at Glenthorne," *Peaceable Table*.

16

With an Act of Pity

IN THE SECOND CHAPTER of Tolkien's *The Lord of the Rings*, Gandalf the wizard tells the hobbit Frodo the story of how the perilous One Ring, the Ring of Power made by Sauron the Evil One, came into his (Frodo's) possession. Centuries earlier, after the Ring had lain for long years in the bed of the river Anduin far to the east, a proto-hobbit named Deagol found it while fishing on the river. Almost at once his companion Smeagol, caught by the Ring's powerful lure, strangled him and took the treasure for himself. The Ring gives its owner invisibility when worn, and long life, but corrupts his (or her) mind. And because Smeagol took possession by an act of violence, his corruption was rapid and deep. Soon hopelessly addicted, he became deceitful, rapacious, and violent, devoured from within by insatiable psycho-spiritual hunger. Hating the sunlight, for centuries Smeagol lived wretchedly in a huge cave under the mountains, eating raw fish and an occasional small goblin he had caught and strangled.

Bilbo's Pity

The next movement in the Ring's journey happened when Bilbo, Frodo's uncle, became separated from his traveling companions during the journey recorded in *The Hobbit*, and lost in that same cave. While crawling down a tunnel in darkness, seemingly by a wild chance he put his hand on a ring, and pocketed it. Soon he encountered Smeagol/Gollum (still unaware of his loss), who engaged him in a high-stakes game of telling and solving riddles: if Smeagol wins he will kill and eat Bilbo; if Bilbo wins, Smeagol will show him the way out of the cave. Bilbo did in fact win, though his last riddle was questionable. He followed Smeagol down a tunnel toward a back entrance, but when they were in a narrow place not far from the exit, Gollum, who had no intention of keeping his agreement, crouched down to ambush him. But Bilbo, invisible with the Ring on his finger, saw what was going on. He was tempted to save himself by killing Gollum with his sword. But filled with a sudden wave of pity for the ruined, wretched creature, he instead took the great risk of leaping over him instead. After a further adventure with goblins near the cave's entrance, he escaped into the sunlight.

Eventually returning home and resuming his comfortable life there, Bilbo reached his 111th birthday with little sign of aging or being corrupted by the evil power of the Ring. Having finally tired of his life in the Shire, he decided to go off and live with his friends the Elves, leaving his home to Frodo. At Gandalf's urging, he included the Ring in this legacy—though parting with it cost him a struggle. We are told that he was the only one in the Ring's history to give it up voluntarily.

Gandalf's Pity

Bilbo would not have given Frodo the Ring if he had realized that it would put Frodo in deadly danger. But some years later, Gandalf returns and tells Frodo what he has learned: that Sauron had later captured Smeagol and, by torturing him, learned that a hobbit named Baggins has it. The Dark Lord is now putting out all his power to find and get it back. The news terrifies Frodo; frantically he asks "'What am I do? What a pity that Bilbo did not stab that vile creature, when he had a chance!'" But Gandalf demurs. "'Pity? It was Pity that stayed his hand. Pity, and Mercy: not to strike without need. And he has been well rewarded. Be sure that he took so little hurt from the evil, and escaped in the end, because he began his ownership of the Ring so. With Pity.'"[1]

Middle Earth, like the Anglo-Saxon culture upon which it was partially based, is a world alive with extraordinary powers. Magic spells were uttered over the forging of wands, swords, special rings, or important entrance doors, giving the owners or users of such things enhanced powers. In the case of Sauron's ring, one such power is the invisibility it bestows upon its wearer, but this capacity is due to the Ring's causing him or her to exist half in the world of dark spirits and energies (and thus to become

---

1. Tolkien, *Fellowship*, 58.

vulnerable to them.) It is no wonder that taking possession of it with an act of violence has such terrible effects.

Into the Light of Common Day?

Our Western postmodern world is not one in which one expects to find such conceptions and powers taught in universities. However, there are subcultures flourishing among us with worldviews comparable to those of Middle Earth. In some of these subcultures, members tend to be poorly educated and may be credulous, but there are others made up of highly sophisticated scholars and scientists who have carried out responsible experiments and carefully recorded and studied spontaneous phenomena. (In rare cases, courses in parapsychology are even taught in universities.) Having assessed the evidence, a good number of these experts have concluded that paranormal phenomena—called psi—really do exist. (For a thoughtful overview of the field, see David Ray Griffin's book *Parapsychology, Philosophy, and Spirituality*.)

One category of phenomena similar to the idea of the influence of acts of pity and of violence is that of cases of "object reading," also called psychometry. A person who practices object-reading can sometimes hold an object such as a garment or piece of jewelry, and receive impressions about former wearers of the item: they may get a sense of good or evil, pain or contentment; they may see partial scenes in the wearers' lives, and feel accompanying emotions such as terror in the case of a violent death. For an example of such a case, a remarkable "reading" of a note found in a bottle five years after the sinking of the Lusitania, see Appendix A, page 197. Until one has studied some of the vast evidence and scholarly studies that parapsychology has amassed on psi, it is not responsible to dismiss such ideas, including the idea that even in our world, taking possession of something with an act of pity might have a protective effect, either marked or weak, on its possessor, just as a contrasting act of violence might have a corrupting effect.

But the issue does not depend wholly on whether or not paranormal powers and influences exist in our world. An act of kindness tends to make the doer a kinder person, just as the opposite act tends to make one more calloused and accepting of violence. It is eminently worthwhile for us to practice pity and kindness for our own sakes, as well as for the sake of the needy and vulnerable beings in our sphere of influence who may need our help.

The Powerful and the Powerless

The word *pity* does not have the positive associations it probably had in the more socially stratified societies of past centuries. The word implies that the person acting is in a position of power, and the recipient relatively powerless; to be pitied is to have to "ask for directions" writ large. The same is true of *mercy*, and probably even of *compassion*, although the last-named word means "suffering with," and in itself has little to do with power or powerlessness. The bad press of *pity* and its synonyms is unfortunate, and not really necessary. It is possible for a person to be pitiable in a particular area of life, but to be strong and even enviable in other ways.

In regard to farmed and laboratory animals, however, there is no question but that pity, mercy, and especially compassion—imagining ourselves in those cages—together with acting on these feelings, are very much in order, and that trapped animals will not resent them or their implications. Anyone, whatever her or his life circumstances, who has driven behind a truck crammed with animals bound for a slaughterhell knows at once that s/he has considerable power compared to these enslaved and doomed beings, guilty of nothing except being who they are. Then why not respond with pity? Many people in such a car probably do, at least temporarily. But if they are going home to a dinner centered on a piece of flesh, they will probably, and conveniently, forget pity as soon as the truck is out of sight.

Seeing and Pitying

Frodo initially responded to Gandalf's objection in a similar way, though his motivation differs. "'I am sorry,' said Frodo. 'But I am frightened; and I do not feel any pity for Gollum.' 'You have not seen him,' Gandalf broke in. 'No, and I don't want to,' said Frodo."[2] But much later, on the gruelling journey to Mordor to destroy the Ring, Frodo does see Gollum, who has been following them with insatiable greed and murder on his mind, When Frodo and his companion Sam capture the evil creature, Sam is the one who is all for killing him in the name of safety. But Frodo remembers

2. Ibid.

his earlier conversation with Gandalf, and realizes that Gandalf, and Bilbo before him, were right. "'For now that I see him, I do pity him."[3] Although killing Gollum seems the only safe thing to do, Frodo refuses to consent.

Because to see the extent of another's suffering really is in most cases to pity (at least for a time), animal activists today, like those working to dismantle human slavery two hundred years ago, have labored to gather and present the painful facts and images to the public who buy the products. And not only do they publicize the terrible truth, they point to action that people who pity can take to help. In late eighteenth century England, this was signing a petition to Parliament to end the slave trade, and boycotting slave-produced sugar (and in the nineteenth-century US, both sugar and cotton). In our times, it has recently meant voting to end agribusiness' callous practice of imprisoning animals in tiny cages, a change that has now occurred (or is in process) both in Europe and in a number of states in the US. Of course, people could do even more by refusing to buy eggs, dairy, and flesh; in fact many are cutting down on the latter and trying meat analogs. This fact has actually reduced meat sales, but as yet only a small minority are willing to be firmly consistent in their commitment.

The chance to take action is crucially important, for otherwise the uncomfortable feelings of pity will be covered over by successive lava flows of other preoccupations. But just as the campaign to end human slavery could not stop with outlawing the trade in 1807, we cannot stop with reduced meat sales and getting some farmed animals out of battery cages and into larger pens; we must work until all cages and pens are empty. We must be willing to take small steps or large, as the way opens.

With Acts of Violence, With Acts of Mercy

Taking Gandalf's advice to be practical even in our world, my family has for many years looked for ways to accompany major (and some lesser) purchases or other acquisitions with acts of mercy. We sacralize a new car, a move to another house, a minor luxury item, by a donation to some life-giving cause or by other action to help the healing of the world. Lacking Gandalf's psychic awareness, we can't be certain how, or even whether, these small acts of mercy bless the new possession and our use of it. But we do know that these acts of giving do good both for the beneficiaries and for us, helping us to remain aware that we are linked to all

3. Tolkien, *Two Towers*, 601.

other beings on earth, and responsible for them especially insofar as our lives actively touch them.

But little purchases matter too. We remember all too well the many years we unthinkingly bought cellophane-and-styrofoam packaged chunks of animal flesh every week, as most people in our culture still do. It is deeply disturbing to think that *every one* of these millions of purchases, every forkful of the flesh they contain, reaches its consumer via acts of hellish violence against the innocent. Do the energies of terror and anguish leave traces in the flesh? If so, what psychospiritual effects might they have on humans at deep unconscious levels?

As our family began to change our ways of eating, we became aware that some of us were psychologically dependent on meat, as most people in our culture are, though our dependence was nothing like poor Gollum's torturing addiction. Our case was more like that of Bilbo; we escaped in the end, thanks to Acts of Mercy, the chief of them far beyond our ken. But there are numberless people who have not yet escaped, many of whom continue to be devoured from within by cancers or other degenerative illnesses. Numberless people and animals are suffering and dying as a result of the cancers animal agribusiness fosters in the body of our mother the earth. And many people in positions of power (small or great) within the industry, together with their supporters, have sold themselves to promote and defend the evil system against compassionate change. Consequently, they suffer from deadly cancers of the soul. We will see in chapter 25, "Whatever One Sows," that their deeds will almost surely follow them, even beyond the walls of this world, and descend upon them with agonizing force.

Seeing them all with the eyes of our spirit, shall we not pity?

17

The Hidden Paradise, the Hidden Hells

> Behind the wild bird's throat
> An Eden, more remote
> Than Adam knew of, lies—
> The primal paradise,
> Lost, yet forever here, . . . [1]

Paradise

The narrator of John Hall Wheelock's poem "The Wood-Thrush" quoted above tells of an experience that once came to him while he listened to the song of the bird: in a single, powerful flash he perceived Paradise at the back of the world, so to speak, paradoxically both lost and forever present. The bird knows of it, yet does not know what he knows.

What might this lost-yet-ever-present Eden mean? The term "Paradise" ordinarily refers to a garden of ideal peace and joy at the beginning and end of the biblical saga of history. But Wheelock is far from being alone in claiming that it is an ever-present reality, largely hidden from our consciousness, but right here despite all the world's evil and suffering. In mystical and other religious experiences, many have spoken of finding themselves in paradise, either in a world-transcending state, or here on earth. For example, George Fox, co-founder of the Society of Friends, in his *Journal* describes experiencing it in a climactic vision: "Now was I brought up through the flaming sword into the paradise of God. All things were new; and all the creation gave unto me another smell than before, beyond

---

1. Wheelock, *This Blessed Earth*, 47.

The Hidden Paradise, the Hidden Hells

what words can utter."[2] This vision apparently referred to paradise being right here on earth, for he could see into the nature of plants, and considered practicing herbal medicine. No one else shared his vision, yet many could see, in his transformed life and remarkable spiritual gifts, outward evidence of the Reality he had entered.

Drawing upon the writings of Fox, other mystics, and romantic poets, I will sketch some of the characteristics of this Paradise.

The Hidden Unity

One of them is, in Fox's terms, "the hidden unity in the Eternal Being."[3] The divine Spirit present in humanity and all creation manifests to some spiritually awakened souls as the magnetic drawing together of all things and beings now separated and alienated. This unifying power is unseen and unfelt by most. Elsewhere, Fox says "[M]ind that which is eternal, which gathers your hearts together up to the Lord, and lets you see that you are written in one another's heart."[4] As we become more and more deeply aware of the Spirit within ourselves, we come closer to all the rest of the universe. As the Inner Love or Hidden Unity is more and more fully manifested, violence and exploitation are diminished and finally excluded. Transformed (and partially transformed) human beings lead this process, but it is not limited to humanity. As more and more human beings are transformed, the harmony increasingly prevails also among animals and the rest of nature.

The concept of a power drawing together all the separated is a major theme of German Romanticism, significantly expressed in Friedrich Schiller's well-known 1785 poem "An die Freude," ("Ode to Joy,") immortalized by Beethoven in his famous Ninth Symphony. The Divine Light is suggested in its imagery of fire:

> Freude, schoener Goetterfunken,
> Tochter aus Elysium,
> Wir betreten feuertrunken,
> Himmlische, dein Heiligtum.
> Deine Zauber binden wieder
> Was die Mode Schwert geteilt
> Bettler werden Fuerstenbrueder

2. Fox, *Journal*, 26.
3. Fox, *Journal*, 28.
4. Fox, *No more but my love*, 11.

Taking the Adventure

> Wo dein sanfter Fluegel weilt . . .[5]

This stanza is translated as follows by Faith Bowman:

> Joy, Elysium's cherished daughter,
> Beauteous spark of Flame divine,
> Drunk with fire, now we enter
> Goddess, thy most holy shrine.
> Thy strong magic binds together
> What Convention's swords divide;
> Beggar is a prince's brother
> 'Neath thy downy pinions wide.[6]

Beauty and Splendor

Another characteristic of Paradise is preternatural beauty and brightness: glowing colors, exquisite shapes, celestial music, intoxicating fragrances. The familiar is strange and wonderful: human beings may seem to be angelic; flowers and leaves to be living jewels. The whole earth, and each thing in it, including natural features such as mountains or rivers, seem intensely alive.

Writings of other mystics and poets support Fox's account of experiencing Paradise as a present, glowing reality. For example, his seventeenth-century contemporary Thomas Traherne, a devout Anglican clergyman and poet, in his book *Centuries of Meditation* describes a childhood in which he seemed

> as one brought into the Estate of Innocence . . . I saw all in the peace of Eden . . . all time was Eternity . . . The [grain] was orient and immortal wheat . . . The dust and stones of the street were as precious as gold . . . The green trees . . . transported and ravished me . . . almost mad with ecstasy, they were such strange and wonderful things . . . Boys and girls tumbling in the street . . . were moving jewels . . . Eternity was manifest in the Light of the Day.[7]

Though Traherne later learned "the dirty devices of the world," and had to unlearn them, he never fully lost his awareness of the presence of hidden splendor: "The world is a mirror of infinite beauty, yet no man sees

---

5. Schiller: *Ode an Die Freude*.
6. Bowman, tr. Ode to Joy," *Faith Poems*.
7. Traherne, *Centuries*, 109–110.

it . . . It is the Paradise of God . . . and the Gate of Heaven."[8] This splendor is probably what the prophet Isaiah meant by the line "The whole earth is full of his glory."[9]

William Wordsworth in childhood also perceived the world of nature as aglow with celestial light, filling him with "aching joys" and "dizzy raptures." As a mature adult he could no longer perceive it, though nature still was lovely to his eyes. Much of his poetry is concerned with bridging the gulf between the life-giving freshness of this paradisal level of existence, and the ordinary plodding or sad existence most people know.

Freedom and Power

The denizens of the hidden Paradise are often portrayed with wings, representing their freedom from the limitations of physical existence, especially from the planet's gravity and the vulnerabilities of physical life. In the vision of God in the temple in Isaiah chapter 6, the supernatural beings called seraphim who attend on the Deity each has six wings. One of them assists the seer, though hardly in a tender way: he purifies him from his dangerous state of uncleanness by touching his mouth with a burning coal from the altar, so that the blazing vision will not destroy him. In other biblical visions, angelic figures, whether winged or not, are so formidable that they tend to begin by saying "Do not be afraid." They then go on to give what is usually good news—promise of the birth of a longed-for child, promise of divine deliverance from enemies and oppressors. The concept of unseen guardian angels is suggested in one of the sayings of Jesus: he urges his hearers not to hold children in contempt, because "their angels in heaven always see the face of my Father." [10]

Post-biblical accounts of visions of angels can be found now and then throughout Western history, but seem to have increased since the late eighteenth century thanks to the writings of Emanuel Swedenborg, to the nineteenth-century Spiritualist movement, and to the widespread interest in Near-Death Experiences in the twentieth. The souls of the deceased are often thought of as becoming guardian angels to their living loved ones. Preoccupation with such stories has intensified in the last twenty-five years or so, so that many more who had angel experiences have told their stories.

8. Op Cit, 15.
9. Isa. 6:3, KJV.
10. Matt. 18:10, ESV.

Taking the Adventure

Modern-day angels tend to be tenderly loving toward those who see them, providing reassurance, guidance, and protection, sometimes giving warnings of impending dangers. Angels are seen both in ordinary settings and in transcendent worlds; they may be in modern dress, or may be robed and winged. (More on this in chapter 20, Return to Eden, Part II.)

Occasionally the idea of a hidden paradise situated above earth, and the angel-like empowerment of a human being to reach it, will appear in song and verse, secular songs as well as hymns. Of the former, some have to do with airplane flight. But perhaps the best known secular song about such a paradise is "Over the Rainbow" from the 1939 film version of *The Wizard of Oz*. As she sings, the heroine Dorothy affirms her faith that such a land without troubles exists high over the world, that it is in color (unlike her drab sepia world of the Kansas farm), and that, like the bluebirds, she will some day fly up beyond the rainbow to enter it.

A Numinous Presence

Not only did Wordsworth know nature as full of a joy-bringing splendor; he also experienced mysterious Presences, not all of them positive. In *The Prelude*, lines 357–400, during an episode in which he stole a rowboat for a moonlight joyride on a lake, he sensed, in a dark mountain that seemed to rear up and stride after him, mysterious, disturbing Forms that blotted out all bright memory-images from his mind for days thereafter. In "Tintern Abbey" he speaks of a lifegiving, infinite Presence:

> a sense sublime
> Of something far more deeply interfused,
> Whose dwelling is the light of setting suns,
> And the round ocean, and the living air,
> and the blue sky, and in the mind of man;
> A motion and a spirit, that . . .
> rolls through all things.[11]

The city-bred Irish poet and artist AE (George Russell, 1867–1935) also perceived a living Spirit and a preternatural brightness in nature as well as in otherworldly visions. In contrast to Wordsworth and Traherne, he developed the gift as he approached adulthood. In *A Candle of Vision* he says that "Such a beauty begins to glow on us as we journey towards Deity,

---

11. Wordsworth, *Immortal Poems*, 258.

... I would cry out to our humanity, sinking deeper into the Iron Age, that the Golden World is all about us and that beauty is open to all ..."[12]

Harmony with Animals

Wordsworth thought of the "motion" and "spirit" as living though impersonal, while Traherne experienced this power as the Creator. But neither of these nature poets is known to have tried to realize the harmony of Eden in harmless relations with animals; in fact, in his long poem *The Prelude*, Wordsworth relates how in his happy, Edenic childhood he even set snares for birds. It seems that one can feel oneself to be living in a state of paradisal unity with nature, and yet engage in monstrous violence against fellow dwellers in the Garden. George Russell was rather more in tune with his fellow animals (human and otherwise); he was a vegetarian, and compassionately worked to bring about a better life for impoverished peasants, but it apparently did not occur to him to call for freedom for all animals.

The Evangelical poet William Cowper (1731-1800) in his long poem of 1785, *The Task*, also does better than Wordsworth and Traherne in this regard. Not only does he perceive signs of Paradise in nature, tracing it to the Creator's Presence:

> The soul that sees Him ...
> Discerns in all things what, with [stuporous] gaze
> Of ignorance, till then she overlooked,
> A ray of heavenly light gilding all forms
> Terrestrial, in the vast and the minute
> The unambiguous footsteps of the God
> Who gives its lustre to an insect's wing
> And wheels His throne upon the rolling worlds.[13]

Cowper also gave emphatic expression to his kinship with animals, especially his anger at their abuse. With prophetic fervor he excoriated sport hunting, the "detested sport / which owes its pleasures to another's pain." He created a mini-paradise of harmony for a few hares whom he befriended, feeding them by hand, and harboring them in his house from "the sanguinary yell of cruel man" and "the savage din of the swift pack."[14] Al-

---

12. AE, *Candle of Vision*, 34.
13. Cowper, *The Task*, 100.
14. Cowper, Op. Cit., 48.

though he unfortunately saw the Bible as justifying meat-eating, he seems to have been sympathetic to vegetarianism, since he lived very simply, and notes that we are only "carnivorous, through sin."

The Beatrician Vision

Support of a somewhat different sort for the hidden paradise is also found in the work of Anglican theologian and literary critic Charles W. S. Williams (1886–1945). In his poems and novels, and his studies of Dante and Wordsworth, especially *The Figure of Beatrice,* Williams proposes that the celestial light that Wordsworth saw in nature is essentially one with the wonder that Dante saw in Beatrice, his Lady. "She did not seem to be the daughter of any mortal man, but rather of a God."[15] This divine glory is what anyone who falls in love perceives in the beloved, says Williams. The lover may be unaware of the beloved's very real faults and sins during this temporary period of openness to the glory; thus the commonplace saying "Love is blind." Or the lover may be more or less aware of them them, but somehow sees his beloved as faultless in spite of all her faults.

After the vision passes, as it nearly always does in a year or two, those faults will probably be painfully apparent, and the lover is likely to agree with the majority opinion that what she or he saw was an illusion. But, says Williams, *it is real;* all along, the glory has coexisted with the beloved's smallnesses and sins. Mostly unseen, it is present in everyone, just as the same celestial splendor remained in nature although Wordsworth and Traherne could no longer perceive it. Williams views this temporary openness to the glory, which he calls "the Flying Moment," as a challenge to deep spiritual awakening: the lover, like the nature mystic, is called to enter the long, hard path of learning to love *all* her or his neighbors as herself. In effect, she is to realize, so far as possible, Edenic harmony, the Hidden Unity, in society as well as in nature. Unhappily, Williams, like Wordsworth and Traherne, failed to apply this principle to compassionate love for nonhuman neighbors; as far as I know, it did not occur to him to reject his culture's system of killing and eating them.

---

15. Dante, *La Vita Nuova,* 4.

Realizing the Inner Love

Clearly, there is tension between different aspects of the Hidden Paradise. Many persons fall in love, and later fall out of love, without heeding, or even hearing, the call to realize the Hidden Unity. Some have felt and yearned after the divine Presence and/or the luminous beauty they perceived, but never questioned the blood on their plates. And animal activists, working to realize their kinship with animals by opposing human violence against them, have sometimes fallen to the temptation of mental or verbal violence against the abusers (a few even justifying physical violence). This stance, needless to say, does not help to realize the Inner Love that unites all the living.

The young Francis of Assisi dreamed of becoming a heroic knight, of attaining honor and fame by doing battle with injustice. But his two knightly expeditions fizzled dismally. He began to hear the voice of Christ, whose message was very different. As Murray Bodo points out in his book *Francis: The Journey and the Dream,* the would-be knight learned that what he must fight was the darkness and fear within himself, especially the fear of touching a leper. Instead of an acclaimed hero, he had to become a despised beggar. Only when he rejected and defeated his own potential for evil, focused in those fears and self-aggrandizing desires laced through his good will, did his mind and soul open to the Hidden Unity, his eyes to the Hidden Paradise. Keeping his face turned to the Presence, he became a man of peace, unable to do violence to any and eager to open their eyes to Love, because he realized that all beings, all creation without exception were his sisters and brothers. Only love for the (seeming) enemy can transform that enemy to the friend she or he in essence is.

The fullness of this Paradise does remain hidden most of the time. But refracted glimpses that offer a touch of happiness, if not a storm of rapture, are readily available to many: in the stars, in blossoming trees against a blue sky, in autumn leaves on the wind, in a strain from Mozart, in the rainbow flashes from a diamond or a dewdrop, in the sight of loving animals snuggling or playing together. Though most of the time we may "miss the many-splendored thing,"[16] Paradise is not hidden altogether.

---

16. Thompson. "The Kingdom of God," 860.

Taking the Adventure

The Hidden Hells

But "The Wood-Thrush" describes not only the narrator's mystical-intuitive perception of the presence of Paradise when he hears the song of the thrush, but of the presence of the world's evil and anguish as well:

> ... Troy lost and Hector slain,
> Judas and Golgotha,
> The longing and the pain,
> Sorrows of old that were ... [17]

The Blinders

Like Paradise, Earth's many hells, of innocent, guilty, or semi-guilty suffering, are partly hidden. One of the factors that hide them is what also hides Paradise: our limitations as incarnate beings. Of the vast majority we remain simply ignorant. Some make their way into history books or into the news: natural disasters, and disasters triggered by greed; street crime and child battering; terrorist attacks; wars of aggression reported in distorted ways that bolster public support. Most of us on hearing of them will wince at the thought of the terrible suffering involved, but the impression usually soon fades, and we turn to something else. Our geographical distance and our differing foci of interest insulate us from the horrors.

There are other insulating factors hiding the hells as well. One is cultural blinkers and blindfolds, which may combine with geographical barriers, or function very effectively on their own to hide a hell in plain sight. For example, before the second wave of the women's movement, it was common for women in our culture who suffered rape or spousal abuse to be isolated by a climate of blame for their victimization: "she must have asked for it." In some cultures or subcultures, having been raped may even make victims "fair game" for further abuse; in the worst instances, they are judged destroyers of family honor, and murdered by their own fathers or brothers. Similarly, in the late nineteenth and first half of the twentieth century, when the Ku Klux Klan and lynch-law ruled in much of the American South, photographers would produce and sell postcards picturing gleeful white mobs surrounding a black figure hanging from a tree, whose crime may have been speaking suggestively to a white woman, making a self-assertive remark, or flaunting an expensive car. Blinded by

17. Wheelock, Op. Cit, 47

The Hidden Paradise, the Hidden Hells

culturally-sanctioned prejudice, people cannot see a horror that is right before their eyes.

A third factor hiding the hells is secrecy and deceit. Example: a transcontinental corporation is wrecking the environment and thus people's livelihoods in a developing country, and suppressing protests by local individuals with deadly violence, but it is able to protect its markets by using its influence on media moguls to suppress the story. Another: an unscrupulous government wins over its people to an aggressive war via concocted stories demonizing the target people, or even by mounting a "false-flag" attack on itself for which it blames the other. Whistle-blowers may face character assassination in the media, prison on false charges, or may suddenly succumb to mysterious illnesses, "accidents" or "suicides." Torture centers may be set up, sometimes in secret locations, for people accused but never tried or convicted.

Readers will recognize a number of these factors and tactics at work hiding the animal hells. For decades most people have been ignorant, protected by geographical distance and more. Our very language sets up a whole system of blinkers, beginning with referring to an animal as "it" rather than the obvious she or he, and a whole vocabulary that demeans animals and presents them as objects, making the exploitation, killing, and eating of them seem natural and normal. Deceit and secrecy make an unholy alliance when the owners of factory-farms give them bucolic names like Clear Run Farms or Happy Valley or Sunshine Farms, but need barbed wire, concrete walls, and laws to keep the public from looking in on all that sunshine and happiness. As a result of footage of horrendous abuse appearing in the media in recent years, several farm states have passed or are considering laws making such undercover photography a crime. Challenged, the powers of this network of hells are trying to consolidate their strength to keep the evil out of sight.

Removing the Blinders

Uncovering the hidden hells to public gaze verbally or pictorially, so that ultimately they may be nonviolently dismantled, is a painful and often thankless task. We continue to pursue this process nonetheless because we feel a powerful compassion, and because of our faith that *compassion's source in Divine Love is more deeply based than the evil rampant in the hells.* One of the ways I have expressed this faith is in referring to "the hells" in the plural, and Paradise in the singular. The hells are pockets, or rather deep pits, of horror; Paradise, centered on the Hidden Unity in the Eternal Being, is the center and the circumference of reality.

As we work toward disclosing and emptying these hidden hells, it is crucially necessary that we never let ourselves concede the last word to the evil of the hells, and consequently give way to depression and despair. Rather, whatever our feelings, we must affirm that the first and last word is with Paradise. From time to time we must refresh ourselves from our work by seeking out and savoring glimpses of this edenic Reality which is our and all other beings' true home.

18

Strength to Love

A Hymn From Yesteryear

When I was a child attending a Protestant parochial school, every morning we sang from a slim, illustrated book of inspirational songs for young people. I remember well one particular song meant to fortify youth against taking the downward path into a life of sin. The music was good, but the poetry was not deathless. It began by urging us little people to "Yield not to temptation, / For yielding is sin . . . .Dark passions subdue . . ." " Temptation to do what? What are the dark passions? We weren't told until the second stanza, which urged us to "shun evil companions" (so some people are evil at their core, children of the devil?) and "Bad language disdain, God's name hold in reverence . . ." "Fight manfully onward . . ." I would never be a man, but apparently I was supposed to try my best to be like one, which never appealed to me. "Be thoughtful and earnest, / Kind-hearted and true,"[1] it exhorted us, reinforcing the suggestions of the first line that if it's lively and fun, it's probably bad for your soul. I could see that to be thoughtful, kind and true was good advice, but it left the initial question unanswered.

Why should I take up space in this book by dealing with second-rate hymn lyrics of yesteryear? To begin with, this 1868 song was addressed to a rather different world, when the middle class had considerable (overt) suspicion of sex. Many evangelicals of the time extended this suspicion to play-going, dancing, liquor consumption, and other recreational activities, partly because they might lower resistance to sexual desire. But in the 1920s, reaction against things Victorian started gathering force, and since then we

---

1. Palmer, "Yield Not to Temptation," *Hymnary*.

have been hearing from every side about how unbalanced this worldview is, about the harm to the psyche done by these inhibiting, anti-worldly attitudes. Is there any point in joining this crowd of voices by calling attention to the weaknesses of "Yield Not to Temptation"?

In fact there is. In the midst of the text's less-than-helpful exhortations were two passages that I've been pondering more and more in recent years, which I will present below. Both of them help us to realize, in Martin Luther King's fine words, the "strength to love."

Temptation to Do What?

The references to evil companions, bad language, and dark passions suggest that by "sin" the hymnwriter, musician Horatio Palmer (1834-1907), may have had in mind youths joining the crowd going to the saloon, talking tough, getting drunk, perhaps falling into the wrong bed. This idea of sin may strike some as the typical anti-worldly-pleasures view, but there is more going on here than meets the twenty-first-century eye. According to historical accounts of nineteenth-century American dietary practices, the male world then was awash in alcohol. This Niagara of liquor was a link in a complex socio-economic situation that blighted many lives: lack of access to education and rampant exploitation of working-class people, alcoholism, resulting wife and child neglect and abuse, the oppression of women, the violent underworld of prostitution and crime—all were intertwined. These actions and situations certainly involve dark passions that should be subdued, not given free rein. But most of us know that individual will power is not an adequate answer to any of them, any more than it will resolve the plight of animals today; broad social and legal changes were and are also necessary.

My focus here, however, is on the decisions and actions of the individual, and the individual's will *does* matter. When do cultural evils become personal sins? At its core, yielding to temptation is sin when the act in question harms a living being: sin is violation of love. "Bad language" may do harm to the hearer, or it may not. One drink in the saloon may be pretty harmless; but when an exploited and exhausted worker drinks down his meager salary to forget his sense of defeat and hopelessness, leaving a dependent family hungry, and especially if he goes home ready to project his anger against himself onto them, the situation is far from harmless to either party.

Strength to Love

Readers will have little difficulty applying to diet this view of temptation and sin-as-harm. We all too often find that those who oppose our message like to portray us as anti-pleasure ascetics. In fact this is almost never the case, and we are rightly eager to refute this view by showing how many tasty vegan dishes we enjoy. But the criticism is a distraction; we should not allow the central issue, harm to sentient beings, to be eclipsed. As Howard Lyman has pithily put it, when we buy and eat animal flesh we are saying to the factory farm and slaughterhell moguls (or animal-raising organic farmers), *"I approve. Do it again."* Likewise with dairy, and commercial eggs from hens caged or free-range: all are laced with blood, drenched in misery. As dealt with above in chapter 3, "We Were Slaves to Pharaoh," the issue surfaces as well in some other products, like non-fair-trade chocolate. Some of the cocoa beans from which it is made are picked by human slaves, and as long as many people buy the product, slavery will be profitable. Much the same is true of products made with palm oil; some of it comes from tropical areas where rainforests and their animal inhabitants are being destroyed to make way for profitable palm plantations. These are situations when the consumer should, emphatically, Yield Not to Temptation.

Strength

This important clarification brings us to one of the insightful lines that made the hymn worth remembering. A major result of taking a firm stand against an indulgence that harms a sentient being is that one's personality becomes stronger in this area. Palmer knew this; his first stanza says "Each victory will help you / Some other to win." By saying a firm *no* to yourself, he was in effect telling us, you build up your psychospiritual muscle tone; next time you are inclined to do that harmful thing, you will face the challenge a somewhat stronger person. It doesn't mean you aren't going to stumble sometimes, especially if you have little support, but it sets you on a trend. (Crippling addictions require additional, expert help; I refer here to common dependencies.) Many of us who years ago stopped eating animals and the milk (products) and eggs stolen from them find that what once seemed so overwhelmingly tempting has long ago become nonexistent for us; we may have to jog our memories in order to sympathize with the novice's struggles. It's good for beginners to know about the empowering effect of sustained practice.

Taking the Adventure

Toughened moral fibre in one area of life is a boon, which may help us in other ways, but it doesn't mean one has entered the Beulah Land in *Pilgrim's Progress* and are about to reach the the Celestial City. In other areas a vegan may still be spiritually flabby—perhaps refusing honest self-examination, or living amid distraction and chaos, or falling apart in crises, or cherishing resentments, or often giving way to out-of-control rages. More is needed; we must have a high capacity overall to cope in a positive way with discomforts and frustrations.

Building Strength

Some people's lives are so arduous and painful that that the world confronts them with make-or-break challenges all the time. But for others, who are used to a certain level of comfort, a good way to develop this coping capacity is additional spiritual disciplines. Like our obligation to free our diet from violence as far as possible, a spiritual discipline must be clearly distinguished from unhealthy, pleasure-despising asceticism. But the discipline is likely to be more difficult in one way than going vegan: there may be no clear-cut moral issue to motivate one. In some cases we may find help for our motivation in environmental or health concerns, which do have moral dimensions, though they aren't always hard and fast.

Disciplines may be put into two categories. One is choosing to say "no" to certain enjoyable things that may be essentially harmless or even good in themselves— e.g., a favorite food (especially a processed one), an unneeded purchase, a comfortable habit. Fasts, of course, come under this first category. The other side is adopting helpful practices that one may presently find unappealing, such as physical exercise, daily contemplative prayer or meditation, eating particular, healthy whole foods. The practice may be either temporary or permanent. It is important to choose disciplines wisely, neither being too easy on oneself nor launching all at once into multiple, demanding regimens, such that failure is more than likely. Specific dividends may vary, but the benefit of a life that is disciplined overall is a personality with strength to spare.

Spiritual-political leaders like Mohandas "Mahatma" Gandhi and César Chávez, both vegetarians (Chávez a vegan) for compassionate reasons, can inspire us. Both of them were in a position to take the discipline of fasting to the point of risking their health and even their lives in order to bring moral pressure to bear on those who resisted their calls for justice. Chávez called his fasts "a prayer for purification and strengthening." Seeing this degree of strength to love broadens our horizons, but most of us should definitely not attempt anything this risky, especially without medical oversight.

Strength to Do What?

Unfortunately, it doesn't follow that becoming stronger necessarily means having strength *to love*. It is well known that a disciplined person living among the chronically self-indulgent will be tempted to a holier-than-thou outlook, which causes others to take offense. (Of course the others may imagine contempt when none is expressed, and become hostile, a painful complication presenting one with further challenges.) The temptation to self-righteousness, which is likely to take noticeable forms in new vegetarians, may become very subtle in later years; it calls for regular and unsparing self-examination.

A potentially worse problem is that those who are severe with themselves may also be hard toward others. Workaholics are firmly disciplined at their jobs, but do so to escape intimacy, family responsibilities, or other obligations. Some individuals labor diligently for causes they once thought good; but long after others see and acknowledge that the cause is badly corrupted, they hang on, lying to themselves and others, becoming more and more like the now-perverted thing they serve. Some—from the family tyrant to the political dictator—exercise their strength by clutching, manipulating, suffocating, and/or attacking others.

This does not mean, however, that all tyrants are self-disciplined. Rynn Berry in his little book *Hitler: Neither Vegetarian Nor Animal Lover*, draws in part upon a biography of Hitler by Robert Payne, who reports that Joseph Goebbels' Ministry of Propaganda depicted Hitler as the ascetic kind of leader, one who abstained from all meat, tobacco, alcohol, and sex in order to pursue his utter devotion to the Fatherland. In fact, however, Payne tells us that *der Führer*, except for a sporadic meatless regimen to combat health problems, was very self-indulgent at the table, relishing Bavarian sausage, liver dumplings, stuffed pigeon, and sometimes ham, as well as cloying quantities of sweet desserts. So the familiar accusation, "Hitler was a vegetarian" originally came from Nazism's Big Lie. But it convinced and still convinces many poorly-informed people, partly because they think it is the ultimate blot on vegetarianism, but also because it was built on an intuited truth that sustained self-discipline builds strength.

Look Beyond

Like Gandhi, Martin Luther King, and Chávez, we must gain the strength to love both friends and foes—especially friends who are acting like foes!—if we are to win hearts and minds to the cause of the animals. Returning (verbal or literal) violence for violence does not work, and does harm to the cause. Disciplines over and beyond veganism definitely help, but as we have seen, disciplines do not guarantee that we will use our strength *to love*. The great majority of us need help from beyond ourselves. Each stanza of Palmer's hymn ends "Look ever to Jesus; / He will carry you through." Jesus as God-With-Us worked for King and Chávez and numbers of their followers, as it still does for many today (including myself). Gandhi was inspired by Jesus' Sermon on the Mount, but wisely remained in his own Hindu tradition, which provided ample transforming and empowering energy, and gave him a spiritual foundation for making common cause with his fellow Indians. In the last few generations, with the appearance of the political activists of Engaged Buddhism, still other language for the empowering Ultimate has been used.

This is not to say that any conception of the Divine is equally valid. The Heart from which all things come is real, more real than any of us; yet, as discussed in chapter 4, "The Work of Human Minds," we must stay aware that every human conception of the Ultimate is limited. When a Goddess like Kali actively demands goat sacrifice, or a Christian God blesses bullfights or grants devotees the right to operate or support CAFOs and slaughterhouses, such a Deity is to that extent crippled by projected human fears, cravings, and violence; such a deity is partly or mostly idol. And there may be other, more subtle projections onto favorite images of God. We must live in tension: asking critical questions about our view of God, yet giving ourselves totally to God, so that Divine strength to love can flow in and through us.

We can live and love beyond our small human boundaries when we open ourselves to the Love that knows no boundaries.

19

No Second Beer for George

A Mystic's Spiritual Awakening

THE PASSAGE IN GEORGE FOX's *Journal* in which he describes his spiritual call had profound implications for Fox's future message and life as co-founder of the Religious Society of Friends. One day when he was eighteen or nineteen, George Fox, together with a cousin and a friend, went into a pub for a glass of beer. After they had satisfied their thirst, his cousin wanted to have another round, and asked George to pay. Fox was deeply disturbed at this insistence on having seconds when no one was thirsty; after paying for his drink he walked quietly out and continued for the rest of the day to be grieved about this scene. Sleepless that night, he heard a voice telling him "Thou seest how young people run together into vanity, and old people into the earth. Thou must forsake all . . . and be as a stranger to all."[1] Not long afterwards Fox began the journeys of search and later of prophetic ministry that were to be virtually lifelong.

At first blush it is hard to see why Fox should have been so exercised about a second glass of beer. Ale and beer were common forms of refreshment in seventeenth-century England, because water was often unsafe; neither Fox nor his guiding voice say anything about alcoholism in this case, and as sins go, this one seems quite mild. Then why does his inner guidance present this situation as the reason he must leave home, breaking ties of attachment to friends and family?

---

1. Fox, *Journal*, 3

Taking the Adventure

Valid and Nonvalid Desires

From the perspective of Fox's later life and witness, and the traditions of mysticism, one can see that there really are important issues here. At their core is, on the one hand, the universal fact of need. Sentient beings have obvious basic needs for shelter, food, drink, fellowship with their kind, including some form of love, sexual expression, and (in many cases) offspring. In the more evolved animals, especially human beings, desires also take symbolic and aesthetic forms—an attractive mate, beautiful clothing, a well-designed and comfortable house, tasty food. Desires are not something bad in themselves; stemming from the fact that we are physical and finite, they make us take care of our bodies. Also, they are part of attached love. They help us care for persons, animal friends, and causes we care about; we want to be close to and involved with the person, social group, or cause we love; we want the best for the beloved or beloved cause, and are willing to make sacrifices.

On the other hand, at some point valid needs begin to express themselves in not-so-valid ways; one may crave a trophy spouse, a home that impresses people with the owner's wealth and good taste, membership in prestigious clubs, an enviably large salary, power over others. (Unhealed psychological wounds may also be involved, notably in cravings for substances and unhealthy foods.) For the young Fox it was clear that the line between the valid and the nonvalid was crossed with the call for that second glass of beer. Later he spoke prophetically against actions that cross the line in other ways: luxurious clothing, insistence on being addressed with flattering titles and deferential gestures from others such as removing the hat. Out of Fox's stance on these issues come the basic Quaker commitments to simplicity of life and the moral equality of all persons, which some are now expanding to include all beings.

Nonvalid Cravings and Violence

Fox also found that when he pressed these points, many people—religious authorities, civil authorities, mobs—responded with violence. He pinpointed violence as having its source in such nonvalid cravings, frequently quoting the Biblical passage "From whence come wars and fightings among you? Come they not . . . of your lusts . . . ?"[2] For Fox, lusts are for the most

2. James 4:1, KJV.

No Second Beer for George

part not sexual cravings but desire for expensive objects that exceed one's essential needs, and are meant to impress others. Because most such things are available only to the rich and powerful, tending toward a situation in which the few have too much and the many not enough, the outcome is often violence—hidden violence done by the oppressed, open violence to enforce the situation done by the rich and powerful . A modern example of systemic violence rising from non-valid cravings is the still-continuing War on Drugs, arising from the addicts' cravings and the purveyors' drive for wealth and power-over (and the refusal of those who support the laws that undergird the war to seek better solutions, preferring to cling to a gratifying us-against-them worldview.) Such cravings, as suggested above in "Seek the Bright Enchanted Gold," can never be satisfied because they are at their root longings for what is infinite.

Nonvalid Cravings and Physical Health

An important aspect of the issue of nonvalid cravings relates to health. George Fox is not usually seen as a health obsessive; he lived an ascetic life, sometimes doing without food or shelter even in winter. But none of the harsh treatment his body endured was (as with some other mystics) self-inflicted in order to "subdue the flesh." It came unsought as a result of following his inner guidance; for example, if he was convinced that the Spirit told him to go speak to people in a certain town, and found that no one there would sell or give him food or shelter, he went uncomplainingly without food and shelter. In fact, he speaks more than once of eating and drinking "for health," and of living with respect for and in unity with God's creation. That the health issue was actually important to him can be seen in the account of his conversion, when he experienced paradise on earth, felt a deep unity with nature, and perceived the inner qualities of "the creatures." He considered practicing "physic," which would have included herbal medicine, for the good of humanity.[3]

Standards for Judging Desires for Foods

It is not always easy to determine which cravings are valid and which are not, but one general principle to follow is the familiar "Live simply, that

3. Fox, Op. Cit., 27.

others may simply live." Many aspects of life are involved in simple living. But since we are concerned here with food, it is clear from these examples from George Fox's life that of the standards by which those who seek to live in harmony with the Spirit should judge desires, two are our health and the health of the earth. From our perspective in another century, we can see a third, the welfare of people living in poor countries exploited by those in rich countries. Fourth, but not least, is compassion and respect for animals.

It is becoming increasingly well known that pesticides, hormones, and antibiotics that threaten human health are concentrated in meat produced by agribusiness, and that agribusiness interests have such wealth and power, especially in the US, that it is virtually impossible to rein them in. Even when animals are raised in the traditional, earth-friendly ways described in chapter 10, "Like the Foul Stable," their products tend to be harmful to those who consume them, a crucial reason being the large amounts and the kinds of proteins and fat they contain. Many studies have shown that the rich Western diet, with its emphasis on meat, dairy, and eggs, correlates with a rise in many degenerative diseases, especially coronary heart disease and certain common cancers. William Castelli, former head of the Framingham Heart Study, T. Colin Campbell, co-head of the massive China Health Study dealing with diet and cancer described in *The China Study*, Caldwell Esselstyn, author of *Prevent and Reverse Heart Disease,* and others have concluded that a plant-based diet is optimal for human health. (It is Castelli who said "When you see the Golden Arches, you're on the road to the Pearly Gates."[4]) More recently, Neal Barnard in *Power Foods for the Brain* cites many studies showing that the meat-heavy Standard American Diet (SAD) contributes in major ways to increasing the risk of the dreaded diseases of aging, Alzheimer's and dementia.

These authorities' conclusions are supported by several of our bodily features. Already in ancient times Plutarch pointed out that, unlike carnivores, we are ill designed to chase prey and rip their bodies apart.[5] Contemporary researchers have refined his insight by pointing out details such as the fact that carnivorous animals not only have sharp teeth and claws, and acid saliva, they have short intestines so that what they eat is processed quickly, for flesh that is eaten decays soon in the heat of the body. By contrast, humans need large amounts of fiber, available only from plants, and have a long digestive tract optimal for processing plant food.

4. Castelli, Physicians Committee for Responsible Medicine.
5. Plutarch. "On the Eating of Animal Flesh," *Ethical Vegetarianism,* 29.

Although we can get nourishment from animal foods, there is much evidence that anatomically we are mostly or entirely vegetarian.[6] These things may mean that not only in the depths of our spirit, where we may sense our oneness with all other beings, but even in our bodies, human beings are essentially nonviolent.

Meat and the Second Beer

If this is true—and readers are encouraged to look into it for themselves—then meat, especially that sourced from agribusiness, is like that second glass of beer that so troubled the teenaged George Fox in the tavern incident. Meat (cooked and flavored) is tasty, people crave it, it has the support of habit and the often the prestige of affluence—but the welfare of the planet and of our bodies (not to mention that of farmed animals) is better met when we awaken from the psychospiritual numbness our culture fosters, listen to the sympathy in our own hearts, and eat foods produced with as little violence as possible. That means plants, grown with respect for the earth. When we feel cravings for meat and products taken by force from animals, as with other nonvalid cravings and dependencies, we do well to seek to understand not only the physical but the spiritual sources of our desires; we need to turn increasingly to the Divine Center.

---

6. Mills, Milton R., MD. "The Comparative Anatomy of Eating." *VegSource*.

20

The Usefulness of Honor

The Mansfield Judgment

IN 1769 A CUSTOMS official named Charles Stewart, from the British colony of Massachusetts, took with him to England one James Somersett, an enslaved African he had purchased in Virginia. Stewart was not pleased when Somersett escaped in mid-1771. He recaptured his "property" that November, and put him in chains aboard the ship *Ann and Mary*, bound for the colony of Jamaica, where Stewart intended to sell him. But Somersett's godparents, Mary Cade, Thomas Marlow, and John Walkin, asked the Court of the King's Bench for a ruling of habeas corpus, claiming that their godson's re-enslavement was not legal.

The case attracted much attention in the press, and by the time of the hearings, Somersett had no fewer than five attorneys. One of them argued that "the air of England is too pure for a slave to breathe," meaning that slavery is incompatible with what it means to be English. The implication is that when Somersett set foot in England he became a free man. After weeks of conscientious deliberation the judge, William Murray, earl of Mansfield (featured in the movie *Belle*), gave his decision in the ex-slave's favor. Although Mansfield based his decision on legal technicalities, he made it clear that slavery was "odious" and could only be maintained under "positive law" supporting it, which did not exist in England. This so-called Mansfield Judgment was to be influential in the campaigns, over the next sixty years, to abolish the British institutions of kidnapping and holding African humans in chattel slavery.

The Usefulness of Honor

Introducing the Honor Code

Two important themes are discernible in this case: an awareness of atrocious injustice, and a sense that (national) honor requires the correcting of that injustice. The latter theme is the topic of a major book by philosopher Kwame Anthony Appiah, *The Honor Code: How Moral Revolutions Happen*. Appiah, who grew up in Ghana, was educated in England, and now teaches at Princeton, analyzes the part that conceptions of honor played in four social revolutions of varying moral weight: the ending of the duel, the freeing of Chinese women's feet, the abolition of Atlantic slavery, and the contemporary campaigns against the "honor" murders of women in Pakistan and other middle-eastern countries. In passing, Appiah mentions factory farming and other evils, suggesting that honor issues may have a part in ending them as well.

Despite having prevailed for hundreds of years (footbinding for nearly a thousand), the first three of these evils each fell within about a generation. The moral objections to them were already known, says Appiah; the main thing that differed was the conception of honor.

Appiah's analysis of honor shows it to be complex; the word applies not only to the *respect* shown to those in the upper ranks of a hierarchy just because of the class in which they were born, but also the *esteem* granted those who meet or exceed the standards of their class or category. This dual meaning implies that a person can both be honorable and be shamed at the same time for closely linked reasons. (An example might be Mr. Darcy of Jane Austen's *Pride and Prejudice*, who is proud of his status as a gentleman of wealth and aristocratic lineage, but also deeply ashamed because, as Elizabeth Bennet rightly tells him, his behavior has been arrogant and disdainful, and thus not gentlemanlike.) Thus a dimension of honor—basic *dignity*—can be claimed by all human beings, including those of low class or poor achievement.

From Honor to Shame

Different but linked aspects of honor stand out in the three successful revolutions. The duel was an institution in which male aristocrats defended their honor against the perceived insults of others of their class, thereby flaunting both their supposed manliness and their superiority to the lower orders, among whom such a killing would be a crime punishable by death.

Taking the Adventure

But the duel's days were numbered when social and political power began to shift from the hereditary aristocrats to the middle class. When bankers, or—even worse—shopkeepers' assistants took to dueling, the institution began to seem ridiculous, and it fizzled out. Thus what the often-heard condemnations of the practice—that is was irrational, violent, and unable to insure justice—could not achieve was brought about by laughter.

Similarly, for centuries Chinese footbinding was associated with upper-class status, though it gradually took hold among lower classes as well. Despite occasional protests against its cruelty, it was so crucial to social acceptability that without it a woman was scarcely thought to be marriageable. Furthermore, the small foot was experienced as erotically charged. Unlike the case of dueling, footbinding's becoming adopted among lower classes did not make it seem ridiculous, perhaps because in essence it served not so much to assert class status as to represent woman's disempowerment: a woman with tiny, deformed feet literally could not choose and go her own way.

What caused it to fall was not an internal shift of power so much as a broadening, so to speak, of the cultural conversation. During the mid-nineteenth century, China's pride and sovereignty were breached by the West, and forced to accept humiliating trade arrangements. Western ideas also entered more quietly, through young Chinese men who returned from studying in universities like Cambridge or Harvard, and through resident Westerners, especially missionaries; both women and men were influential in condemning footbinding. Finding that Westerners considered bound feet grotesque, those Chinese who cared about their country increasingly felt that the little "golden lotuses" were not a woman's pride but China's shame. In such an atmosphere the institution could not long survive.

Appiah makes a case that honor was also involved in the movement to end British involvement in the slave trade and, later, slavery itself. One argument used by William Wilberforce, the devout Evangelical statesman who led the campaigns in Parliament for decades, was that slavery was incompatible with Britain's claim to be Christian, and was thus a blot upon its honor. It also helped that many Christians, who believed that to be preoccupied with one's own honor was selfish and unworthy, could espouse national honor, because that could enable one to get beyond oneself and sacrifice for the greater good, thus wielding moral power.

Furthermore, group honor understood as basic human dignity was a particular issue in the involvement of the working classes in the anti-slavery movement. Many voices, including some defending the status quo, pointed

The Usefulness of Honor

up strong analogies between the abuses and exploitation that English mine and factory workers suffered, and the ones undergone by slaves. A sense of identification took root among workers: like the slaves, they were mistreated and held in contempt because they labored. But they increasingly came to hold that because of their basic dignity as human beings, labor deserves respect. Workers in northern manufacturing cities competed with one another by city to gain the greatest number of signatures on petitions to Parliament and on pledges to boycott West Indian sugar. And Parliamentarians began to accept the idea of basic dignity, which implied that they had to listen to the "lowly" instead of only talking down at them.

Appiah insightfully points out an analogy between ongoing present-day campaigns against the "honor" murders of women in certain Muslim countries and the anti-slavery campaigns: activists claim their nation's religion as ally, so that the widespread flouting of its principles is a source of shame. There is broad (if not entirely unanimous) agreement, in Pakistan and elsewhere, that honor murders are incompatible with Islam, one of whose central assertions is "Allah is compassionate." A similarity to the anti-footbinding movement is found in the presence of a broadening of cultural conversation, facilitated by the Internet, leading to an alliance between vulnerable Pakistani women and empowered women in other countries. As British workers identified with abused slaves, many foreign women today see honor murders as an evil practice assaulting their own dignity.

Basic Dignity and the Divine Light

When honor (as catalyst for change) is understood as the basic dignity of all persons, it is implied that there is something in every person worthy of respect. Our country's founding fathers, many of them Deists, asserted this in speaking of self-evident truths that all men [sic] are created equal, and endowed by their Creator with inalienable rights to life and liberty. In previous chapters I have mentioned that the Jewish and Christian belief in the image of God in every person is another foundation for basic dignity, as is is the Quaker affirmation of the presence of the Divine Light or Spirit in every person. This concept has been influential, even though Quakers are relatively few, because Friends have been active out of proportion to their numbers in the anti-slavery movement, prison reform, and other justice movements, thanks to this belief. Of these three foundations (there are still others), I believe the Inner Divine Light is the strongest. Without arguing the case,

Taking the Adventure

for the moment let us consider its possibilities as the source of a changed conception of honor that may hasten the moral revolution that we seek.

Early seventeenth-century Quakers were in fact much concerned with the meaning of honor. They lived in a society polarized by class, in which people of lower classes (to which most Friends belonged) were expected to bow and (if male) to doff their hats to richly-dressed aristocrats, addressing them, when spoken to, by title and honorific terms. But on the basis of their experience of the Light as one in all persons, conferring the only true honor on all, Quakers rejected such practices, keeping their hats on, using only the title "Friend" (derived in part from the line attributed to Jesus, "No longer do I call you servants . . . but I have called you friends."[1]) This rejection of titles essentially continues among Quakers today. The presence in every person of the equalizing and unifying Light was, and is, also the basis for Friends' opposition to exploitation, war, and other forms of violence. In the last few decades Friends have increasingly come to affirm the presence of the Light throughout the cosmos, and as a result have become active in environmental efforts. Many other spiritually aware people as well are affirming that human treatment of nature must change radically. But for most religious persons, including Quakers, this expanded vision has obviously not yet led to a stance of opposing violence toward animals.

Honor and the Revolution for Animals

The majority of people who care about animals probably are not in the habit of thinking of a Divine Light present in every heart, but most probably would agree that both animals and people are due the respect, or even reverence, that would be appropriate if there were in fact Something of God in them. How might this conviction help activists and their supporters communicate better with the unconvinced?

The way the duel ended—by being shown as embarrassing and ridiculous—is definitely not the way for us to take. Many meat-eaters already see vegetarians as looking down on them from their moral high ground, accusing them of dark deeds, and holding them in contempt. In fact flesh-eaters are born into a system that does make them complicit in terrible cruelties to animals, whether knowingly or not; and informing them of these unwelcome facts is a necessary part of our message. But it must be presented

---

1. John 15:15, KJV.

in ways that will awaken their compassion. Trying to shame them for their complicity would in most cases make them more defensive.

It is more profitable to stress the positive potential of honor. The general view justifying the status quo—that a "food" animal is a dimwitted, lumpish object, identical to every one of "its" kind—must be corrected by information that supports animals' basic dignity. Such information is increasingly available thanks to ethologists and other observers: animals are complex and sensitive beings, able to experience both keen pleasure and terrible suffering; many are capable of what we must in honesty call love.

It is also good to stress the basic dignity—the true honor—of the human beings we are seeking to awaken. Whether as bearers of the Light, or of the Divine Image, or as endowed by their Creator with inalienable rights, they have the potential for manifesting gleams of the divine love to "the least of these." A small percentage of persons do evil deliberately with no apparent compunctions, but most intend to be decent, caring folk. Yet they are entrapped by custom, and their consciences have gone numb. Faith claims that in their innermost being, probably unknown even to themselves, is something wonderful that is incompatible with the evil system that they are defending.

We must not forget that with the help of the Spirit of God, they can become free of the trap, so that their—our—actions are more and more in keeping with their and our true honor.

21

The Prophet From Nazareth

"What Would Jesus Do?"

ONE OF THE ISSUES debated among religious vegetarians and animal-eaters is the question "Was Jesus a vegetarian?" It is true that for some animal advocates, the question is unimportant; Jesus has played little or no role in their lives, and there are other looming contemporary issues that take up their time and attention. But in fact the question matters for all of us who care about our animal cousins, because the figure of Jesus, and its roots in the Bible, are pivotal for millions of Christians. Thus, how one interprets the texts about him that deal with this issue makes a huge potential difference to the progress of the animal concern.

For Christians who hold that every part of the Bible presents models for human life, the answer to the vegetarian question is a confident *no*. They find scenes in the gospels that show Jesus helping some of his followers to make a successful catch of fish, or multiplying fish (and bread) to feed thousands of people in the wilderness; cooking fish for his disciples in one Resurrection appearance, and eating a piece himself in another. They conclude that because Jesus by his actions affirms fish consumption, the Bible gives its stamp of approval to meat-eating.

But those from the Christian tradition who do not see every passage of the Bible as historically accurate, or necessarily authoritative for our lives, may come to different conclusions. Keith Akers, in his books *The Lost Religion of Jesus* and *Disciples*, has pointed out that there were many vegetarians among early Christians; Jewish Christians, the core of the primitive church, included vegetarians. Jewish followers of Jesus were centered in Jerusalem

The Prophet From Nazareth

until the destruction of the city in CE 70, and their first leader was Jesus' brother James. The later Ebionites, who lived in the same general area and who had some significant continuities with them, claimed that both James and Jesus were very much opposed to the temple and animal sacrifices, and embraced poverty and vegetarianism (the latter two tended to go together; meat was eaten by the well-off). Akers makes a significant and arguable case.

But even if the mainstream tradition is correct when it describes Jesus as accepting fish-eating, his stance was not necessarily applicable to us; there are major cultural differences between his situation and ours. He was ministering to peasants who were near the edge of subsistence or being pushed over it as a result of heavy taxation by Roman authorities and the Temple priesthood; in many instances they were losing their family farm plots to wealthy city-dwellers as a result of crushing tax debt. Those who earned a living by fishing were also being exploitatively taxed; but if peasants who lived near the lake could catch a few fish just for their families, it might help them survive.

Our situation as mostly middle-class people in the twenty-first century is entirely different. We have many kinds of plant foods available, and we have access to biological information indicating that fish are sensitive to pain in ways quite similar to ourselves. Furthermore, not only do we not need to fish (or hunt) to survive, we should know that both commercial wild-catch fishing and fish-farming are destroying the oceans at a frightening rate, just as factory-farming of land animals is bringing havoc to soils, water sources, and the atmosphere, and is contributing substantially to climate change. Thus Jesus' stance regarding fish-eating in a severely oppressed subculture is no more binding on us than is his manner of dress. In fact, the pervading biblical theme that the world belongs to God, whose tender mercies are over all God's creatures, would rather require that we abstain from foods that threaten the earth and cause unnecessary suffering to animals.

Jesus' Focus

In the canonical gospels, Jesus occasionally speaks caringly of animals; he says that God is conscious of the fall of every sparrow; he compares God's (and/or his own) longing to renew disordered Jerusalem with a hen's desire to gather her chicks under her wings. The fourth gospel depicts Jesus as developing the ancient God-is-our-Shepherd image with a dramatic new turn to express the depths of divine love: "The good shepherd lays down his life for the sheep."[1] This image greatly enhances the dignity of physical sheep, but as a metaphor, its focus is human beings. And human beings are the primary focus of Jesus' prophetic preaching and actions. He denounces oppression by the powerful (although God loves even them); he has good news for the poor and exploited; he teaches listeners to be compassionate as God is compassionate. *His central theme is that the Kingdom of God is in their midst.* Thus animals are not the primary objects in his prophetic message. This chapter will be devoted chiefly to sketching the history of the idea of the Kingdom of God as focussed on oppressed humans; however, Jesus' Good News of the Kingdom does contain the seeds of the liberation of animals, as we will see in the last section.

Roots of the Kingdom of God

Many readers may not be aware how far back in Hebrew tradition the Kingdom of God theme is rooted. According to *The Prophetic Imagination* by Old Testament scholar Walter Brueggemann, its roots are found in the account of the establishment of the Covenant between God and Israel at Sinai, and even before that, in the Exodus, Israel's foundational story. God is the Liberator who brings Israel out of Egypt, out of the house of bondage ruled by a foreign emperor; and this God, who cares for the lowly and the oppressed, is to be Israel's only ruler. The nature of the Covenant is complicated, with laws of many sorts, not all of them life-giving, formulated at various times over centuries. But the provisions that were almost surely central in the oral scriptures of the peasant villagers aimed at economic justice: to safeguard each family's inherited plot, and prevent poor families from being ruined by indebtedness and exploitation. Their themes were based on God's loving and liberating compassion for the least among God's people.

In a later century, the prophet Samuel speaks out of this theme when the elders of the people ask for a king to lead them in war against the invading Philistines. Samuel resists, reiterating that God is to be their only monarch, and warning them that a king will become an exploiter, a taker: "He will take your sons . . . he will take your daughters . . . he will take your fields . . . he will take the best of your fields and vineyards . . . the best of your cattle and donkeys . . . he will take a tenth of your flocks, and

---

1. John 10:11, NIV.

The Prophet From Nazareth

you yourselves will become his slaves."[2] But God, with evident reluctance, tells Samuel to give the petitioners what they request. Brueggemann holds that "the people" who asked for a king probably did not include everyone; many of them may have been suspicious of this risky innovation, but got overruled.

The second king, David, is described as "a man after God's own heart," and a royal/messianic theme arises in which justice is established through human kingship (as seen, for example, in some of the Psalms), a theme naturally promoted in royal and aristocratic circles. But this theme exists in tension with many of the common people's commitment to the original state of affairs, a realm ruled by God only. And with good reason; already with David's son Solomon, who established a mini-empire, oppression had returned. Samuel's warning that "he will take. . . he will take . . . he will take . . . " in fact characterizes many of the kings as they are described by the chroniclers: they become the new Pharaohs of their day. In such situations, prophets arise to denounce, among other things, the oppression of the poor by the ruling royal and aristocratic powers of their time, and call both king and people to return to God. If they refuse, says the prophet, they will meet disaster.

The disasters that do in fact befall Israel over several centuries, namely, being conquered and exploited by one rising empire after another, are interpreted by later prophets as the result of earlier sins. They seek to find meaning in these catastrophes and sufferings by tracing them to covenant-breaking acts; they call the people to return to God. In certain passages they denounce the imperial oppressors, promising a new Exodus and a renewal of broken Israel. In some passages this renewal is to take place under an ideal Davidic king, sometimes under the compassionate and just rule of God only.

Jesus' Renewal of the Kingdom Proclamation

Jesus' ministry must be seen as a part of this long kingdom-of-God tradition. He appears as a prophet in a situation in which the Roman rulers, their governors or client-kings such as Herod Antipas, and the collaborating priests of the Jerusalem temple (the High Priest was the Roman governor's appointee) all demanded shares of the of the produce of subsistence farmers who made up perhaps ninety percent of the population. Under

2. I Sam. 8:11–17, NIV.

this crushing triple tax burden, the village life in which most Galileans and Judeans lived was disintegrating. Unable to pay mounting tax debts, pursued by anxiety, many formerly self-subsistent peasant families were losing their farm plots to the wealthy, and becoming day-laborers or worse. One of Jesus parables, in Matthew 20:1–16, reflects the situation by describing more and more day-laborers collecting in the marketplace over the day, desperate to find work for pennies on one of the great estates—ironically, they may find work on one that swallowed up their own property.[3]

Many of Rome's oppressed subjects elsewhere may have fallen into despair and apathy, but because of the Jews' tradition of a compassionate and liberating God, there was strong resistance: they would not accept this situation as simply the Way Things Are. Festering frustration and rage were expressed in various ways, some covert, the most conspicuous being banditry and periodic violent revolts. These the dreaded Roman soldiers/goon squads, the Legions, smashed with merciless ferocity: burning villages and even whole cities, enslaving or crucifying the fleeing inhabitants. The glorious *Pax Romana* was based on a protection racket and state terrorism.

Jesus' prophetic renewal of the ancient message that a compassionate and just God is Israel's only king is thus politically and economically subversive. It means that Caesar, who takes . . . and takes . . . and takes . . . and claims he is Son of God and therefore divinely authorized,[4] *is neither god nor king.* Jesus message was that the kingdom of God comes when the faithful and unfaithful alike find God's giving, forgiving, and liberating presence in their midst. By implication, they need not resort to the corrupted Temple, no longer a house of prayer but (as in Jeremiah's day) a headquarters of robbers (namely, the priests). Where the stresses of hunger, anxiety, and loss of farms have led to alienation and in-fighting in the villages, he calls for renewal of Covenant principles: share your bread (in communal meals); forgive the debts your neighbor owes you; lend to your neighbor in trouble; embarrass the hostile neighbor, who insulted you with a slap on the face, by turning the other cheek. Reach out even to the Roman soldier who demands that you carry his gear for a mile by carrying it for two miles.

The stories of Jesus also show him proclaiming the Kingdom of God by his actions. When he casts out multiple demons called Legion (!) from a homeless, psychotic man, and the Legion flees into pigs who rush into the water and drown, his hearers would understand that God would cause the

---

3. Korb, *Life in Year One*, 86.
4. Crossan, *Jesus: A Revolutionary Biography,* 1–4.

The Prophet From Nazareth

shock-troops of the Roman Pharaoh to meet the same fate as the horses and soldiers of the Exodus. story. (Since pigs can in fact swim, this part of the story is probably not literal history.) Stories of sea-crossings followed by the feeding of thousands in the wilderness also proclaimed that their one and only Monarch, who had once brought them out of slavery in Egypt and through the Red Sea, fed them in the wilderness on manna, and given them the land, was at work through a new Moses. Stories of healings and a raising of the recently dead proclaim the presence of a new Elijah, renewing God's rule in a time of apostasy and royal tyranny. (In confirmation of these connections, Moses and Elijah appear together with Jesus in the Transfiguration story).

The Cost of the Kingdom Proclamation

During his traveling ministry among the peasant villages of Galilee Jesus has skirmishes with the scribes and experts in the written Scriptures who function as retainers for the wealthy Temple elite (Jesus' message is probably based on the oral Scriptures of the illiterate poor, says Brueggemann). But when he goes to Jerusalem and makes a public, symbolic attack on the corrupted Temple itself, he is speaking Truth to Power—loudly. As a result, the Romans, together with their bedfellows the chief priests, put him to the horrible, tortured death of a subversive: namely, public crucifixion.

Some authorities think that the fact that no attempt was made to round up his followers is probably because Jesus' message was nonviolent.

One of the reasons the political-economic dimensions of this message are hard to discern in the gospels is that the oral traditions that preserved it were probably not recorded until after the huge, hellish catastrophe, the destruction of Jerusalem and the Temple, that crushed the Judean revolt of 66-70 C.E. (Mark was perhaps written down just around 70). During the succeeding years, Rome used its shining victory over the uppity Judeans in a blame-the-victim propaganda campaign. In this paranoid atmosphere, it became dangerous to identify with or support anything Judean; and the message of a crucified Jew was highly suspect by its very nature. Thus the subversive nature of the Kingdom of God proclamation was muted and downplayed in the gospels; Roman centurions look pretty good, and elements of the period's victim-blaming become part of the gospel story. For example, the brutal, ruthless Pilate (recalled by Rome six years later for ill-judged and excessive

Taking the Adventure

violence[5]) is presented as a well-meaning sort who wanted to release Jesus, but was pressured by a Judean crowd easily manipulated by the chief priests (whom the common people in fact hated) to demand his crucifixion—both very unlikely. Needless to say, this questionable defensive strategy was to bear the poisonous fruit of antisemitism for many centuries.

The Prophetic Principle and Animals

The concept of the Kingdom of God was preached to villagers who might have been more or less capable of governing themselves, if only the Roman gougers and the minority of Jews they employed would leave them alone. But though their small, partially self-subsistent communities would then have been much better off then than under the heel of Empire, they would still have been suffocatingly oppressive to women and animals.

However, the work of the prophets, and in this case that of Jesus, does contain the seeds of liberation for both women and animals An example of this important prophetic principle is seen in the Kingdom teaching "And call no man your father on earth, for you have one Father, who is in heaven,"[6] which implies a profound critique of patriarchal control not clearly evident in earlier prophetic writings. The prophetic principle in question is that all social interactions are to be judged by the criteria of God's justice and compassion *for all*. But no single prophet can speak to all situations. Any one prophet may denounce a pattern of injustice and its attendant violence without seeing or acknowledging others. As Chapter 3, "We Were Slaves to Pharaoh," points out, in the Exodus narrative the Israelites' lambs and the horses of the Egyptians are disposable; yet. "the core of the prophetic critique goes on, a divine gift out of which later prophets are called to develop, correct, and deepen the message of earlier ones." In Moses' prophetic demand to Pharaoh, "Let my people go," are the seeds of the liberation of many oppressed groups in later centuries—of children, of serfs, of enslaved Africans, of women, of animals.

By calling for the enactment of God's compassion, justice, and liberation for our oppressed animal cousins, and especially when we ourselves *demonstrate* compassion for all parties, we are showing ourselves to be true daughters and sons of the prophets—for Christians, most especially of the great prophet from Nazareth.

5. Crossan, *Jesus: A Revolutionary Biography*, 138-40. Kalechofsky, "Pontius Pilate," 7.
6. Matt. 23:9, ESV.

22

Stranger at the Table

ABOUT IN 1628 THE twenty-something Rembrandt Van Rijn painted the climactic scene of the resurrection narrative in Luke 24 in high drama. The story tells that two disciples of Jesus were walking from Jerusalem to their home in the village of Emmaus (a journey of about seven miles) on Sunday afternoon, two days after the crucifixion of Jesus. As they talk over the shattering event, a stranger overtakes them and asks what they are discussing that makes them so sad. One of them, named Cleopas, tells the newcomer about Jesus, the prophet of mighty word and deed from Nazareth whom their hopes had cast as the one who was going to liberate Israel, but who had been seized by the authorities and, horribly, crucified. They add that

Taking the Adventure

that very morning, women of their group had reported finding his tomb empty, and angels announcing that he was alive; but others going to the spot did not see anything.

The stranger responds by explaining to them that this all happened in accordance with God's plan, in fulfillment of various Scripture passages from Moses and the other prophets. When the two travelers reach their home, the stranger shows signs of going on, but they urge him to spend the night: "Stay with us, for it is getting toward evening . . . " He accepts the invitation, and joins them for supper. At the meal he takes the part of the host, breaking the loaf of bread and distributing the pieces. As he does this, suddenly they recognize that he is Jesus; and he vanishes. Electrified, the two disciples get up and go back to Jerusalem (a two-plus hour walk, mostly in the dark) to tell their friends that Jesus had appeared to them, and became "known to them in the breaking of the bread."[1]

The Breaking of the Bread

That the recognition took place in the context of a shared meal is significant; it identifies the stranger, connecting him with the main concern of Jesus' ministry, the Kingdom of God. As we saw in the previous chapter, this Kingdom is an ancient theme in Israel's history, the minority position of those who hold that God's highest will for us is not royal rule but a society of equality and thus of fairness. As described in chapter 3, "We were Slaves to Pharaoh," this concept is rooted in the Exodus, Israel's founding story, whose theme is that God, unlike many other nations' deities, is against exploitative rule; God wills to liberate its victims, via human action, into a life of happiness and plenty. Later prophets renewed Exodus for their own times. They denounced (among other things) the rapacious rule of contemporary overlords, whether they were Israel's own rulers, or those of a new foreign empire. They promised renewal and abundance to all who Returned to God as their king. One of the major symbols of this new life of plenty is the shared feast: "On this mountain the LORD of Armies will prepare for all people a feast with the best foods, a banquet with aged wines, with the best foods and the finest wines."[2] Of this more later.

In his own day in which Roman greed and cruelty were driving the common people into tax debt, loss of farms, hunger, and misery, Jesus'

---
1. Luke 24:35, ESV.
2. Isa. 25:6, GW.

teachings gave particular emphasis to the shared-meal image, in his parables and sayings as well as in actual meals to which all were invited. It becomes not only a symbol of future freedom and plenty, but a present reality of enough to eat for everyone. (The technical term is *open commensality*.) Furthermore, it means acceptance and friendship for those at the bottom of society instead of rejection and contempt. In virtually any human society, some have much while others have little or nothing, and, correspondingly, most people will dine with those on their own social and financial level, but not with those they consider beneath them. This applies not only to the aristocrats, who scorn peasants, but to self-supporting peasants, who scorn beggars and prostitutes. But the feast Jesus promotes is one of compassion, equality and plenty for *all* who will to share. The God of unstinting love, *not* Caesar, rules.

Cleopas and his companion were almost surely among the poor; if they had substantial means, one would expect them to be riding in comfort, not walking nearly five hours in one day. According to Scott Korb's *Life in Year One*, many first-century Jewish peasants who still had homes lived in dirt-floored, thatch-roofed hovels made of stones mortared with mud, and their food was likely to be scanty. The rough stone and board wall behind the dining figures in Rembrandt's painting, the small table with only just enough food to go around, reflect this probability (although not the high ceiling and spaciousness, which the artist probably chose in order to convey a sense of the numinous). Yet they invite the homeless stranger to share what they have for the night. In doing so, they enact what they have learned from Jesus: and they find that he is not dead, but right there at their table. They are stunned, rapturous.

A wonderful golden light, many times brighter than any oil lamp could cast, illuminates Rembrandt's table and diners, except for the figure of Jesus, who is silhouetted in it. (For a color reproduction online, see http://www.artbible.info/images/rembrandt_emmaus-open_grt.jpg .) To my mind the amber glow represents the Divine Light, which, largely unseen, suffuses all things and sometimes radiates out of the darkness in dazzling splendor: "The whole earth is full of thy glory,"[3] says Isaiah. It is the impersonal aspect of God made visible. This promised feast of the Kingdom of God is also described in the hymn "God is There" by Faith Bowman:

> While the world was wrapped in silence,
> Winter night's swift course half-run,

3. Isa. 6:3 KJV.

Taking the Adventure

> God's almighty Word of Wisdom
> From her heavenly place leaped down!
>
> To a people battered, bleeding,
> Ruled by rapine, fire, and fist,
> Came a pledge of peace and healing,
> Of God's Kingdom in their midst.
>
> Where we call no man our master
> But are kin and equals all,
> Rich and homeless feast together—
> God is there to grace the hall . . . [4]

In the homeless stranger at the table and the light surrounding him we see a glimpse of God, the unknown Someone who offers life and abundance to all, who cannot be defeated by violence and death, the Someone from whom all somethings and someones come, and to whom they return.

A Welcome to All?

Does this mean that *all* someones, however lowly, are in fact welcome at the table in the Kingdom of God? It is evident that, historically, most human actions to make sure that everyone has enough to eat have fallen sadly short. Perhaps the term "Kingdom" contributes something to the problems; despite the term's intent to abolish tyranny, its identification of God with a male monarch (even if the only one) influences our thinking. Suggested alternatives, like the Commonwealth of God, don't carry the same emotional weight.

Particular instances of the Feast fall short in different ways. For example, even this marvelous Rembrandt painting shows that the artist seems to assume that the Kingdom of God is a male-centered society. The three diners (one is on his knees before the figure of Jesus) are all male, whereas, in the background, a woman is doing the work. It is unlikely that Rembrandt's contemporaries, and thousands of people of faith viewing the painting since then, have seen any problem here. (The figure of the maid is, however, ambiguous; suggestively, her body is also silhouetted in a small circle of golden light, and inclined at the same angle as that of Jesus.)

---

4. Bowman, "God is There," *Faith Poems*. See also Wisdom of Solomon 18:14-15.

Furthermore, when we seek to provide a table and shelter for all, inviting the destitute from the "highways and hedges," we find that we must have not only generous, open hearts, but caution, prudence, and toughness as well. Those in greatest need do not necessarily welcome the Kingdom; a mentally disturbed or addicted or mean-spirited few may sabotage the program for many. And the program may even perpetuate the problem, if supportive services such as therapy and job counseling are not part of it. These necessary precautions tend to creates a two-class situation: those who bring the food and make the rules, and those who receive and obey. This pattern tends to blunt the sensitivity of the well-intentioned folk who plan and carry out the dinners. Sometimes when I have participated in serving at dinners for homeless people, I found that the "hosts" ate at their separate table, which the homeless "guests" did not feel free to join. (I must confess that, having little small talk and thus being ill qualified to recommend myself to strangers, I was much tempted to join the hosts. Perhaps some of the others there felt the same.)

The View From Beneath the Bottom

It is probably in regard to our oppressed animal cousins that historic efforts to welcome the stranger as a guest have failed most dismally. Most of the time people of faith have continued to regard "food" animals as beneath the bottom, if they are aware of them at all. Absent as conscious subjects, as Carol J. Adams says in *The Sexual Politics of Meat*, they exist only as things on the platter. They remain strangers, not recognized even after death.

It is true that in some places on earth, social conditions may make this problem very hard to remedy. One example is a program to feed homeless people who live on the vast city dump in Managua, Nicaragua. I visited this place in 1995, and was horrified. Adults, children, whole families spend their lives combing the trash for not-too-decayed scraps to eat or items they can sell for a few *cordobas* on the streets; when a truck arrives to dump its trash, desperate people swarm over, and fights may break out. Because this situation especially reached my heart, I contribute to an organization called Pro-Nica, supported by a group of Florida Quakers, which works with a Nicaraguan NGO group (among other groups) to provide one meal a day to some of these destitute folk, especially the children. And the local people who plan and serve the meals, wanting these hungry children to have the best at that one dinner, include "meat."

Taking the Adventure

I made inquiries from one of the Pro-Nica members working for the program: wouldn't it be more compassionate and Friendly to make the meals nonviolent? My correspondent, herself a vegetarian, agreed, but said it is hard to do. It seems that much of the country is a "food desert" when it comes to vegetables (which agrees with my earlier experience there in 1986). Money for the program is limited, veggies are scarce, meat is more available, so that is mostly what the children get with their rice and beans. I keep hoping for a way to open to a truly peaceable table.

Of course there are food deserts in the US as well, but the middle-class people of faith who plan meals for homeless people are not confined to these deserts. Most of them center the meals on animal flesh because they have always eaten that way themselves, and never thought of anything else. I know one or two of these meal providers who have even heard the message of compassion for animals, but rejected it, and later drew attention to how much the homeless appreciated their meat dish. Instead of working toward an Exodus for the animals, most people of faith have unthinkingly participated in enslaving them. Instead of healing and freeing them, we have paid to have them live in filth and misery, and die in terror and agony. Instead of sharing fairly at the planetary table with free animal nations, we consume products of giant firms that take over their living spaces, extinguishing nation after nation.

Returning

Like his forbears the earlier prophets, the prophet from Nazareth called people of all classes to repent. The word "repent" has become a caricature suggesting a stuffy outlook and imaginary misdeeds, but its original intent, as I tried to show in "He Came to Himself," is profound, and is highly relevant here. One of its primary meanings is to turn away from corrupt social structures based on ranking and exploitation, and Return to the God of compassion and fairness. Both society and the individual must be transformed, until we love our neighbors as ourselves on both individual and socio-political levels. We rejoice that some in our day *have* heard the prophetic message in regard to animals; no doubt some readers of this essay are involved in shared-meal programs where the tables are genuinely peaceable. I know of one or two church groups whose members not only served homeless persons vegetarian meals, but decorated the tables with candles and flowers in honor of the stranger-guests.

In the stranger we have invited to the table, whatever her or his race, class, or shape, we must recognize the divine Face, God with us.

23

"All Animals Are Equal . . ."

". . . But some are more equal than others," goes George Orwell's familiar line from *Animal Farm*, a satire on betrayed sociopolitical revolutions. In the language of Quakers, the line might be "All bearers of the Divine Light are equal, but we human animals are more equal than the others." "More Equal" is of course nonsense that shows up the bad faith of a speaker who has betrayed his or her commitment to (distributive) justice. No one who seeks to live a true spiritual life would seriously make such a claim; those who defend the status quo of animals-as-food would simply say that the cherished value of Equality does not apply to them, and never has.

But equality is a complex and ambiguous concept, and it is not surprising that even Friends, for whom it is a cardinal principle, often do not see the issue clearly. People who openly defend hierarchical social structures have pointed out that in fact all people are *not* equal, let alone all beings. There is a great mental gulf between Einstein and the badly brain-damaged, a moral/spiritual gulf between Gandhi and the torturer. This obvious inequality of capacities in individuals, applied across the board to oppressed groups, was once used to deny equal rights to women, Jews, African-Americans, children, and others. Traits that appeared in some partly as a result of particular conditions of oppression were turned into stereotypical descriptions of the whole group. Thus (valued) women are modest and nonassertive, attractive to men and fertile, physically and mentally weak; but women of despised categories are only good for one-night stands or heavy labor. Blacks are lazy, highly sexed, musical, and prone to crime; Jews are dishonest gold-diggers who will try to take advantage of

Taking the Adventure

(more spiritually-minded) Christians. It follows, obviously, that these inferior beings must be subordinated to their betters, or society will degenerate.

As a result of the movements for racial, gender, and ethnic liberation (assisted by certain wars) in the nineteenth and twentieth centuries, such bigoted ideas are, for the most part, no longer openly accepted in our culture. But the pattern of abusive stereotyping is still in place for animals almost everywhere, and contributes to keeping them in chains. People who would never think of using "Jew-moneylender" or "lazy nigger" as an epithet don't hesitate to use animal words as terms of abuse against fellow humans: "bitchy" or "hoggish" or "birdbrained" or "bovine." Or, to describe those who commit atrocities, just "animals."

Surprising Discoveries

Just as with these other liberation movements, the heightened concern, in the last thirty or forty years, with animals as beings with rights and interests of their own, who deserve our care, has brought to light a great deal of information that challenges the stereotypes. Ethology, the study of animals in their own societies and environments, best known as a result of Jane Goodall's work with chimpanzees, has revealed much that can't be discovered by cutting up the bodies of animals identified by numbers and kept in cages. Among the historic discoveries of her long-running Gombe project are the fact that chimps make and use tools; that communities establish their own cultures, sometimes adopting practices from others; e.g., a particular tool-use that was part of the culture of one chimp community took root in another after a chimp emigrated from the first to the second. Chimps, can, alas, also make war. Goodall was right to (unknowingly) violate scientific protocol when she first began her study by giving the animals names rather than numbers; chimps have been seen to have diverse personalities, complex emotions and social relationships, ranging from the bully and the political opportunist to the devoted friend and the compassionate foster parent.[1]

Yet in Africa they are still widely regarded as food!

We are shaped rather like chimps (or vice versa), and we share with them 98% of our DNA, so perhaps these discoveries shouldn't surprise us. But scientists studying cows—kept not quite in their natural habitat but with respectful regard for what it might feel like to be a cow—have also made some surprising discoveries. For example, researchers Donald Broom

---

1. Miller, "Crusading for Chimps and Humans," *National Geographic*.

and Kristin Hagen carried out a study in which they devised a control panel in a paddock that required young cows to figure out how to open the gate admitting them to a food treat. Broom and Hagen fitted out the heifers with brain and heart monitors to measure their level of excitement. The heifers mulled over the situation for a time. When some of them figured out the solution and opened the gate, they had a "Eureka!" response: their hearts raced, their brainwaves altered, they jumped for joy, and trotted happily over to the food.[2] Their responses were definitely stronger than those of control cows simply admitted to the food reward.

John Webster, a professor of animal husbandry at Bristol University and a welfarist, reports that cows in a herd form small friendship groups of up to four animals; they spend their time together, often grooming each other. They will be careful not to hurt one another with their horns. Cows may also demonstrate that they dislike certain other cows, and bear grudges for months, even years.[3]

Keith Kendrick of Brabingham Institute reported parallel capacities among sheep. They can remember as many as fifty faces of other sheep, recognizing them even in profile; they can become strongly attached to particular humans, becoming depressed by being separated from them, and greeting the long-lost person enthusiastically after separations of up to three years.[4]

Not so bovine—or ovine—after all! When we take in this kind of evidence that "farm" animals have complex lives and viewpoints, our human practices of casually incarcerating them in revolting conditions and killing them for food begin to seem more and more like the organized enslavement and massacres of humans in the grimmest periods of human history.

Wherein Lies Equality?

What if these studies had come up with different results, tending to support common prejudices that animals are mindless carbon-copies of one another? Suppose our only signs that animals have feelings was their pulling back, trembling and screaming, while facing deadly violence?

---

2. Hagen, "Emotional Reactions to Learning in Cattle." *Applied Animal Behavior Science*.
3. Leake, "Cows Hold Grudges, Say Scientists," *The Australian*.
4. Trivedi, "Sheep Adept at Recognizing Faces," *National Geographic News*.

Taking the Adventure

Does their claim to equality depend on their mental capacities and psychological complexity?

The discoveries do strengthen our ability to identify with them, increasing our motivation to change the human treatment of them. But it can't establish their equality, because humans can still be "more equal," i.e., more intelligent, more capable, more complex. It is on a different level: it is a moral rather than a descriptive concept. Thomas Jefferson saw this point clearly in regard to racial equality (though his performance did not measure up to his insight): "whatever be their degree of talent it is no measure of their rights. Because Sir Isaac Newton was superior to others in understanding, he was not therefore lord of the property or person of others."[5] Most people would agree that subjecting a brain-damaged human being to painful experiments—or killing him for food!—is no more justifiable than doing the same to a human genius.

Moving Toward Moral Equality

Then how can we justify supporting the psychological violence of tearing a cow away from her friends, or a calf from his mother, so that we humans can consume her milk—let alone supporting physical violence so we can eat her flesh? Most people, including most socially concerned people of faith, don't try to justify these massive violations of moral equality; they just go on eating their steaks and their cheese. And the wealthy, politically powerful meat and dairy and egg industries go on supplying them and raking in profits. The dead hand of tradition and habit is heavy indeed.

Needless to say, it will not do. We must continue to examine our lives. We must "speak Truth to Power"—even when the powerful are not only politicians and CEOs, but ordinary, obscure human beings, including ourselves. After all, we have the choice to reach for that chunk of flesh in the supermarket, or to choose a nonviolent alternative—a power infinitely beyond that of the cow under the blade.

---

5. Jefferson, Letter to H. Gregoire, *Teaching American History*.

24

The Animals and the Angels

Innocence and Experience

> The sun descending in the west.
> The evening star does shine.
> The birds are silent in their nest,
> And I must seek for mine.[1]

THE COMMUNITY IN WHICH I live is located in an open, parklike area of great beauty, a space we share with many birds, lizards, rabbits and ground squirrels. Each time I take a walk, I will see some of them—flying or perched, eating, on sentry duty, singing or giving alarm, emerging from or disappearing into dens and nests. I often stop for a brief moment of wonder and delight as I look into their dark liquid eyes and bless them.

But at night, and occasionally also in daylight, there are also the coyotes. Sometimes there are howls which I always feel are expressions of hunger, not only of the body's hunger for the food that perishes, but the soul's hunger for the food that leads to eternal life. (For where did they come from, if not the divine Source? Is it not possible that at some deep level they feel it and thirst painfully for the fullness of that Life?) And occasionally there will be a fierce outburst of many coyotes yammering together as (I suppose) they tear apart a rabbit or squirrel they found abroad or dug out of his or her underground nest. Then what can a compassionate listener do except grieve and pray—pray that the consciousness of the terrified victim be received into the Light, that the coyotes will evolve beyond the bloodlust that curses them as well as their victims?

1. Blake, "Night." *Poems That Live*, 404.

Taking the Adventure

I find that William Blake's poem "Night," the first stanza of which is quoted above, gives voice to these very concerns. The setting is evidently a rural scene in England's green and pleasant land; a living moon watches the beautiful landscape and smiles with delight. The innocents are birds and sheep, the predators are wolves and tigers. (English tigers? Oh, well.) But there is another, major party in this scene that is probably seldom in the thoughts of friends of animals today, and that is angels. (This is, after all, William Blake.) After birds have gone to nest, sheep to fold, and other animals to caves, bright angels move unseen through the fields, blessing the buds and flowers and the sleeping creatures, comforting any who should be sleeping but are crying instead.

The angels know the predators too, and grieve when they attack and kill. Then the angels convey the souls of the slain animals to a Peaceable Kingdom, where the lion will become a compassionate guardian of the flock.

There certainly are problems in finding practical meaningfulness in this poem.

> When wolves and tigers howl for prey
> They pitying stand and weep,
> Seeking to drive their thirst away
> And keep them from the sheep.[2]

How can angels possibly drive away the wolves' hunger, their bloodthirst? I cannot imagine any means except spiritual evolution, which seems likely to take a very long time. How can the angels keep them from the sheep? The narrator implies that they succeed at times and at other times fail. The dreadful rush, the terror, pain and killing take place; the angels weep.

So far, Blake's concept of angel guardians of animals seem merely fanciful. A visionary, he may have himself seen these figures, but whether they are real apart from his highly original and creative mind apparently makes no difference to the real-life tragedy. After this turn in the story, however, the question of the reality or otherwise of Blake's spirit beings becomes very significant indeed for real life. "The angels, most heedful, /Receive each mild spirit / New worlds to inherit." The narrator, whom I assume to be the author himself, perceives the angels conducting the surviving spirits of the victims into what is unmistakably the Peaceable Kingdom. "And there the lion's ruddy eyes / Shall flow with tears of gold. . . " The great beast is filled

2. Op. Cit., 405

The Animals and the Angels

with compassion, becomes the guardian of the sheepfold, and declares that he can now lie down beside the lamb.

Whether or not there is life beyond death for any or all sentient beings potentially makes a great difference overall to the problem of evil and suffering. It's not that surviving death in itself solves that problem, however; as philosopher C.D. Broad pointed out, injustices might go on just as merrily after death as before. We can't count on the afterlife providing a suitable Reward for every being, or indeed that it includes a Peaceable Kingdom of any sort. But if survival *is* a reality, whatever its nature, it would expand the stage of action exponentially. If the horrible deaths of billions of farmed animals does not mean the end of them, it makes a huge difference both to them and to activists.

This possibility may seem scarcely more meaningful to some readers than the idea that angels exist and interact with living beings on earth. In the minds of many people of faith in the mainstream who work for peace and justice, life beyond death is associated with an other-worldliness that irresponsibly abandons concern for earth in order to gratify the desires of the individual human soul. The concept is generally thought to stem from wishful thinking. This assumption, however, is far from being true; in fact the survival of consciousness beyond death is supported by evidence.

Philosophical Background

Blake's narrative, likely to be seen by many as sheer fantasy, has implications for the nature of reality that are worth examining. As philosopher of science David Ray Griffin has shown in *God and Religion in the Postmodern World*, the confident assurance of many educated people in our culture that death is extinction of consciousness is not, as they assume, a scientific finding. It is a cultural belief, part of a materialistic worldview that evolved out of the philosophical ferment in the seventeenth century during the birth of science. The dualism associated with Descartes that separated mind and matter as two different realities was adopted not only by scientists throwing off the stifling rule of religious authorities, but by religious thinkers who actually intended thus to safeguard the reality of God and the immortal human soul, both of which were under challenge at that time. But in the next centuries, this plan backfired, because it is hard to understand or imagine how two totally differing realities can interact at all. Thus the soul—or consciousness—came to be seen as less than real, a mere byproduct of the brain, or even nothing but the brain. In either case, a materialistic worldview implies that consciousness is extinguished by death.

There are serious problems with materialism which philosophers are increasingly recognizing, mountains of evidence of different kinds that it cannot account for. Of particular interest to us is the abovementioned evidence (not proof) that human consciousness survives the body's death. This evidence is of various kinds, including veridical (truth-telling, evidential) instances of apparitions, of reincarnation-type claims, especially by small children, of communicators that take the initiative appearing in the trances of mediums, and of Near-Death experiences (NDEs). The whole issue is extremely complex; for a longer discussion see my 2001 book *The Uttermost Deep: The Challenge of Near-Death Experiences*. Here I can hardly do more than provide a very rough sketch with a few examples.

Near-Death Experiences

Of the different types of evidence of life after death, NDEs come closest to the pivotal action in Blake's poem, in which the angels as welcomers of the dying or nearly-dying persons in NDEs correspond to those who convey the animals' souls to paradise in the poem, and the gold tears and bright mane of the lion, and especially the "immortal day" which the animals enter, suggest the supernormal light seen by Near-Death experiencers. Many contemporary examples of NDEs that include welcomers and extraordinary light could be given; I will refer to a few cases from the nineteenth century. Accounts from the past, especially if they are confirmed by other witnesses and/or were written down soon after the event, do not lose their value with the passage of time.

It is remarkable that the brilliant Anglo-Irish writer Frances Power Cobbe (1822-1904), the tireless nineteenth-century activist on behalf of both laboratory animals and oppressed people, was also a pioneer in Near-Death studies. In 1882 she published a book entitled *The Peak in Darien* (the name is taken from John Keats' sonnet "On First Looking Into Chapman's Homer"), presenting a number of cases she had witnessed or collected, which include both welcomers and extraordinary light at deathbeds. In one of them, an extraordinary light was seen by two attendants at a deathbed. This is rare; usually it is only the dying (or apparently dying and then returning) person who tells of seeing a wonderful light. In another of Cobbe's cases, a dying person shows surprise at the appearance of a welcomer she

The Animals and the Angels

had thought was still alive, but who, it was later learned, had died shortly before this date. She concludes that her study strongly suggests that the death of a human being is not extinction but rather *expansion* of consciousness. For more details on these cases of Cobbe, see Appendix B1, page 200.

There are a few out-of-the-ordinary cases from other sources in which welcomers have been seen by deathbed attendants as well as the dying. In one case, three relatives caring for a dying aunt named Harriet Pearson saw an apparition of the aunt's beloved deceased sister Ann walking toward the sickroom. In another case, an accurate apparition of a distinctive-looking male welcomer was seen at the deathbed of a Mrs. Rogers by a nurse-attendant who had never known the man in life, and who was uncomfortable at the idea of communication with the dead. The cases strongly suggest that deathbed welcomers are more than images projected by dying persons hoping for reunion with loved ones. For more details, see Appendix B.

Unlike the above examples, most NDE cases are not subject to any confirmation, but many are impressive nonetheless because they include themes common to other NDEs, and present examples of afterlife concepts prevalent in cultures distant in time or space, themes which the experiencers neither knew of nor expected. For example, occasionally themes similar to material in the ancient Egyptian Book of the Dead or the Tibetan Book of the Dead will appear. Another notable factor is the evident power of NDEs in many cases to lead to extensive and often liberating life-changes, especially a new outlook centering in love for one's neighbors, an intense thirst for knowledge, and disappearance of all fear of death.

Other Kinds of Evidence

There are other categories of evidence for survival of consciousness: cases in which someone senses a presence, hears inexplicable voices or footsteps, or detects scents such as perfumes or tobacco favored by the deceased person; electronic phenomena such as inexplicable voices on recordings or on the telephone, and electric lights going on or off of their own accord at significant times; two or more people sharing a vivid, realistic dream of the deceased at the same time. One survey shows that about half of bereaved spouses have such experiences, but most keep quiet about them out of fear that others will think they are deluded or mentally disturbed.[3] Many cases are not evidential, but in a small percentage of them, especially when two

3. Rees, ""Hallucinations of Widowhood," *British Medical Journal.*

or more persons have virtually the same experience at the same time, the impact is increased, and it becomes less likely that the explanation is wish-fulfillment (or fear) on the part of the bereaved.

Animal Survival?

So much—or so little rather—about human experiences that suggest human survival of death. But how about animals? There are a number of collections of cases of this kind, and it is significant that they are quite similar to the categories suggesting human survival: apparitions, sometimes seen by more than one person, a sense of presence, characteristic sounds (barks, miaows, jingling tags, feet padding along or jumping down from furniture), unexplained familiar scents, vivid and coherent dreams about the deceased animal, or a definite feeling by a bereaved guardian of an invisible furry body settling down in bed against her or him. Some are experienced by more than one person at a time. Most have to do with animal companions, but before automobile travel, apparitional horses were occasionally seen as well.

As in human cases, many such experiences, though comforting to the bereaved, are not evidential. But they do not all happen to bereaved guardians. Author Kim Sheridan in *Animals and the Afterlife* tells of a case in which an apparition of a deceased dog was seen, not by the dog's bereaved guardian, but by her chiropractor, who had previously dismissed all such accounts as nonsense. For details, see Appendix B4.

The question of whether angels comparable to those Blake describes really do come as welcomers to dying animals is, of course, going to remain very hard to settle one way or the other. I recorded a suggestive case of a man who saw a vision of his deceased wife carrying away the spirit of the his cat who had recently died. The case is not evidential, but the resemblance to human NDE cases means that the idea is worth taking seriously. See Appendix B5.

These few comments, and the many accounts on which they are based, can hardly do more than encourage readers to question received notions and look into the evidence for themselves. But if in fact the more highly evolved animals, at least, do survive death, the implications for ethics are profound.

Cautions

In this last section, I will proceed "as-if"—supposing it were established that nonhuman animals of many sorts and conditions *did* survive death, what would be some implications for our treatment of them?

It must be admitted at the outset that such a state of affairs would not necessarily lead to an elimination of humans' casual killing of animals. There have been many cultures that took survival of both animal and human consciousness for granted, but manifested this belief in cruel and exploitative ways. For example, in some tribal cultures, animal sacrifice was based on the belief that the spirit of the slain beast would go to the other world and there be accepted by the deity as a gift. In regard to human beings, there have been found ancient burial sites of powerful men that included the remains of many other persons, probably slaves and wives killed at his death in order that they might serve the great man in the next world.

Several ancient peoples in the Near East held that survival was a curse for all, whatever their rank; there was a widespread view of the human afterlife as a gloomy, meaningless existence in a dusty underground realm. The early Hebrews' belief in an underground realm called Sheol falls roughly into this category. The Latin poet Lucretius wrote his long poem *De Rerum Natura (The Nature of Things)* in part to reassure his readers that the universe runs by purely physical principles; consciousness is extinguished at death, so they need not fear the gods or dread the afterlife. (So much for the widespread modern notion that all ideas of survival are wish-fulfilment!)

It is true that the majority of Near-Death Experience narratives to be found in the literature are happy or peaceful. But we cannot safely deduce from the evidence that, if animals (and people) do survive death, they will surely be compensated with joy and peace for unjust suffering on earth. There are certainly many NDE accounts, especially those from children close to death, that tell of entering a paradisal realm and being met by a joyful, bounding dog or cat the child had loved and lost. These comforting, happy visions are seldom evidential; their main significance is that there are many of them, and were not expected by the child experiencers. There are stories of Edens with contentedly grazing deer or horses; there is a wonderful account by experiencer Audrey Harris of a woodsy Peaceable Kingdom. I had the good fortune to hear the story from Ms. Harris herself; it is also available online and in print. For details see Appendix B4.

But it must be acknowledges that there are NDEs (their percentage of the total being unknown) that are dismal, distressing, disturbingly meaningless, or terrifying, and in many cases no reliable connection can be traced to the moral/spiritual character of the human experiencer. We cannot assume that things would be different for our fellow animals.

These depressing generalizations do not, however, mean that the possibility—even likelihood—of life after death for sentient beings has nothing to offer those of us who defend animals. It expands the stage; after each physical life it places, in Gracie Allen's well-known image, a comma rather than a period. We cannot be certain what might be on the other side of that comma, but continued or expanded existence of consciousness would give increased weight and value to any animal being, as John Wesley, vegetarian and co-founder of the Methodist movement, showed in his remarkable 1781 sermon "The General Deliverance"). An animal is a she or he, a subject and not an *it,* no mere object to be disposed of at the whim of a supposed owner. There is *more.* And though there is no certainty of happiness in this *more*, there are good reasons for hope.

Evolution and Survival

At first blush, evolutionary theory would seem to be one of the blocks to survival, but this idea is not necessarily true. The moral wall discussed in chapter 2 that is customarily drawn between human beings and animals—such that killing a human is murder, killing an animal is "slaughter" or even "harvesting"—is shown up by evolution to be an artificial construct: all we animals are of one blood, we are kin. If humans survive death, animals very likely do too, either as individuals or perhaps, as with social insects like bees, as part of a group consciousness.

But how about the reductionist outlook of materialism often thought to be implied by evolution, the apparent dethronement of the soul resulting from the principle that when a new form of life arises, physical adaptability to the environment is of first importance, with the development of consciousness being secondary? This would seem to make evolution rule out survival. But this apparently fundamental element is not, in fact, a necessary part of evolutionary theory. As mentioned above, it is rather a philosophical assumption that tends to be part of the Darwinian version of evolution. In fact there are several other philosophical frameworks for evolution that are more congenial to survival, in which intelligent design and evolution (to use contemporary politicized terms) make very comfortable bedfellows.

The Animals and the Angels

Among them is the theory of the evolution of consciousness toward an Omega Point of super-consciousness that Roman Catholic paleontologist Teilhard de Chardin theorized in his book *The Phenomenon of Man*. The process philosophy of Alfred North Whitehead, partially inspired by developments in early twentieth-century physics, also makes consciousness primary in evolutionary process, and has been found compatible with (human) survival by some of its proponents (see *Parapsychology, Philosophy, and Spirituality* by David Ray Griffin). There are other forms of evolutionary theory in which survival is even a crucial part of the theory: see, for example, a Theosophical work influenced by Eastern thought by E. Lester Smith and others, *Intelligence Came First*, and the similar systematic philosophy of involution and evolution by Hindu Vedantan mystic Aurobindo in his book *The Life Divine*.

Why Reasons for Hope?

Despite the fact that some NDEs are distressing, even painful, and serve no evident moral purpose of correction or reward, there are reasons to consider the likelihood of life after death as a decided plus. The most important reason is a framework of thought which represents the total existence of a living being as an initiatory journey of adventure climaxing in transformation. Many people who have had NDEs, including some who had painful ones, show this outlook in their subsequent life. As mentioned above, such an experiencer cannot go on as before; s/he feels s/he is not the same persons. Previous values—prestige, power, wealth, or a possessive marriage relationship—now seem suffocating and empty. Now s/he thirsts for God and for knowledge; s/he devours books; s/he gives away wealth and property; s/he explores different religious practices, or deepens her original faith commitment; s/he embarks on a life of service. S/he may receive guidance from a guardian angel; gifts of healing, telepathy, or clairvoyance may appear. While these changes often bring joy and fulfilment, they also result in the pain of misunderstandings, disruption of intimate relationships, loneliness, longing, the sense of being a stranger in a strange land.

These changes are in many cases similar to those reported by mystics, whose spiritual awakening leads to a lifelong search for God that takes them through trackless deserts and cosmic loneliness, including "dark-night-of-the-soul" experiences, some of which are remarkably similar to certain painful NDEs. The journey, described by scholar of Western mysticism

Taking the Adventure

Evelyn Underhill as consisting of five major stages, ultimately leads to the inexpressible joy of empowerment and union with the Ultimate.

Perhaps this long hero-adventure recounted in many versions and many cultures— awakening, growth, ordeals, and fulfilment of a person of destiny—is also the Eastern and neoplatonic mystics' journey from the One as potential, out into a far country to gain a treasure, and ultimate return to the One as Love realized. Perhaps this journey is something every living being is engaged in, for God surely loves all whom s/he has brought forth, and intends to return to her- or himself. This claim is a matter of faith, for we see glimpses only, moments of it in our life (or lives) on earth, and the vast majority of it must be hidden from our sight. The sense of profound unity with all beings, including animals, that many mystics and Near-Death Experiencers describe, seem to support such a faith.

Benefits and Liabilities

I find this framework of existence as a Great Adventure, going out from God and finally returning to God, profoundly encouraging when I am overwhelmed with the vast extent of human and animal suffering and the stubborn, opposing power of the forces of ignorance, greed, and callousness so often fueling it. I feel supported in my prayers for my fellow animals living or deceased, for their and our evolution beyond violence and back to the divine Heart. (This sketch of the Adventure, necessarily brief, is supported and developed further in my 2001 book *The Uttermost Deep*.)

Those who claim that interest in life after death is world-abandoning are not always wrong. It is true that when a whole culture takes for granted a view of the afterlife as retribution or reward and refuge, a certain percentage of the population will take that concept as an excuse to limit their interest to their social circle and their own spiritual progress, closing their hearts to the suffering of their fellows. This kind of complacency explains the aforementioned conviction of many liberally-inclined people of faith that belief in an afterlife leads to a pie-in-the-sky outlook. However, those who have experienced near-death, and are convinced of and interested in life after death, are in many cases much more deeply engaged in healing this world than they were before. Furthermore, belief in human survival of death is not the only culprit in world-abandonment; despair resulting from belief in reductionistic materialism can also lead to spiritual numbness and closed hearts.

The Animals and the Angels

Thus it is eminently worth our while to consider carefully the very considerable reasons for hope that this life is not all there is, both for our human sisters and brothers who are bone of our bone and flesh of our flesh, and for our dear animal cousins. To be convinced, or more than half convinced, of the reality of survival of death opens a substantial possibility that we can be of help both to abused animals and to human beings even after their deaths; this awareness can help us overcome the temptation to burn out or despair. It can also change our view of our own prospective deaths from extinction into the next event in the Great Adventure which God sends us.

25

Whatever One Sows

"Do not be deceived: God is not mocked, for whatever one sows, that will [she or] he also reap."[1]

WE HAVE SEEN THAT some of the narratives cited in "The Animals and the Angels" strongly suggest, in Frances Power Cobbe's image, that human consciousness does not becoming extinct at death, but expands. There are other cases suggesting that this may be true of companion animals, and perhaps all animals with some degree of individuality as well. Assuming for the present that survival is a reality, the present chapter will explore some of the profound implications that one of the (human) near-death phenomena have for our relationship with animals here and now.

The Life Review

The key phenomenon is a highly developed form of what is usually called the Life Review. Almost everyone has heard of the idea that "a drowning person sees his whole life flash before his eyes." In fact the phenomenon of seeing such images of one's life is not limited to victims of near-drowning. For example, a soldier injured in the Vietnam war by six rounds of machine-gun fire tells how he entered a peaceful state in which "my life began to become a picture in front of me, [beginning with] the time when I was still a baby, and the pictures seemed to progress through my whole life. I could remember everything; everything was so vivid . . ." He found the review to

---

1. Gal. 6:7, ESV.

be a completely positive thing; he had "no regrets."[2] For a similar but more detailed case from the nineteenth century, see Appendix C1, page 204.

For other experiencers, however, there have been definite regrets. In some, the encounters with their past took place in a heightened state of spiritual sensitivity in which they felt surrounded by a loving Light or Presence, and realized that love is the standard for judging all one's thoughts, words, and actions. Stripped of rationalizations and self-flattering excuses for certain things they had said and done, they recognized how harmful various of their actions were. One said, "After I could see the mean little things I did as a child, . . . I wished I could go back and undo them."[3]

Empathy

A limited number of those who returned from the brink of death had a still deeper level of encounter with their own pasts. Not only did they perceive everything they had done, and realize that some or even much of it had harmed others; they seemed to be living it all over again, not only from their own perspective, but with a consciousness expanded to include the feelings of everyone else upon whom they had had an impact. I have named this the Empathic Life Review. P.M.H. "Phyllis" Atwater says of her life review in 1977:

> For me, it was a total reliving of every thought . . . every word . . . and every deed . . . plus the effect of each thought, word, and deed on everyone and anyone who had ever come within my environment . . . (including unknown passersby in the street); plus the effect . . . on weather, plants, animals, soil . . . No slip of the tongue or slur was missed . . . If there is such a thing as hell, as far as I am concerned this was hell . . . The old saying "No man is an island," took on graphic proportions.[4]

The empathic life review of Betty Eadie involved not only feeling the impact she had had on others, but also the effects these others had on still others. "I was shown the "ripple effect" . . . I saw how I had often wronged people and how they had often turned to others and committed a similar wrong. This chain continued from victim to victim, like a circle of dominoes

2. Moody, *Life After Life*, 62-63.
3. Op. Cit., 60.
4. Atwater, *Coming Back*, 36

Taking the Adventure

.... My pain multiplied and became unbearable."[5] But this dreadful circle was not the last word; her life review took place in the presence of a loving Christ, who had compassion on her in her severe self-judgment. Furthermore, she found that the ripple effect also worked in situations of goodwill and kindness, spreading further goodwill and kindness.

For two further cases, one involving considerable detail, see Appendix C2 and C3.

Reflections

Although the Near-Death Experiencers who have undergone empathic life reviews do not seem to be many in proportion to all cases on record, there are some thinkers and spiritual teachers who assert that all of us can expect to undergo such an encounter at some point after death. Perhaps the biblical image of the Great Judgment is a symbol of this encounter with one's self, showing in total detail just how totally we are part of the web of the living.

If this is the case, the empathic life review idea is not so rare after all. Not only traditional Christianity and Islam, but strands of folk Buddhism and concepts about the afterlife in records of ancient Egypt present varying versions of a Judgment. Their main difference from the empathic life review is that in contemporary NDE narratives, the judgment is seldom if ever made by an impersonal power or an authority figure, but by oneself; and no outside punishment or rewards are given, for experiencing the effects of one's impact on others provides its own punishment or reward. The empathic life reviews strongly suggest that, eventually, we will know this interconnectedness concretely with every fiber of our being. The druglord who controls many people, body and soul, and doesn't hesitate to order killings; the tycoon who plans and builds a meat empire, complete with factory farms and slaughter-hells; the lying politician who frightens the public into supporting an ethnic pogrom, a war of aggression, or even genocide, in which millions die and many survivors suffer for the rest of their lives—all are throwing themselves into the hell of the terror and anguish of *every one* of their countless victims. Being convinced of the reality of this principle can deliver an activist from feelings of futile rage and hatred against perpetrators of massive evils, and may even arouse feelings of compassion for them.

On the other side, the Gandhi or Martin Luther King who teaches and acts to bring about peace and reconciliation experiences the healing

---

5. Eadie, Betty, *Embraced by the Light*, 113.

and fulfilment, generation after generation, of the millions his or her life touches. Most of us, of course, will fall somewhere in between, touching fewer lives directly than the great monsters and the great saints, with lesser good and lesser evil.

In his book *Whole in One,* British philosopher David Lorimer relates the empathic life review to better-known psychic phenomena such as telepathy, and to many mystics' sense of participation in the life of all things. Lorimer sees such phenomena as evidence of a universal "empathic resonance," the basis of an "ethic of interconnectedness." In other words, if conscience tells us that callous or sadistic treatment of other beings is wrong, it is because we sense at a deep level that we participate in the pain we cause to other living beings—though in ordinary incarnate life we may not feel that pain. If "Love your neighbor as yourself" and "Love your enemy" are good advice, it is because we participate in the blessings and benefits we confer on our enemies and our neighbors, *including* our animal neighbors and the planet as a whole. There is no wall restricting moral principles to one's own group, or even to humanity.

This means that those who see "nature red in tooth and claw" or "hit the other guy before he hits you" as the ultimate principle of life, justifying a stance of violence and exploitation of others as "realism," are in fact being extremely unrealistic. It's true that the moral world is not neat; there will always be painful situations when one has to choose between two actions that are both harmful, and situations where one does harm accidentally. But there are many more situations in which we can opt to reject a culturally sanctioned evil, and instead choose to treat our fellow animals—furry, feathered, or human—with respect and tenderness. This way is in keeping with the deepest nature of the universe.

26

Divine and Feline Grace

I HAVE ALWAYS LOVED cats, and have enjoyed having them in my life for decades. They're beautiful and graceful, it's a delight to cuddle them and feel them vibrate, it's interesting to watch their widely varying personalities develop. Two of those I've lived with over the years have helped me become a better seeker of God and lover of my fellow beings, and as it happens, they're both in residence now.

Angelique: No Good Deed Goes Unpunished

In the summer of 1994 my friend Doris and I stopped by her mother's house for a few words. On her front yard were two scrawny, neglected kittens, a ginger and a tortoiseshell, mewing pathetically. We offered them some water, but had no way to feed them then. The ginger kitten let us pick him up, but the tortoiseshell wouldn't allow us near her. They "belonged" to the next door neighbors, who had a long history of failing to feed, alter, or otherwise care for their cats. Doris' mother, suffering from dementia and not her usual caring self, threatened to "kick them into the next county." I wanted very much to take them both home, but unhappily wasn't in a position to do so at the time.

As soon as possible I went back, together with my son Richard, taking with us a small doll-bottle of goat's milk. The ginger kitten, to our sorrow, was gone, but the tortoiseshell was still there. She fled from us and hid in a bed of rose bushes, from which it took about forty-five minutes to lure her. While I drove home, Richard cuddled her and fed her the bottle, from which she sucked desperately. The threats of my friend's mother made me

Divine and Feline Grace

think of the passage in Hebrews, "Do not neglect to show hospitality to strangers, for thereby some have entertained angels unawares."[1] I named her Angel, which morphed into Angelique.

We knew that an infant so severely neglected would take some time for psychological healing. It took some time all right; now, an old woman of about ninety in human years, Angelique is still an unhappy orphan. She has a loud, strident voice and a demanding personality: she wants her (vet-recommended) baby food, or wants her treat, or wants fresh water in her bowl, or wants grooming and cuddling, and she wants it an hour ago, and who do I think I am to be doing other things first? Almost every time I enter the bedroom I'm treated to resentful-sounding, sometimes high-decibel miaows. Much of the time she seems to be tense, with her claws out, so that picking her up to give her the desired cuddling is a dangerous enterprise; I've learned to hug her while letting her back feet remain on the bed, so that when she decides to jump out of my arms, she won't leave ribbons of skin behind. If I'm not yet awake when she's ready for attention, she occasionally bursts out with an abrupt, eardrum-breaking *miaow* that slams into me and practically makes me leap up from the bed.

I used to get some relief from my frustration by calling her Mary Musgrove, after the reproachful, chronic complainer in Jane Austen's *Persuasion*, who lost her mother at age nine and never grew up. But I have stopped that, because I came to realize that Angelique really is an angel in the word's original sense of a messenger of God. She was sent to help me develop the strength to be patient, to say "May you find peace, Angel" instead of shouting "Shut *up*," to remember that it is the prickly and difficult one who most needs to experience the Divine compassion that never gives up until it touches and releases the sufferer's Inner Light. After almost twenty trying years, I really am learning these lessons, a little . . .

Taliessin: "Because He [She] First Loved Us"

In the spring of 2008 my spouse Robert and I decided to adopt a kitten from our friends Barbara and Clark, who were taking in pregnant stray cats, supervising the births, and finding homes for most of the kittens. In the spring of 2008, studying a picture of the kittens in the most recent litter before meeting them, I asked Barbara if anyone had claimed that cute gray one who lay on her back making bunny-paws in the air. Amazingly, no one

1. Heb. 13:2, ESV.

had; she was to be mine. I named her Pearl, but when she turned out to be a he, the name was changed to Merlin. Not wanting precious Merlin to be any more frightened or lonely than necessary in his strange new home, I also took one of his litter mates, a slim, rangy, very short-haired tabby with narrow black-and-gray stripes. (I prefer solid, rounded tabbies with wide stripes and longish hair, but none were available.) Merlin's add-on brother I named Taliessin, Tali for short.

In his early years Tali turned out to be a keen hunter, a habit which tended to cool the faint warm feelings I had for him. But after a time I made an effort to avoid letting him see how much I preferred his charming, Professional-Cute-Kitty brother; I took the trouble to cuddle Tali and pretend I loved him. To my dawning surprise, he responded as though my forced "love" were real. As time went by, he became very affectionate, climbing into my lap when I was reading, or eating, or in contemplative prayer, sometimes extending a paw toward me, favoring me with his quiet purr, and cuddling with me at night. When I go out to call him, he will often come bounding joyfully toward me as though I were the summit of all his desires. He follows me on my walks like a dog, with many side excursions to check out interesting smells.

To my mind, Tali is also an angel, a messenger of God, demonstrating the meaning of Divine Grace: we are surprised by love we did not ask for or deserve. I used Tali, I offered him a pretense of love—and he responded with genuine love. I am so grateful. I love Tali "because he first loved [me]."[2]

And What If . . .

I believe that all animals with whom we interact are messengers from God—an office so exalted that the thought of how millions of them are treated, by people totally ignorant of their mission, is enough to make one shudder. (*Kyrie, eleison!*) As Shakespeare's devout Isabella says, "proud man" is "most ignorant of what he's most assured, / His glassy essence, [and] Plays such fantastic tricks before high heaven / As make the angels weep."[3] Perhaps by "glassy essence" she means that in every human's innermost being, like a mirror or glass ball, there is an image of God.

And what if every animal—at least every "higher" animal—also has that glassy essence from which God shines for those who have eyes to see?

2. I John 4:19, KJV.
3. Shakespeare, *Measure for Measure*, Act 2, Scene 2.

Divine and Feline Grace

Of course many a beast, like human beings with "a little brief authority," will still carry on in an unpleasant way at times, "an angry ape" pounding his chest, and we must learn to love them anyway; love them sensibly, actively, persistently.

But there are other beasts who, like Tali, are very different, and prove capable of loving us before we love them. Many rescued from the horrors of the factory-farm and slaughterhell systems, or other situations of terrible abuse, forgive the species that treated them so satanically. They accept healing, they offer love not only to their caretakers, who deserve it, but to any new person who visits them. Each such animal being is more wonderful than a miracle. Each is a bearer of divine Grace, a manifestation of God's unutterable Gift of love.

27

Jonah, the Big Fish, "as Well as Many Animals"

The Supposed Problem

It is one of the ironies of religious history that many people dismiss the rich book of Jonah because they cannot see beyond the unrealistic nature of the fish story. Their kind of reaction is summed up by the "sermon" of the cynical character Sportin' Life in the Gershwin and Heyward opera *Porgy and Bess*. The Bible may present Methuselah as having lived nine hundred years, and Jonah as living in a whale, or rather as making "his home in that fish's abdomen," but Sportin' Life's take on it is that the stories "ain't necessarily so."

That Jonah survived being devoured by the fish isn't the only credibility problem in the story. Most of the events in the plot—that God sends a violent storm on the sea to awaken the heart of the runaway prophet; that the storm ends abruptly when he is thrown overboard; that God summons a huge fish (often carelessly referred to as a whale) to swallow him; that he lives three days in the fish's belly; that God speaks to the fish, who then vomits Jonah out on dry land; that the inhabitants of Nineveh (arrogant with unchallenged imperial power and wealth) immediately change their ways at the preaching of a nobody from one of their conquered countries—these things are not the stuff of history as we know it. But to reject the story for that reason is to miss completely the profound points this tale, as a parable, is making. (Those not very familiar with the story might do well to check it out now; reading the whole thing takes only about five minutes.)

Jonah, the Big Fish, "as Well as Many Animals"

Background: The Sea Monster

Ancient Hebrews shared with several of their Middle Eastern neighbors some form of a myth about a vast dragon-like monster living, in most instances, in the sea. The formless sea represented the dangerous forces of chaos epitomized in this monster, threatening to invade the land and overthrow structured human community. The hero-God fights with the monster and defeats her (e.g., the Babylonian Tiamat) or him (Yamm of the Canaanites, Lotan of Ugarit, Leviathan or Rahab to early Hebrews)[1], thus assuring his people's survival. The image appears in many other cultures as well. In some forms of the hero story, the resemblance to the central action of the book of Jonah is fairly explicit; the hero is swallowed by the monster in apparent death, and either breaks out or is otherwise expelled in symbolic rebirth. (This apparently primitive scenario is far from dead; in the nineteenth century Longfellow used it in his epic poem *The Song of Hiawatha*; Walt Disney used it in *Pinocchio*, and James Cameron strongly echoed it in *Titanic* when Rose descends into the seemingly endless corridors of the growling, deadly ship.)

As the Hebrews over centuries came to understand their God to be creator and lord of all the earth, Leviathan/Rahab ceased to represent the threat of chaos to human society; for example, in the late book of Job he is described in detail as one among other wonders of God's creation. By the time the book of Jonah was written, perhaps 400-200 BCE, the terrifying sea monster has dwindled into a big fish, one who is obedient to the motions of God's mysterious but compassionate purposes. The fish, it might be said, has taken a longer journey than Jonah has! As a symbol the fish is a positive figure; instead of the devouring sea-dragon he appears to be, he is a lifesaving (albeit uncomfortable) place of refuge and a means of partial turnaround for Jonah. But no, he is not a real animal.

Nineveh and Assyria

Our story is set in the Northern Kingdom of Israel in the eighth century BCE, when Israel, along with other lands in the Near East, was threatened, and later devastated, by a new rise of the ancient Assyrian empire. "Jonah, the son of Amittai" is the name of an apparently real prophet who is mentioned briefly in Second Kings 14 as having made a political prediction

---

1. See Ps. 74:13, Isa. 27:1, Isa. 51:9

prior to the Assyrian invasion of Israel, but nothing more is known about him as a historical figure; our parable is simply woven around his name.

Much, however, is known about Assyria, and useful summaries can be found in encyclopedias. Centered in what is now northern Iraq, it had existed for somewhere between a thousand and two thousand years before the historical Jonah, boasting extensive development of art and other signs of high culture. Several times over this long period it invaded other nations, devoured them, and swelled into a large empire, notably in its last blast during the ninth to seventh centuries BCE. In the lightest cases of conquest, its kings demanded protection money, i.e., tribute; in the not-so-light cases, Assyrian armies besieged, pillaged, took captive and deported many of a country's inhabitants, replacing them with deported peoples from elsewhere, in order to undermine a country's self-identity and thus prevent revolt. Skillful bas-relief murals in palaces and public buildings in its capitol city Nineveh depict some invasions as featuring massacres, with piles of severed heads. The gruesome treatment of those who resisted, or were thought to have resisted, included gouging out eyes, cutting off limbs, impaling, flaying, or burning alive. And it was not only the victims of their conquests that the powerful in Assyria enjoyed killing; they were also fond of hunting and murdering animals, with the king specializing in canned lion hunts. No doubt the one kind of thrill-killing supported the other.

By the time the book of Jonah was written, the Assyrian empire had been extinct for centuries, and no longer posed a threat to Israel. But once-conquered peoples can have long memories. When the prophet finally obeys God's command to preach doom to Nineveh because "its wickedness has come up before me," he resents God's later decision to spare the city because the people repented. Jonah's feelings did not arise merely from a tendency to be suspicious of foreigners (though there was in fact such a spirit in post-exile Israel), as commentaries such as *The Interpreter's Bible* claim. We can begin to put ourselves into Jonah's head if we imagine the scenario of the story reset during the twentieth century: "Now the word of the Lord came to Rabbi Goldstein of New York in 1941, saying, "Arise, go to Berlin, that great city, and cry against it, for its wickedness has come up before me." The unhappy rabbi would have no great expectation of his preaching being met with success, or his life being very long, if he obeyed. (One could well imagine his being tempted to sail for New Zealand instead, though, unlike Jonah, he would have no illusions that he could escape from God's unbearable presence by such a flight.) Kurt Mitchell's wonderful 1983 children's picture-book version of the Jonah story, showing the prophet as a mouse and the Ninevites as cats, gives the reader strong sympathy for Jonah's attitude.

The Standoff

It is the very people who perpetrated the atrocities sketched above that Jonah's God wants to see repenting—that is, turning away from the power-madness and runaway greed that had fuelled these horrors, and taking up lives of justice and compassion such as are the natural expression of the Image of God within. The prophet, understandably, would much rather the Ninevites get what they deserved, but after his harrowing adventure with the storm and the huge fish, poor Jonah knows he has no choice; he turns his reluctant steps to ancient "Berlin." What he threatens the Assyrians with is not specified beyond the vague "In forty (or was it three?) days, Nineveh shall be overthrown." Was Jonah thinking of a gruesome military attack of the sort the Assyrians had themselves specialized in? That would seem appropriate. A rain of fire and brimstone from heaven like the legendary one that destroyed Sodom and Gomorrah? We aren't told, but when Jonah has walked the length of the city preaching doom and emerged, probably surprised that he's still alive, he puts down his "The End is Near" sign and sets up an observation post outside the walls in hopes that he will get to see the catastrophe happen.

The overthrow, of course, doesn't take place, and Jonah's sense of justice is outraged. Not only that, he is probably still anxious; very likely he is convinced of the falsity of the rumors he's heard, that these demons in human form have changed their ways, As long as the city is intact and functioning, it's likely to continue its atrocities against its neighbors—and of course he is thinking of his own victimized people. He has survived the big fish and his dangerous preaching mission, but he may still end up devoured by this cruel Assyrian monster. But God, in seeming naïveté, takes their repentance to be genuine. Thoroughly angry, Jonah argues with God (a long Jewish tradition), saying, in effect, "I told you so! I knew you were a merciful God who dislikes vengeance, and that you'd let these devils off the hook after all. This is maddening! Stop the world; I want to get off."

Taking the Adventure

What Kind of Compassion?

Apparently Jonah thinks that God's stance is a mushy mercy that obliterates all justice and common sense. Is this the case? It's worthwhile for us to look carefully at God's answer, because real animals have an important part in his explanation, as they had in the Ninevites' expression of repentance. When the king made his proclamation ordering that everyone fast and put on a hairshirt in order to show that they had all truly changed their ways, he included animals: "Let neither man nor beast, herd nor flock, taste any thing: let them not feed, nor drink water: But let man and beast be covered with sackcloth, and cry mightily unto God . . . let them turn every one from his evil way, and from the violence that *is* in their hands."[2] And God, explaining to Jonah at the end of the story why he has decided not to destroy the city, says ""Should I not have compassion on Nineveh, the great city in which there are more than 120,000 persons who do not know the difference between their right and left hand [small children?], as well as many animals?"[3] In other words, "those who do evil and the innocents are all bound up together; if I summoned an enemy to torch the city and massacre its inhabitants, I would be doing a terrible injustice to the little ones and the beasts."

Here the author of the parable is roundly rejecting an earlier conception of the organic unity of a family or a people, in which the sins of the fathers may appropriately be visited on the children (and on sacrificial animals); that is, all members of the group are united in guilt, and subject to punishment when their forebears have done evil. Jonah has taken this view for granted in his hope to see the catastrophe, and so apparently have the Ninevites, as seen in their insistence that the animals participate in the fast and the sackcloth. But the author of Jonah is not the first in post-exile Israel to reject this idea in favor of the responsibility of the individual for his or her own deeds only.

So far so good. But what about all those in Nineveh whose hands still drip with innocent blood? We can't help but share some of Jonah's feeling that their repentance is cheap; it shouldn't get them off scot-free after the sickening atrocities they've committed. Couldn't an omnipotent God have devised some "smart" fire-and-brimstone for them? Judging from the end of the story, apparently not. And even if that were possible now, there

---

2. Jonah 3:7–8, KJV.
3. Jonah 4:11, NASB.

would still be the problem of all the earlier imperial goons, going back (intermittently) over more than a thousand years, who lived in undisturbed possession of their arrogance, their bloodied weapons, and their loot throughout their lives.

One might say that the parable doesn't even speak to the crux of the problem of evil. Further, it doesn't acknowledge the fact that accountability is usually necessary both to stop evildoers in their tracks, and to give pause to future would-be looters-torturers-killers. The Pinochets, their henchmen, and their colleagues at the court of present-day Pharaoh have to be brought to trial and face consequences for the horrors they perpetrated in Chile in 1973 and the twenty following years, or future Pinochets will follow in their footsteps, confident of immunity. The story doesn't solve the knottiest problems.

"The Bundle of Life"

But we can be grateful for what the parable does give us. It emphasizes that we—human animals of all ages and moral levels, *and* the scaled, furred, and feathered sorts—are indeed all bound together, but in a somewhat different way from what primal peoples thought. We are bound up together in God's infinite love and compassion, which is stronger than vengeance, which never gives up even on the most depraved killers. That boundless love calls on us who are daughters and sons of the prophets to urge and encourage the violent to change their ways, and Return to their true selves and to God.

God's wonderful mercy is not recent news; in fact even the earlier "sins of the fathers" passage (in Exodus 20 and Deuteronomy 5) acknowledges it: God says "I lavish unfailing love for a thousand generations on those who love me and obey my commands,"[4] especially the central command to love their neighbors as themselves. When we show love in action to both victims and victimizers, however small our actions may seem, their effects go on for a thousand generations.

---

4. Exod. 20:6 NLT.

28

Narnian Paradise

"Narnia, Narnia, Narnia, awake. Think. Love. Speak."[1]

So says the great Lion Aslan, the creator of Narnia, at a critical point in the plot of *The Magician's Nephew*. In telling this tale of the origin of his magical land, C. S. Lewis draws primarily upon aspects of the story of Creation and Fall in the first three chapters of Genesis, and Milton's *Paradise Lost*. The story is magnetically captivating and sometimes funny as it portrays the wonderful goodness of the natural world, highlighting the harmonious relations of animals to one another and to humans. It also treats of the nature of evil and suffering, and climaxes in a joyous *eucatastrophe*, i.e., a sudden and well-earned turn to a happy ending. Two important themes in the story feeding into the eucatastrophe are the dismantling of oppressive social class barriers carried over from other, fallen, worlds, and the concept that the Divine power does not work alone, but welcomes the cooperation of both humans and animals in accomplishing its life-giving purposes.

Digory, Polly, and the Magician

This is a story for children, and thus its treatment of evil and suffering must be restrained, but its initial scene presents the central child character as being in great psychological pain. Two youngsters named Polly and Digory, who live in adjacent row houses in Victorian London, meet in Polly's back yard. Polly sees at once that he has been crying, and evidently rubbing his eyes with very dirty hands. He tells her that he is miserable because he has

1. Lewis, *Magician's Nephew*, 103.

been pulled out of his much-loved home in the country, and is now trapped in stifling London staying with his Aunt Letty and Uncle Andrew (sister and brother). His uncle looks sinister and behaves oddly; his aunt keeps trying to hush her brother up about something. The underlying reason Digory has been uprooted is that his father is working abroad, and Digory's mother, who is very sick and approaching death, needs the care of his aunt.

The two children become friends. While exploring the joined attics of their row of houses, Polly and Digory open a door and find themselves in Uncle Andrew's forbidden study, lined with books on (ceremonial) magic. Andrew offers Polly a beautiful golden ring among several he has crafted. When she touches it she vanishes, transported to what he believes is another world, but turns out to be a kind of inter-world Grand Central Station, the Wood Between the Worlds. There Polly emerges from a small pond, of which the Wood contains many. Meanwhile, Uncle Andrew—a coward who won't go into another world himself—pressures Digory to take a similar ring and follow her, carrying in his pocket two green rings which will bring them back.

The First Temptation

Digory figures out that the ponds are like gateways to different worlds. Before returning to Earth wearing their green rings, at Digory's urging Polly agrees to venture first into one of the other worlds. They arrive in what is apparently the courtyard to a long-ruined and crumbling palace; exploring the ruins, they come to a hall full of what appear to be statues of splendidly dressed royalty. The last figure is the most impressive of all, a woman of great size, beauty, and fierceness. In the center of the room is a short pillar, atop which sit a small golden bell and hammer. Below it an inscription tells the reader to make a choice: strike the bell and deal with the danger that will result, or forbear and be driven mad with wonder about what would have been.

This first Temptation occurs in a world very different from the biblical Paradise, but is akin to that of the Eden story in that it deals with action that will give (increased) knowledge of good and evil. Digory, who has a great thirst for knowledge, is vulnerable to it as the more easy-going Polly is not. The action is not explicitly forbidden as eating the fruit in the Genesis story was, but Digory has good reason to know it is wrong for him, because in order to do it he has to grab and thereby injure Polly, who has objected and is about to don her ring and leave. Here we have the seed of Narnia's Fall. It is

Taking the Adventure

sparked by a male, not a female character as in the Bible story; and the evil act is not disobedience to an authority figure, but disrespect for and harm to another person. The bell he rings awakens the last seated figure, Jadis, the final queen of the country of Charn. Jadis turns out to be an archetypal image of evil; not only is she arrogant, ruthless, and power-hungry, she has magical powers that enabled her to destroy physical objects and all other human beings in Charn with a word.

The children manage to put on their rings to return to London. They soon find that the rings operate like a magnet, because the queen, who is holding on to them, is drawn along. As a result, she is set loose in our world, which she means to conquer. Digory and Polly manage to forestall her plans, however. During an accident to Andrew's and Jadis' hansom-cab in front of Aunt Letty's house, Digory catches hold of her foot, and Polly, holding his other hand, puts on her gold ring. Not only do they succeed in going to the Wood Between the Worlds and bringing her along, they find that the Cabby, his horse Strawberry, and Uncle Andrew have all been pulled along too. But the children's plan to return Jadis to her own world goes astray, and instead the whole party ends up in yet another world—empty, dark, and silent.

Appeal and Response

Shortly after the six unwilling visitors arrive, the creation of Narnia begins. This appears to be pure coincidence, usually a sign of a weak plot. But examined more closely, the text strongly suggests that three of the six unknowingly invite the process, thus co-operating with the Creator. The Cabby had taken the lead; generously concerned for everyone's well-being, he asked if anyone was injured, and expressed thanks that no one was. Amusingly, he proposed that they pass the time by singing a "ymn." His seemingly incongruous choice was "a harvest thanksgiving hymn, all about crops being 'safely gathered in.'"[2] The children joined their voices to his.

The text of the hymn is not given, but clearly the one meant is "Come, Ye Thankful People, Come," by Henry Alford. It is true that the bare world in which they stand is hardly a scene of harvest; however, the hymn is more relevant than it first seems. I will quote the first and last stanzas, assuming that the Cabby sang them both, since this was the hymn "he could remember best":

2. Op. Cit., 86.

> Come, ye thankful people, come,
>> raise the song of harvest-home;
>> all is safely gathered in,
>> e're the winter storms begin.
>> God our Maker doth provide
>> for our wants to be supplied;
>> come to God's own temple, come,
>> raise the song of harvest-home . . .
>
> Even so, Lord, quickly come,
>> bring thy final harvest home;
>> gather thou thy people in,
>> free from sorrow, free from sin,
>> there, forever purified,
>> in thy presence to abide;
>> come, with all thine angels, come,
>> raise the glorious harvest-home.[3]

The word "come" is repeated no fewer than seven times in these stanzas. In the first verse, the hymn's narrator uses it to invite other persons to join in the song of thanksgiving, and expresses confidence that the Creator will supply all their needs. In the last stanza, the word twice invites God to come, with all his (probably not her) angels, be present with his people, and celebrate with them a feast of the abundance he has provided. These sentiments are clearly relevant to the characters' situation in the pitch-dark, disorienting world in which they all suddenly find themselves. Singing the hymn, the Cabby and the children implicitly affirm the hymn-writer's faith that they are not abandoned; the Divine Being is aware of them and will care for them in their present straits. They call upon him to manifest and bring them what they need to flourish.

Thus Aslan's appearance to begin creation shortly after they finish the song is apparently a divine answer to their reiterated appeal. Furthermore, Aslan creates by means of an answering song that does much more than fulfill their needs; he brings into existence a paradisal Narnia, one feature after another, including "angels." First come the stars, who join Aslan in song. They are actually conscious beings, as we learn in a later story, a concept that alludes to the text in Job about creation, "when the morning stars sang together, and all the sons of God shouted for joy."[4] Then comes the sun,

3. Alford, "Come, Ye Thankful People," 545.
4. Job 38:7, KJV.

rising and dispelling the darkness. The different features of Eden—the grass and other plants, the trees (including a number of nut- and fruit-bearing kinds which can feed them), the animals, who, like Milton's newly-created beasts, push up out of the ground—all appear in response to particular sequences of notes in Aslan's song. The climax of creation, now enacted via the spoken word, is the Lion's gift of rationality and speech to some of the animals, including the London cab horse, Strawberry.

To Speak or Not to Speak

As I mentioned in chapter 9, "I Am a True Beast" about *The Horse and His Boy*, the gift of speech Aslan gives to selected animal characters satisfies a deep human longing to communicate freely with animals. It is most unfortunate that Lewis made the distinction between speaking and nonspeaking animals, however, and it doesn't work in the later stories, in which talking animals show little or no sign of distress or anxiety at humans' hunting or killing their own non-speaking kind for "sport," as we humans certainly would if a powerful race moved in among us and picked off mentally defective human beings for fun and food. Furthermore, most of the few characters who hunt show no concern about the danger of unintentionally killing a speaking animal.

Lewis puts far too much weight on the capacity for human speech. Some of the abilities that Aslan tells the talking animals are theirs because they can talk—"Jokes as well as justice come in with speech"—have in fact been reported in recent years among the "dumb" animals in our own world. One example of a joke, occurring among animal companions living in the same household, is seen in the true story of an (animal-companion) rooster who loved to sneak up behind a sleeping cat, suddenly crow loudly to jolt him awake, then run off. Furthermore, Marc Bekoff in his co-written book *Wild Justice* reports behavior patterns among wolves based on intra-group justice: members of an extended family engage in play with agreed-on rules. For example, one may pretend to bite, or pretend sexual advances, but no real biting or sex is allowed during the game; a wolf who repeatedly breaks the rule is ostracized from the group. There is no doubt a gradation of intelligence, fellow-feeling and communication abilities among Earth's animals, but they certainly are not, as Aslan describes those lacking human speech, "witless" beings.

Lewis thought that rationality, especially as expressed in speech, was the crucial capacity making humans morally valuable, and which set them apart from other beings, whom speaking beings could legitimately kill for food. Variants of this notion were common in Lewis' day, and in fact the root idea goes back to the ancient Greeks. Lewis seems to have set up the nonspeaking/speaking distinction for several reasons. He believed the convenient fiction that butchering could be humane; he approved of hunting (although he himself didn't hunt); he seems to have been largely unaware of animal bonding, which means that butchering one animal may cause grief in another.

Perhaps the root reason is that he didn't want to give up meat. In other of the Narnian books, humans, speaking animals, and Dwarves eat flesh with the narrator's approval; in *Prince Caspian*, he even calls a meal of the flesh of a bear (killed in self-defense) "glorious."

But *The Magician's Nephew* is different: the Narnian Paradise, like the biblical one, is vegan and innately nonviolent. Not only are there no meat-eating scenes in this new world, vegetarianism is unmistakably implied in Aslan's charge to the talking animals: "'Creatures, I give you yourselves . . . I give you forever the land of Narnia . . . and I give you myself. The Dumb Beasts whom I have not chosen are yours also. Treat them gently and cherish them . . .'"[5] There is no doubt that killing other animals for food is ruled out.

Good and Evil

The Cabby, the children, and the horse find this whole creation scene one of wonder and joy. "'Glory be!'" said the Cabby. 'I'd been a better man all my life if I'd ha' known there were things like this.'"[6] Uncle Andrew and the Queen/Witch, however, respond very differently. Uncle Andrew sees Narnia chiefly as a place where he could get rich, not a place to find new kin or friends; therefore, he resists the wonderful evidence of his ears that Aslan and some of the animals can speak, and he talks himself out of being able to understand them. As a result, instead of joy he reacts to what they do and say with fear, and would like to shoot Aslan. The Queen resents Aslan and all he is doing because his magic is different from her own, and stronger. She actually does try to kill him by flinging at his head an iron bar she had

---

5. Lewis, Op. Cit., 205
6. Op. Cit., 88

Taking the Adventure

wrenched off a lamp-post in London, but he shows no sign of even noticing that he was struck. She shrieks and runs.

With the arrival of the Witch, who is the embodied evil Digory has awakened and brought into this new Paradise, come Narnia's Fall and its potential consequences in hunger for power as control, violence, and suffering. But Aslan gives Digory a second chance: "'as Adam's race has done the harm, Adam's race shall help to heal it.'" The Lion instructs Digory to travel to a garden far to the west of Narnia, pick an apple from the central tree there, and bring it back. Strawberry, who is given wings and renamed Fledge, will carry him (and Polly) to the garden. Aslan tells them he will use the apple as seed for a tree that will protect Narnia from the Witch for hundreds of years.

The Second Temptation

The scene is set for Digory's second Temptation. Following their flight on the back of Fledge across the beautiful new world of Narnia and the Western Wild, the children arrive at the Garden, finding it walled and obviously private. A sign on the gold gate tells all comers to enter only by the gate, and to take fruit only for others.

This Eden-within-an-Eden has no tree of the Knowledge of Good and Evil, but it does have an extraordinary tree in its center, one bearing silver apples that casts light rather than shade. Without doubt it is the Tree of Life, and Digory's target. He picks an apple. Its fragrance tempts him to eat it, but he reminds himself that that it must only be taken for others, and manages to resist the desire.

But the Witch is in the garden too, having already leaped over the wall to enter, and has eaten an apple. Digory runs out of the garden, but cannot escape her. She tempts him to decamp to his own world with the apple, if he loves his mother, and use it to heal her. Compared to his mild desire to eat the apple himself, this wish is agonizing. But the witch makes the mistake of suggesting he leave Polly behind so that his theft will never be recognized. Knowing Polly can easily return with her own magic ring, Digory finds his mind suddenly clearing: the witch can't really care about his mother, and must have some dark motive. He manages to resist, and hold to his mission. The two children mount Fledge and fly back; Digory is silent throughout the return journey.

Narnian Paradise

Under Aslan's guidance Digory plants the apple, having now sadly given up all hope of saving his mother's life. But the new Tree of Life which will protect Narnia for centuries grows up to full size and bears fruit within the hour; and from it Aslan freely gives him an apple that will heal. The later scenes in which, returned to London, we see him cutting up the apple and feeding it to his mother—a poignant reversal of the more usual mother-feeding-child relationship—and feel his joy at her ensuing recovery are deeply moving, particularly to readers who are aware of how desperately the eight-year-old C. S. "Jack" Lewis had longed to heal his own mother dying of cancer. The death-dealing fruit of the Eden story has become the fruit of life.

Implications

A good case may be made that *The Magician's Nephew* is the most moving thing C. S. Lewis ever wrote. The plot is well-crafted and absorbing, and its climax can bring tears of joy. The beauty and splendor of an unfallen earth is conveyed in several scenes, especially in the flight to and from the Garden. (C. S. Lewis was well qualified to describe paradisal vistas, being a sensitive observer of nature, and fond of taking long walking tours in his adopted England.) There is of course no predation among the animals, and no fear of humans. The conversations of the talking animals show a delightful mixture of good-will and naiveté, leading to a kind of humor particularly appealing to children. The underlying concept of the genre of fantasy that there are many worlds, some old while others are new, expands the reader's consciousness.

It must be admitted that, regarding gender, especially among adults, the story is anything but mind-expanding, as we can see when we compare the two queens in the story. Jadis the reigning queen from Charn is a cruel monster, as is her sister who challenged her right to the throne, whereas Helen, the kindly consort queen of Narnia, is modestly silent while trustworthy males make the important decisions. The message is clear: women cannot be trusted with authority, and should stay in their place.

Class Revolution

But the book has profound and refreshing implications about the evils of human social class and about the value of animals. The human characters, none of them native to Narnia, fall into the traditional old-world categories of aristocrat, gentry, and working class. Most are gentry, and morally may be classed as good, bad, or some-of-each. Aunt Letty is a responsible, caring, rather unimaginative person who has put up with her ne'er-do-well brother Andrew for a long time at considerable financial loss, and is now devotedly nursing her slowly-dying sister Mabel. The sketch of Mabel after her miraculous recovery shows glimpses of an exuberant, beauty-loving, youthful spirit, who plays "such games with Digory and Polly that Aunt Letty would say 'I declare, Mabel, you're the biggest baby of the three.'"[7] The two children are taken seriously as human beings, sympathetically drawn yet flawed, whose words and actions have huge potential for wonderful good or horrifying evil.

The powerful figures, who can work magic, are on a different level. Uncle Andrew is of course a member of the gentry too, but likes to present himself as upper-class: "'Not exactly royal. The Ketterleys are, however, a very . . . old Dorsetshire family, Ma'am.'"[8] Furthermore, as an Adept in magic, he sees himself as unfettered by moral rules; he has "a high and lonely destiny." But the consequences of his actions show him to be a selfish, self-deceiving fool. (He always remains that, but he is not damned; we are told at the end that he learned a lesson and improved somewhat in old age.) Jadis, the much more powerful magician who also claims a High and Lonely Destiny, is not only an aristocrat, but at the zenith of aristocracy, a queen; physically strong and extraordinarily beautiful, but a monster of evil. Unlike Uncle Andrew, she is unredeemable.

But perhaps the most impressive character is the Cabby, Frank, "obviously the bravest as well as the kindest person present" in the scene where the hansom cab is wrecked, and he is a member of the working class. (I suspect he was inspired in some small part by C. S. Lewis' remarkable Cockney friend Charles Williams, a self-taught and highly original novelist, critic, and theologian.) One of the Cabby's appealing traits is his affection and respect for Strawberry. He is delighted when the horse becomes one of the talking animals: "'Strike me pink! I always did say as that 'oss 'ad a lot of sense, though.'"[9] He had viewed Strawberry essentially as a partner rather than a slave even during their London days: "'We 'ad our living to earn, see,' said the Cabby. 'Yours as well as mine. And if there 'adn't been no work and

---

7. Op. Cit., 164
8. Op. Cit., 63
9. Op. Cit., 104

no whip there'd 'ave been no stable, no hay, no mash, and no oats. For you did get a taste of oats when I could afford 'em, which no one can deny.'" He had sympathized with the discomforts and pains Strawberry now recalls: "'It was a hard, cruel country,' said Strawberry. 'There was no grass. All hard stones.' 'Too true, mate, too true!' said the Cabby. 'A 'ard world it was. I always did say those paving-stones weren't fair on any 'oss. That's Lunn'on, that is. I didn't like it no more than what you did. You were a country 'oss, and I was a country man. Used to sing in the choir, I did, down at 'ome. But there wasn't a living for me there.'"[10]

The Cabby's respect for Strawberry is increased now that the horse can speak. When Digory urges that they go quickly over to where Aslan is standing in council with some of the talking beasts, so he can ask for a healing fruit, the Cabby asks Strawberry's permission before lifting Digory onto his back.

When the Cabby (and Polly) join the council group, Aslan asks him if he is pleased by Narnia and would like to stay permanently; the answer is an enthusiastic yes, except that his wife isn't there. Aslan deals with this minor problem by bringing the wife Nellie into the scene with a single call. We readers' hearts are so warmed to the Cabby by this time that when Aslan informs the couple that they are to be King Frank and his Queen Helen of Narnia, the dramatic overthrow of social class ranking delights readers: we feel it couldn't have happened to a better man.

Human-Animal Caste Revolution

The change in Strawberry's status, from the enslaved London cab-horse to an active participant in the journey to get the saving apple is, if anything, even more drastic than that of the Cockney cab-driver to King Frank. We in the twenty-first century who work toward liberating animals are used to the language of slavery and abolition, but C. S. Lewis anticipated us (in a restricted way): several times he has Aslan refer to the animals of our world as slaves. As we saw, the Cabby was the most considerate and reluctant of slave-owners, but a slave Strawberry was, if much better off than most; England prior to the twentieth century has often been referred to as "a hell for horses." After he enters Narnia, Strawberry is not only liberated but is changed to a "talking animal and free subject," and is even one of the animals Aslan invites to join the council to develop a plan to safeguard the

10. Op. Cit., 109-10

country from the Witch for hundreds of years. Finally, he is given wings, the ultimate symbol of freedom, and invited to become the one who makes possible the life-saving journey to the Garden. Conscious cooperation with the Divine is for animals as well as humans.

The highest status an animal in this story holds is of course seen in Aslan. As mentioned in chapter 9, "I Am a True Beast," Lewis claimed that he did not intend Aslan to be a literal Christ-figure; rather, he is an instance of what the incarnation of God might be in a world belonging to animals, namely, the God-Animal: "Touch me. Smell me. Here are my paws, here is my tail, these are my whiskers. I am a true Beast."[11] Aslan's powers are called magical in the story: like Uncle Andrew and Jadis, he can make changes in the physical world directly by the power of his mind and speech. But the differences outweigh the resemblances. He can *create*, can bring the things he imagines into physical existence, whereas the other two can only change what is already there. Even more important, unlike the blight and suffering their magic causes, his Magic is generous, life-giving, and life-affirming.

How to Return to Paradise?

The Narnian paradise, like other images of the world in its deepest reality of harmony and oneness, is remote from us; often it seems hopelessly out of reach. We who cherish this vision of a world in which perfect beauty, love, and peace reign, and want to make our own soiled and anguished world a little more like it, are often called sentimental, unrealistic, impractical. In fact, the truth is usually the other way around: those who work to save and empower the despised, especially animals, are the ones who are realistic about these beings. It is the exploiters, who think of other animals only as things—experimental tools or walking meat—who are pretending, are trying to erase from their minds and hearts the obvious facts that animals are *not* things but individuals with their own agendas and feelings. Even better, they are our kin, and potential friends.

Retellings of the Paradise story such as this, especially those climaxing in a eucatastrophe that affirms the ultimacy of healing and love, can bring to fuller consciousness our longing for the healing of the world and its suffering victims; they can strengthen our faith that we can co-operate with the Divine in bringing it about.

11. Lewis, *Horse and His Boy*, 170.

Narnian Paradise

There is another way that those of us who are Jews and Christians can enlarge our awareness of Paradise at the center of things, and at the same time refresh ourselves from our arduous task; that lies in bringing out the vegan potential of Judaism's and Christianity's weekly holy days, the Sabbath and Sunday. Both have traditional obstacles to making the day meatless, but more importantly, both also have links to Eden, that of Judaism more explicitly. And both anticipate a return (or increased realization) of Paradise, when God's Peace reigns on earth. Of this more in the two final chapters.

29

Return to Eden, Part I: The Garden Feast

"THEN GOD LOOKED OVER all he [she] had made, and saw that it was very good! ... And God blessed the seventh day and declared it holy, because it was the day when he rested from all his work of creation."[1] So ends the first version of the Bible's creation story.

It is ironic that Christians who cling to meat-eating like to cite verse 28 of this account, in which God gives the new man and woman dominion over the animals, to defend their habit. Many animal advocates know that in fact Eden was vegan: in the very next verses, God assigns both humans and animals a plant-based diet. Furthermore, the text tells us that God created the humans in God's own image—and no Jew, Christian or Muslim would claim that God's dominion means that God created humans or other animals in order (metaphorically speaking) to fatten us up and eat us! Jewish tradition interprets the word translated "dominion" to mean guardianship; just as God's rule is generous, life-giving, and empowering, so must be the dominion exercised by all who bear the divine image.

The Garden and the Holiday

This rich myth, presented in two versions (roughly, chapters one and two of Genesis), is a seedbed for all three Abrahamic faiths. God's best dream for our planet, the story says, is a garden-earth, its care assigned to humans, where all living beings breathe the divine breath and live together in peace, where humans and animals alike dine well on the garden's bounty. The

---

1. Gen. 1:31, 2:3, NLT.

Return to Eden, Part I: The Garden Feast

second version has problems regarding gender. However, for those deeply concerned about our imperiled Earth today—dangerously poisoned and full of want, excess, evil, and suffering—it inspires with its vision of what we are to work for: a world of beauty, peace, and plenty for all species.

The first version climaxes with the Creator in effect taking a holiday to savor and enjoy the beauty and goodness of the newly-made universe, and declaring the day hallowed and blessed. It implies that here is the origin of the Jewish custom of observing the seventh day, the Sabbath, as a holy day. Later in the saga of Israel's history, in the giving of the Ten Commandments or Ten Words through Moses on Mt. Sinai as recorded in Exodus, the link is made explicit. The people of Israel are to "Remember the sabbath day, to keep it holy . . . you shall not do any work,"[2] and the basis given is God's resting and hallowing the seventh day in the first creation story. It implies that this weekly celebration, as a remembrance and recapitulation of God's holiday to enjoy his garden-earth, would include feasting on the abundance the garden provides.

The second passage in which the Ten Words are given, Deuteronomy chapter 5, repeats this Sabbath command almost word for word, but offers a different foundation for observing the day. After instructing that servants and domestic animals are to rest as well as the householder, it says "You shall remember that you were a slave in the land of Egypt, and that . . . your God brought you out from there with a mighty hand and with an outstretched arm; therefore . . . God commanded you to keep the sabbath day."[3]

Taken together, these two rationales for Sabbath observance have a strong potential for furthering the cause of peace and amity between humans and animals, as we shall see.

The Celebration of Creation

Biblical texts give few specifics about how the Sabbath is to be observed. but among the few are: to refrain from lighting a fire, collecting fuel, carrying loads, and striking bargains or otherwise carrying out one's regular business. The day was rather to be one of refreshment and delight.[4] According to the saga, while the Israelites sojourned in the wilderness they were not to gather manna, the daily food from heaven, on the Sabbath morning; extra

---

2. Exod. 20:8, 10, KJV.
3. Deut. 5:15, ESV.
4. Exod. 35:3, Num. 15:32, Isa. 40:13, Isa. 53:13, Jer. 17:21.

manna had to be gathered the previous morning.[5] This led to the general principle that food preparation should be done before the Sabbath begins.

Over the centuries, certain positive actions such as attending a synagogue to pray and hear a portion of Torah read, and eating certain foods, became a regular part of the day's observance. Jews of late biblical and later Roman times typically ate fish, which was not considered to be meat, on the Sabbath. Over time a large body of specific prohibitions accumulated, classed in thirty-nine categories about 200 BCE. They were important to Jewish identity, but for many they also became a burden that tended to overwhelm the day's delights. Other Jews felt that the detailed prohibitions were beneficial by enabling them to focus on study, prayer, and enjoyment of family fellowship.

Perhaps the most ancient and basic work prohibition is that against lighting a fire, which has been interpreted as foregoing human mastery over and manipulation of nature. Opinions differ, especially in our technological society, as to which actions today are covered by this rule. Traditionally observant Jews see it as including starting a vehicle, because that means igniting gasoline. For example, ex-senator Joe Lieberman, in his book *The Gift of Rest*, noted with some amusement that when his Senate duties detained him until sunset on Friday, his observance of this prohibition meant a long walk to his home, even in heavy rain, trailed by dutiful secret service people—all in the interest of Sabbath rest.

But in favorable weather a walk, especially in a pleasant area, makes for a more enjoyable and healthful Sabbath activity than a car ride. Despite some ironies and inconveniences, Lieberman, like many Jews, finds the Sabbath a happy and refreshing gift, a celebration that he and his family look forward to during the week, as they keep an eye open for special treats for the Sabbath dinner. He brings home fresh flowers for the table, which will also be adorned with a tablecloth, the family's best china, and the Shabbat candles lit shortly before sunset. Family members dress up. The meal is leisurely, with enjoyment of food, conversation, and fellowship.

A cherished poetic image for the coming of Shabbat is the welcoming of a bride. Correspondingly, in keeping with the this-worldly nature of Judaism, which affirms harmless pleasures as gifts from God, married couples are encouraged to celebrate the day (or rather night) by making love. The ordinary marriages of ordinary people, whether made up of exemplary,

---

5. Exod. 16:26.

mildly flawed, or thoroughly selfish persons, on this holyday symbolize the joyous and unsullied union of Adam and Eve in the Garden.

Of course not all devout Jews consider the traditional Sabbath, with its many specific ordinances, to be an inseparable whole. Many congregations affirm and celebrate the heart of the event as they interpret it, feeling free to dispense with individual prohibitions; e.g., they drive their cars to synagogue or temple for Shabbat services, or turn on the oven to heat dinner. But it will remain a day off from the week's work, and a day for happiness, following the model of God's celebration of God's good creation.

Freedom for All

The other base of the Sabbath is liberation. Roberta Kalechofsky points out in the introduction to her co-authored *Vegetarian Shabbat Cookbook* that the idea of a weekly day off from labor for everyone—householders, slaves, animals—was unheard-of in ancient Pagan cultures. She cites Rabbi Michael Lerner's comment that there was nothing to stop slaveholders and animal owners from forcing those they controlled to labor long hours every day, day after day, until they dropped or dropped dead. A weekly day of rest for all was revolutionary. Reactions to it in ancient Rome were mixed, the mixture decidedly affected by class. Intellectuals like Seneca, Tacitus, and Juvenal thought Sabbath rest irresponsible, a waste of valuable time, and felt that it marked Jews as lazy and shiftless; patricians feared its subversive influence on slaves. Unsurprisingly, slaves and workers thought it was a wonderful idea, and as a result of it, were attracted to Judaism.

Sabbath equality—the fact that rest is for animals too—has even more radical implications, which are firmly in keeping with the vegan diet of Paradise. Considering the negative associations of "diet," it might also be called the Eden Feast or the Practice of Paradise.

Interest in this Practice has increased in recent years. Traditionally, most Sabbath menus have not followed it but have included meat, which has long been associated with festivity and abundance. However, occasional saintly figures such as Abraham Isaac Kook (1865-1935), himself a strong supporter of vegetarianism, have anticipated the Practice in a general way: he cites the nonviolent way of eating that God prescribed in Eden, and held that in the future, individuals fulfilled with the divine Light would shun meat-eating altogether out of compassion for animals. He sees this development as taking place especially in the Messianic Age. Present-day Jewish animal activists are developing the idea more concretely, with a potentially greater response now that more people know how pleasurable vegan eating can be. Roberta Kalechofsky, having described in her abovementioned introduction the enormous harm that animal agriculture is causing the earth, tells her readers

> "Celebrating Shabbat with vegetarian food continues the revolutionary spirit in which the Shabbat was first conceived of as a gift of freedom for human beings. It becomes a gift for all the creatures which God blessed; it restores our harmony with that first miraculous Shabbat when God looked at the created world, found it good, blessed it, and rested on the seventh day."[6]

Exodus, Judaism's founding event commemorated weekly in the Sabbath and yearly at Passover, is indeed a great gift to the world's oppressed and enslaved, the gift that keeps on giving. Roman workers and slaves were by no means the last to be inspired by its message that God desires freedom and refreshing rest for all, including the lowest and last. Antebellum Southern pro-slavery legislators passed laws to prevent enslaved people from learning to read, partly because those who did often became preoccupied with Exodus, composing and singing subversive songs like "Go Down Moses." Latin American liberation theologians applied Exodus to the abject condition of peasants and city slum-dwellers, who caught the spark and began to study this and other biblical passages with big socio-political changes in mind. Jewish and Christian feminists of the Second Wave saw the freeing and empowering of women as a further working-out of the exodus principle.

Today some Jewish and Christian animal activists are finding divine inspiration in this story underlying the Sabbath as we work to liberate our animal cousins. Who is it that needs to come out from under the lash of Pharaoh's overseers, if not the wretched chickens and cows and pigs and turkeys reduced to property, trapped on hellish factory "farms," doomed to the execution planned for them before their births? For them to join humans liberated from Pharaoh's rule of greed is to return to and begin to realize the harmony of Eden, and enrich the human Practice of Paradise.

---

6. Kalechofsky & Schiff, *Vegetarian Shabbat Cookbook*, viii.

30

Return to Eden, Part II: The Emmaus Feast

Observing Sunday

MARGARET TOBIN, WHO LIVED with her parents and five siblings in a tiny house in Hannibal, Missouri in the years after the Civil War, had a dream: she decided that when she grew up she would marry a rich man. But Maggie was not the kind of poor girl whose head was full of nothing but jewelry, rich clothes, elegant dinners and glittering balls; she was a generous, deeply compassionate person. The riches she longed for were not primarily for herself but for her dear father, who worked long hours six days a week firing coke furnaces at the Hannibal Gas Works for a very small salary, and was almost always bone-tired. One can only imagine how John Tobin looked forward to Sunday, when he could get some real *rest*, partially during Mass at the local Catholic Church, and all afternoon and evening. For his sake, his daughter must also have been very glad to see Sunday come.

In her late teens she and a sister moved to Colorado, and Maggie Tobin, after joining the local Catholic Church, looked around for her rich man. Inconveniently, at a church picnic she met and fell in love with a poor man named J. J. Brown, and he with her. She labored with herself over the longed-for wealth to rescue her father, but finally decided it was better to marry for love.

Maggie was unusual in many ways: one of them in that, although she deliberately gave up her dream, it came true after all. Some years later, in the course of his work for a mining company, J. J. Brown discovered a rich vein, and was rewarded with 12,500 shares in the company and a seat on

Taking the Adventure

the board. The Browns were millionaires, and Maggie had the satisfaction of seeing her beloved father retire and finally get plenty of rest.

Maggie enjoyed being rich, including living in a big house in Denver and wearing jewelry and fine clothes, but her chief interest lay in her projects to improve the status of women, help the poor of the city, speak up for exploited miners, set up schools for poor children, and other compassionate causes. She also took classes and private lessons to educate herself, and traveled widely; thus she was not a tough-talking backwoods gal but a highly cultured woman.

She was already something of a celebrity at the time she was caught in the *Titanic* disaster, when she gave one of her garments to a fellow survivor in Lifeboat Six suffering even more from cold than she was, resisted the sour, defeatist crewman in charge, and kept up her freezing and frightened companions' spirits all night. (Most people now think of her as the Unsinkable Molly Brown, but during her lifetime she was always Margaret or Maggie.)

She never rested on her laurels. No sooner had all survivors been taken aboard the *Carpathia* than she set about collecting a fund on behalf of the poor immigrants from third class who had lost everything. Margaret had her follies and failings, but she continued her good works on behalf of the poor (along with various cultural activities) throughout her life, which suggests to me that Maggie Tobin Brown never forgot about what Sunday rest means to an exploited, chronically exhausted worker. The story of her life is well told by Kristin Iversen in her *Molly Brown: Unravelling the Myth*.

From Margaret's early experience of her father's plight, one can see why in many families of yesteryear, especially the working poor, Sunday was so special. It was prepared for by the weekly Saturday-evening bath; on Sunday morning, one donned one's best clothes for church, to be followed by the week's celebratory dinner unfortunately centered in meat (for the poorer families, the week's only such meal). Grandparents, aunts and uncles and cousins might all gather to participate. Church attendance was usually taken for granted, both among devout people like the Tobins and non-religious families, but either way, the Sunday feast was the done thing. Obviously, it was a welcome day, but the return to Eden and to its nonviolent delicacies were never thought of.

In my family of origin, very involved in our Dutch Calvinist church as we were, we always knew that Sunday was a celebration of the Resurrection of Jesus, a splendid and wonderful event, but we never thought about it as

Return to Eden, Part II: The Emmaus Feast

leading to the restoration of the Edenic world, or considered celebrating it with Garden-feast meals either. Both my parents, working-class people raised on farms themselves, appreciated Sundays, but would have seen vegetarianism on any day as undermining their whole way of life. I started out loving Sundays. Until I was six, we attended a church with a Sunday school, which included storytelling, the singing of wonderful songs (one was about precious jewels, and once we sang about a little light within each child, with some of the children, thrillingly, getting to hold burning candles). There was always a child-sized picture card for each of us to take home, featuring a scene in the weekly Bible story. It was all very magical. Unfortunately for me and my siblings, however, during that year, when our family moved to a farm, we transferred our membership to a church that made no attempt at all to reach out to children's hearts. We little people were almost totally invisible, and Sundays became long and boring.

Hymns and sermons in our church spoke of Sunday as a day of rest, but for farm families, the official release from work didn't translate into a lot of rest. Except in winter, my parents labored long hours on the farm, and were often very tired. My mother's responsibility for cooking meals for six was the same as on the other days of the week, fifty-two weeks of the year. For my brother and father, there were the essential jobs of feeding, milking, egg-gathering, and generally caring for the cows and chickens (which of course is true for Sabbath-keeping farmers as well). Still, there was less work for them on Sunday than on most other days. My sister and I didn't have to clean and case scores of eggs that day, but we couldn't forget that there would be twice as many on Monday.

Among middle- and upper-class people with no great experience of physical labor, there was some chafing at the day thanks to ill-conceived blue laws and customary social restrictions of pleasurable activities. But for obvious reasons, most of the poor saw it differently.

These sketches of Sunday-observance of yesteryear tend to show that an appreciation of the day of rest, and a celebrative spirit—though less conscious than in Judaism—were in many cases not lost for Christians with the holy day's move to the first day of the week.

Easter Stories

But why did the move take place—what was the event behind it all about? Can there be any meaning today to the concept of Resurrection? Is there really any link between the reports of Jesus' disciples seeing and speaking to him after his death, and our own work to support or liberate animals, or the work of people like Margaret Tobin Brown to make life easier and more worthwhile for the most oppressed human beings of society?

The Easter stories are seldom seen as having anything to do with animals, beyond mistaken conclusions sometimes drawn from the mention, in two of them, of Jesus' eating and cooking fish (see chapter 21, The Prophet From Nazareth). But the stories are crucially important to the condition of all oppressed or enslaved beings, including animals, that are in any way influenced by Christianity, because they point implicitly to the goal of the Christian saga of history, the end of exploitation and suffering, and the return to the human-and-animal harmony of Paradise here on earth. This chapter is intended to explore the meaning of Resurrection, to make the link clearer, and suggest a way to celebrate it every week.

The first followers of Jesus, mostly impoverished peasants who, as we saw, were being pushed to the edge and beyond by exploitative Roman policies, were all faithful Jews; they had always observed the Sabbath, and remained faithful Jews throughout their lives. But the Sabbath that began the evening of Jesus' horrible death marked the worst day in their lives. Most of them would not have stood vigil near his cross, which could have gotten them killed, or even have seen it; but, living as they did in a police state that practiced terrorism in the way it executed subversives, they knew only too well what his agonizing, prolonged death would have been like. Crucifixions were always located in public places, such as along main roads, to frighten the populace into submission. Not only were Jesus' followers terribly traumatized by losing him, their hopes were shattered for a renewal of Israel, especially for an abundant life for the poor which he had taught and put into practice in shared meals. Sabbath would never be the same for them again.

But then, the stories say, the day after that Sabbath, the first day of the week, some of these broken people began to report unbelievably wonderful experiences: they had seen Jesus alive and spoken with him. His aliveness meant that God's promises of truly renewed hearts and a renewed society which Jesus had taught and embodied, were after all stronger than the worst Caesar could do to stop it. It meant that love and liberation win the day over power-hunger, sadistic torture, and killing. So the Resurrection is very relevant to justice issues, and celebrating it nonviolently follows naturally.

Return to Eden, Part II: The Emmaus Feast

In fact, for Christians to celebrate it by eating the flesh of enslaved and violently killed animals is a travesty of the worst sort.

But anyone who tries to figure out just what happened on that long-ago Sunday faces a challenge. To begin with, harmonizing the Resurrection stories told in the four gospels cannot be done; there are hopeless conflicts about who saw Jesus when or where. For example, in Matthew's gospel, on Easter day Jesus tells his followers to return to Galilee, where he will see them again; but in John's, he continues to see them in the Jerusalem area. Some of the conflicting elements are influenced by differing claims by followers of this or that major disciple that he or she was Jesus' delegated leader of the new movement. The stories as told in the gospels imply that, e.g., Mary Magdalene (alone in John, with companions in Matthew) saw the risen Jesus first; or, in another case, that Cleopas and his companion apparently saw Jesus first, but before they could open their mouths to tell the other disciples about it, one of the others present quickly spoke up to say that Simon Peter had seen him, supposedly bolstering later claims that Peter is the one Jesus' disciples are to follow now. (In fact, James, Jesus' brother, became the first leader of the church in Jerusalem.)

Paul's Collection of Cases

Paul of Tarsus, who never saw Jesus during the latter's physical life, is actually the strongest witness to the existence of reports that some of Jesus' disciples saw him after his death. Paul visited Jerusalem several years after Easter and interviewed Peter and James on the subject, thus becoming a second-hand witness to their experiences. In chapter 15 of his first letter to the Corinthians, Paul lists the experiencers, which include an appearance to the twelve disciples at once (including, apparently, Judas) and one to several hundreds of followers at once. He includes James as having had a late appearance, and, finally, himself also (making him a first-hand witness), though he doesn't say it happened on the road to Damascus. There is no mention here of women as experiencers. Paul also presents his summary in this X-saw-him-first, Y-saw-him-second approach, which I confess does not impress me.

But some of the appearances he cites are not mentioned in the gospels. Those that *are* included there were told and retold for almost forty years before any of the gospels were committed to writing, which means some of the stories may have changed a great deal. At the same time, because several of the Easter appearance stories in the gospels were to women, it is unlikely that they would have been made up out of whole cloth; in the ancient world such reports would have been less convincing than if the seer had been a man, because women were not considered reliable witnesses. So there is very likely some historical truth in them. But we can be quite sure, primarily from Paul's summary, that a number of appearances did indeed take place, and to specific persons. Apart from specific reports, it seems evident that something extraordinary must have happened to galvanize the leaders among those first followers, changing them from fearful people in hiding lest the Romans would hound them down and kill them too, to people who spoke and acted with power.

It is clear, however, that Jesus was no longer physically present among them from day to day. Whatever the resurrection means, it doesn't mean a return from death like that of a Near-Death Experiencer, in which the person resumes ongoing physical life; the Jesus of these stories appears and disappears unaccountably. The idea of the revival of bodies of the deceased, derived from passages in several earlier scriptures, was a live issue in Judaism at that time, and the visions of Jesus told in the gospels were interpreted as such a revival, creating a source of confusion ever since.

In the language of parapsyschology, what seems to have actually taken place on Easter and thereafter was the perceiving of apparitions, originally a neutral term which, roughly, means "that which appears." In rare instances, such cases have included touching or other apparently physical contact. Throughout history there have been hundreds, perhaps thousands of accounts of apparitions of the dead, and some of the living; there have also been clusters of appearances of a single deceased person. Many such stories are still told and recorded in modern times.

They can be placed in two main categories. The first is "haunting ghosts," nearly always silent figures usually seen in particular locations, and surrounded by an atmosphere of chill. In some instances the figures show no particular feelings, but many show signs of neediness, hostility, or other disturbance. Some ghostly figures seem to be mere images, others to be responsive to the perceiver[s].

The second category is "crisis apparitions," which are themselves of two kinds: *announcing figures,* who convey to the perceiver the news of the crisis (often the death) of the person whose apparition is seen, and *empowering figures* who appear to a perceiver who is her- or himself in crisis. Empowering figures are strong, caring, and wise, coming to warn of an

Return to Eden, Part II: The Emmaus Feast

imminent danger, or bring a healing energy or a comforting and life-giving message to one or more persons who need it desperately. Apparitions of this kind, though they may be wingless, dressed in modern clothes, and recognized as deceased persons, are sometimes called angels. The nature of the two major kinds of apparitions, haunting ghosts and empowering figures during a crisis, could hardly be more different. Considering the acute crisis that Jesus' death brought to his followers, and Jesus' life-giving words and actions in the resurrection stories, it is needless to say that the figure seen in all the resurrection accounts is an empowering crisis apparition. (We might add that St. Paul's interpretation of the nature of the resurrected Jesus as having a "spiritual body" comes close to this modern-day interpretation.)

Apparitions of Ramakrishna

It is helpful to see the stories of Jesus' after-death appearance in this context of similar stories, some of them evidential, throughout history. The context is the first reason I am inclined to take Jesus' appearance stories seriously as a whole, despite the historical problems of the ones in the gospels. It may be useful to compare them with a cluster of apparitions that occurred to the followers of the Indian devotional saint Ramakrishna (mentioned in chapter 4) after his death in August of 1886. The two main sources of these accounts are highly detailed books by two of his disciples, *The Gospel of Sri Ramakrishna* by Mahendra Nath Gupta, and *Sri Ramakrishna the Great Master* by Swami Saradananda. Many of the happenings in the books were recorded shortly after they took place. Overall, the details of these 1886 and 1887 apparition accounts resemble the cluster of resurrection narratives, but they are much better attested than those in the gospels' Easter stories. For a sketch of the Ramakrishna apparition accounts, see Appendix D1.

I bring up these apparitions of a spiritual leader not only because of their overall rough resemblance to the stories of Jesus' appearances, but because they took place in modern times, and were recorded in detail not long after they occurred. They provide an anchor of sorts, showing that the cluster of stories of Jesus' appearance after his death is not unique, nor need the biblical accounts be dismissed out of hand as incredible. But, although written down soon after the events they describe, the Ramakrishna stories are less impressive in one important way than the bare summary of Jesus' apparitions by Paul, because the latter included two appearances to a large number of followers at once.

Taking the Adventure

It should also be said that the Ramakrishna accounts are essentially private messages to an order of devotees, and do not, like those of Jesus, serve to reawaken faith in God's program of the transformation of society into the Kingdom of a generous, life-giving God rather than of a life-sucking Caesar. Not only that, it tells those who seek justice and equality for all the oppressed that divine power transcends the massive and violent power-over of the few. Thus the Ramakrishna stories are much less significant spiritually, socially, and politically.

Historically, of course, the Kingdom of God that Jesus proclaimed and died for did not spread through the whole of society, nor did it last; within a few generations, Jesus' vision of equal sharing of God's bounty by the rich, the oppressed, and the outcasts was largely being spiritualized away, as patriarchs and rich householders increasingly took control of the churches. And thanks to the co-optation of the church by the emperor Constantine in the fourth century, it even abandoned its centuries-long opposition to violence taught in Jesus' Sermon on the Mount. The church was looking more and more like the Roman empire that had essentially taken it over, with the ascended Jesus understood as a co-emperor at the right hand of the imperial God. This sad scenario is perhaps not surprising; few periods of (relatively) healthy, just society endure very long. But every flowering of the Dream, however brief, is valuable in itself, and deserves to be cherished and learned from by those who mean to see it realized again. "The light shines on in the darkness, and the darkness has never put it out."[1]

Apparitions and Life Beyond Death

The resurrection appearances obviously are profoundly meaningful, whether or not one considers them to be historical. But a related question that must also be considered is this: is a crisis apparition what it seems? *Is seeing and speaking with such a figure a genuine contact with the surviving consciousness of a deceased person?* This issue has been dealt with at a little greater length in chapter 24, "The Animals and the Angels," though that too is a mere sketch, and the issue is a very complex one; only a few aspects of it can be mentioned here. For one thing, a study of many apparitions or other forms of apparent contact with the deceased strongly suggests that the unconscious mind of the perceiver contributes

---

1. John 1:5 ISV

Return to Eden, Part II: The Emmaus Feast

something, little or much, to the experience; and with multiple perceivers, things become extremely complex.

An apparition is likely to be very convincing to the perceiver[s], but the critical observer will have many concerns to address first. Her or his answer to the crucial question is more likely to be "Probably so" (1) if there is more than one perceiver in a given case; (2) if there is an animal present who is obviously reacting to the apparition seen by the human[s], (3) if the perceiver is not bonded to the deceased, was unaware of her or his death, or did not know her at all, but whose description closely matched her; or (4) if the perceiver learned something from the experience that she or he couldn't have known normally. A case also gains in credibility (5) if the perceiver took action as a result of it. There are cases on record that include one or more of all these characteristics; I describe two such cases in Appendix D2 and D3, page 208.

"The Mystery of the Eighth Day"

I said above that applying the idea of the revival of bodies of the deceased to interpret the Easter appearances of Jesus has long been a source of confusion, which is true, but there is another sense in which, when seen in light of the earlier biblical sources, the interpretation is in fact spiritually fruitful. The passages in question, in Isaiah, Ezekiel, and especially that in Daniel,[2] present the resurrection idea as part of the righting of terrible wrongs of the past, something that will take place in the messianic age to come, the age of renewal of the whole earth, and even, somehow, of the past. In Judaism the human (or animal) self is not an essentially spiritual being tied to a physical body, but a spiritual-physical whole; thus if violence and other unredressed wrongs against a good person are to be righted, it seemed necessary that the person must be physically revived.

The revival-of-the-body idea was an effort of faith to make sense of the conflict behind God's sovereign love and goodness on one hand, and on the other, the long history of the wrongs and violence of the powerful of the world against the defenceless. Unfortunately, such a physical revival doesn't really work, as a philosopher with a fertile imagination and a critical consciousness could soon figure out. (Philosophers like to come up with problems like "If cannibals eat a foreigner entering their tribe, and are themselves later eaten by other cannibals, how can all be physically

2. Isa. 26:19, Isa. 66:24, Ezekiel 37:1–14, Dan. 12:2

resurrected?) But all faithful members of the Abrahamic religions, whether or not they affirm a bodily resurrection, hold as an article of faith that God is just, generous, and compassionate, and lovingly affirms human beings who are or try to live a caring life; further, that God desires the repentance and transformation of the violent and evil. How the horrors of the past can ever be resolved, forgiven by God *and all victims,* and seen as part of God's providential plan, seems impossible to our time-bound state of consciousness; it must remain a profound mystery. We who live by faith and hope know only that we are charged to do what we can to make the world a more just and generous and compassionate place during the time given to us.

For many traditional Christians, Jesus' victory over evil and death is the beginning of this movement back to the renewed earth: the first, so to speak, of the Last Things, a movement that climaxes with the new Eden on earth. The Eastern Orthodox churches are particularly clear that Jesus' incarnation and especially his resurrection eventually lead to the transfiguration of the whole cosmos, which is already, though invisibly, filled with the Divine Light, and which at the Last Day will shine out to be seen by all. God's perfect, nonviolent paradisal world will be restored. The anticipation of this wonderful event, on Easter and indeed every Sunday, would seem to require living and eating both joyfully and nonviolently; as we noted before, it makes no sense to celebrate the triumph of life and love over the cruel death of the innocent Jesus by eating the body of a cruelly killed innocent today. There are in fact many days on the Orthodox churches' calendar on which the faithful are encouraged to abstain from meat, but regrettably, they are of a penitential nature rather than a celebrative one.

Despite its strong theme of the coming of the transfigured cosmos, in the Orthodox churches a prophetic voice calling Christians to work toward increasingly realizing that cosmic transfiguration by political-social action on behalf of humans and animals is rather hard to find. The accepted avenue to bringing the new earth nearer is through becoming a saint, a person whose union with God releases spiritual power that can transform the humans around him or her. In the case of a few saints such as Seraphim of Sarov (1754–1833), and Francis of Assisi, such life- and love-giving energy can even transform flesh-eating wild animals, and thus (re-)create a small Eden around the saint, inspiring others to follow his or her path. Such saints are indeed powerful, both in the lives of others and (probably) in their effects on human and animal spiritual evolution, but to become one is likely to seem out of reach for most ordinary Christians.

Return to Eden, Part II: The Emmaus Feast

However, there are two kinds of things ordinary Christians of any denomination can do. The first is to work in ordinary social and political ways to help in healing and empowering our distressed fellow animals and our wounded planet. The second is to anticipate the transformed cosmos as a realization of Eden every Sunday by celebrating the presence of God in the the living Christ here in our midst, bringing closer God's life-giving and world-renewing power.

The Supper at Emmaus

I will conclude this chapter by suggesting one way for Christians to enact such a celebration, drawing upon a Resurrection appearance, the Emmaus story considered in chapter 22, "Stranger at the Table." Recall that two followers of Jesus, walking from Jerusalem to their home in the village of Emmaus on the afternoon of Sunday two days after his crucifixion, are joined by a man they do not recognize, who explains to them at some length that this event was part of God's plan as foreshadowed in various scripture passages. When they reach Emmaus, at their invitation he enters their house to spend the night. During "the breaking of the bread" they recognize him as Jesus, and at that same moment he vanishes. They set out to go back to Jerusalem that same evening to tell the good news to Jesus' other disciples.

Historical Jesus scholars Marcus Borg and Dominic Crossan have pointed out that this story shows definite signs of being a parable. In the years after Jesus' death, his followers, reading the scriptures, found many passages they interpreted as foretelling his death and resurrection. They were convinced that he was still present empowering them, though mostly unseen. They remembered that he had taught them to share meals, "the breaking of the bread," with any in need, anticipating and acting to realize the Kingdom of God where there is plenty for all.[3]

These are valuable insights, but I believe the story will carry even more weight if we consider the possibility—or probability— that it has a historical core (like the narratives that show women as perceivers). I see a clue in one odd and seemingly very improbable feature: the fact that the two companions don't recognize Jesus during most of the experience. This strange forgetfulness of the identity of someone so important to them suggests that, without being aware of it at the time, they were in an altered state of consciousness. A similar odd forgetfulness in perceivers turns up in a

---

3. Borg, *Jesus,* 285-86; Crossan, *Jesus,* 197.

few accounts of apparent contact with the deceased in our own time; for descriptions of two twentieth-century cases, see Appendix D4, page 209. In a comparative study, two parapsychologists theorized that the peculiar selective amnesia of the perceivers in such cases serves the purpose of enabling them to remain calm and relaxed, as they would not be if they realized that they were in contact with a beloved friend who had died; thus the experience could continue longer. Most experiences of spontaneous apparent contact with the dead last only a few minutes or even less, with half an hour the longest known. It is unlikely that there would have been time for Jesus' biblical exposition and the preparation for even a simple meal.

Supposing then that something like this Emmaus account, something this wonderful, really did happen on that Sunday evening, an event that serves as a foretaste of the divine Feast of the Kingdom in which even the least and last are welcome, and of the transformed, Edenic cosmos of harmony between humans and animals—what would be more appropriate for Christians today than to celebrate it with our own weekly Emmaus dinner? The original meal, assuming there was such, was almost surely a simple and perhaps scanty meal in a rough dirt-floor peasant hovel. But we need not try to re-create these circumstances, any more than the Sabbath celebration of an Edenic world means that celebrants must go naked and picnic in a garden; we need only make it a happy and special meal.

For several months, my family has been experimenting with such an Emmaus dinner, and it has become the high point of our week. Borrowing from a Sabbath dinner, we lay the table with our best tablecloth and napkins, set a bouquet of flowers flanked by candles as centerpiece, and set wine goblets. (Our silver candlesticks and crystal goblets are from a thrift shop—this feast isn't an example of conspicuous consumption!) One person breaks a chunk of bread, giving a piece to each diner, and another says a grace composed of two or all three stanzas of the Eucharistic hymn "Be Known to Us" by James Montgomery and Faith Bowman:

> Be known to us in breaking bread,
> But then do not depart;
> Abide with us, Beloved, and spread
> Thy table in our heart.
>
> May we enjoy ambrosial food
> And drink the finest wine;
> Relish thy Garden's highest good,
> And on thy heart recline.

Return to Eden, Part II: The Emmaus Feast

> From this rich bounty on thy board
> May all thy creatures feast!
> May purple-flowing streams afford
> Pleasure to first and least.[4]

We clink our glasses with the toast "He is risen!" "He is risen indeed." And then we enjoy our dinner. Dessert is a piece of fruit, an obvious pleasure of the Garden of God; those of us with a sweet tooth also have a special treat. My favorite is soy ice cream with (fair-trade) chocolate sauce, which tastes all the better because I try to avoid refined sweets during the week as I anticipate our feast.

I heartily recommend this celebration, which is, of course, nonviolent, Peaceful. That very appropriate aspect of the Emmaus dinner does not set it off from the rest of the week for our family, who have been vegan for some years, but for Christians who are just beginning to take the adventure of Peaceful dining, adopting the weekly Emmaus feast is a splendid way to start. God wants all her/his beloved beings to be free, to flourish, and to rejoice. "They are refreshed from the abundance of your house; You cause them to drink from the river of your pleasures."[5]

---

4. Bowman, "Be Known to Us," *Faith Poems*. May 9, 2014.
5. Ps. 36:8, ISV.

Appendix A to Chapter 16

Reyes de Zierold Object-Reading Case

GUSTAVE PAGENSTECHER, A PHYSICIAN of German extraction living in Mexico in the 1920s, discovered that one of his patients, a Maria Reyes de Zierold, had a remarkable gift under hypnosis: when an object was placed in her hands, she would begin to describe scenes and express emotions corresponding, more or less accurately, to elements of the life of a person who had held or worn the object.

In 1921 Pagenstecher's friend Mr. H. who had heard of Sra. de Zierold's gift sent him a letter with two enclosures, a small paper triply folded and secured with three seals, and a sealed envelope, and asked that the small paper be given to Sr. de Zierold in trance. Before starting, Pagenstecher contacted the American Society for Psychical Research, who sent seasoned investigator Walter F. Prince to provide guidance. Three other persons, including a note-taker, were also present in Pagenstecher's office when Sra de Zierold was hypnotized and given the small paper.

At first she could see nothing, but felt movement and seasickness; she concluded that she was on a ship; it was night, between two and four o'clock. Then she saw many people (evidently on deck), who were very frightened, some screaming. In front of her was a tall, stout Spanish gentleman with fair skin, full black beard and moustache, and a large scar over his left eyebrow. He tore a page from a little book and wrote on it against the wall. She heard an explosion, officers giving commands, passengers donning life jackets, great confusion. She became excited, and speaking rapidly, she described the bearded man adding more to his note, then rolling it up and putting it in a bottle he took from his pocket, driving in a cork. He threw it overboard. Then a much louder explosion and a rattle like a machine gun. Giving several terrified screams, Sra. de Zierold gasped out "I'm

Appendix A to Chapter 16

drowning!" and "They have all drowned!" At this point Pagenstecher took the paper out of her hand.

After calming somewhat, she described the scene more fully, adding that the ship was enormous, that rockets had been sent up, that the ship sank after the second explosion. She said that after experiencing drowning, she found herself afloat again, alone on a quiet sea that covered all sign of the tragedy. She added that she might have seen some survivors in life jackets if the paper hadn't been taken from her hand then.

At this point the sealed envelope Mr. H. had enclosed was opened. It contained an account of the background of the case. During a layover of several days in Havana, Mr. H. and his companion had met a woman whose husband had disappeared on a journey, the husband's last letter having been sent from New York not long before the sailing of the *Lusitania* on May 1, 1915. He wrote that he intended to sail to Europe, but gave no details of date or ship, perhaps because she had feared for his safety if he did so. His name could not be found on the manifests of the ships sailing from New York sunk by the Germans around that time, but it was thought that he might have embarked under a pseudonym. His appearance was almost exactly as Sra. de Zierold had described it, except that he was not stout, merely broad. He did have the scar over his eyebrow, which he owed to a would-be political assassin. The bottle had been recovered by fisherman on the Azores; they passed it on to someone who sent it to Havana; and because it contained the writer's and his wife's names, an official of the Cuban government had delivered it to her about a year before Sra. de Zierold's vision.

The small paper was then unsealed; it was about half the size of a normal book page, and appeared to have been torn on a perforated line out of a notebook. Translated into English, it read "Goodbye, my Luisa, take care that my children do not forget me. Your Ramon." These lines are straight, then in steeply slanting lines, "Havana. May God protect you and me also." The next day Pagenstecher put Sra. de Zierold into a trance of a different kind, in which she received information from unidentified intelligences. "They" reported that the Spaniard was a political refugee staying in Cuba with his family and brother under the assumed name of "Ramon P____."

He was on his way to Spain to try to claim an inheritance. His true name should not be published, they said, because it would endanger his brother, also a refugee. (Ramon's dangerous situation as a political refugee would make his sailing under a false name likely.)

Appendix A to Chapter 16

Pagenstecher wrote to the widow Luisa and asked whether this information were true. She confirmed nearly all of it. She was grateful for his work with Sra. Reyes; she had been worried that perhaps her husband was being held incommunicado for years in a Spanish prison. But her story of how the note reached her differed somewhat from that which Mr. H. had given in the sealed envelope.

W. F. Prince also wrote to her, asking her to let him see another letter from her husband so that he could compare the handwriting. She obliged him with a letter dated January 10, 1915, and Prince was satisfied that the handwriting matched perfectly. The letter had a black border because of the recent death of Ramon's mother.

The shipwreck that Sr. de Zierold described so graphically corresponded most closely to that of the *Lusitania* on May 7, 1915, a few miles south of Ireland. The ship was indeed "enormous," and it sank in a calm sea between two and four o'clock. But this was not at night but on a sunny afternoon. There was indeed an explosion, perhaps two (reports differ) and a fusillade-type sound as pipes broke. The great confusion and distress were partly because the ship almost at once listed sharply to starboard, making it hard to launch lifeboats, then tilted with the bow downward and the stern rising, so that avalanches of furniture and equipment fell on swimmers and killed many of them. It sank in only eighteen minutes, leaving a half-mile-wide circle of wreckage, lifeboats, corpses and survivors. Sr. de Zierold did not mention these grotesque movements of the ship, and afterwards she saw the sea covering every trace of the wreck. Her perception of a night scene may have been due to a projection from reports of the wreck of the *Titanic* (which sank at night, also bow first at about two o'clock, with deck equipment falling on and killing swimmers) scarcely nine years previously.

This case was carefully recorded, with experienced and responsible witnesses. Correspondence between the vision and historical event is not perfect, but it is, overall, very impressive. First published in the *Journal and Proceedings* of the American Society for Psychical Research, it is retold in chapter 10 of my 1971 book *Psychic Visits to the Past*.

Appendix B to Chapter 24

1. Cobbe's NDE Cases

"At the last moment so bright a light seemed suddenly to shine from the face of the dying man, that the clergyman and another friend who were attending him actually turned simultaneously to the window to seek for the cause." But the light was definitely not coming from the window.[1] Such a perception of awe-inspiring supernal light has been reported since then by many persons who came close to dying but returned. Many returnees were unfamiliar with its association with death. Only rarely, however, do bystanders also see it. In many accounts the light is felt to be not only alive and conscious but full of intense love. However, in a minority of reports, experiencers saw a bright light they found distressing, even frightening, and tried to evade it.

In another case from Cobbe's collection, involving a spiritual welcoming party akin to Blake's angels, a dying woman in joyful surprise told of seeing by her bedside her three deceased brothers, then described a fourth thought to be alive in India. This "excited such awe and horror in the mind of one of the persons present, that she rushed from the room." In time the news came that the brother had in fact died before that date.[2] (This kind of account, evidential in that a welcomer not known to be deceased appears to a dying person, is now known as a "peak in Darien" case.) In biblical tradition, angels are a category of beings distinct from humans, but in popular literature from the nineteenth century onward, there is a tendency for angels, both as guardians and welcomers to the surviving personality, to be identified with the spirits of the beloved deceased.

1. Cobbe, *Peak in Darien*, 296-97.
2. Ibid., 297.

Appendix B to Chapter 24

2. Pearson Deathbed Case

Another example of a welcomer at a deathbed, seen not only by the dying person but by three living persons, is found in *Human Personality and Its Survival of Bodily Death* by pioneer psychical researcher F. W. H. Myers. An Englishwoman named Harriet Pearson, on her deathbed in December 1864, told of seeing her much-loved deceased sister Ann at her bedside. But before that, no fewer than three of her caretakers, then in other parts of the house, reported that they had seen an apparition of diminutive Ann Pearson, in her distinctive old-fashioned wig, black cap, and shawl, walking past their rooms towards Harrier's room. The house was searched, but with no results. One of the three attendants, Harriet's niece Emma Pearson, wrote a detailed account twenty-three years later, which was seconded by another attendant, housekeeper Eliza Quinton, who was asleep in her room at the time the apparition was seen and did not see it/her, but was soon awakened by the others.[3]

3. Mrs. Rogers Deathbed Case

There is another important case of a deathbed attendant seeing an apparent welcomer, a case much stronger than any of those cited above, because not only is it evidential, a record of it was made by the experiencer very shortly after it took place. (As a pioneer, Cobbe was unaware of parapsychology's principles, developed later, prioritizing cases of psychic events promptly recorded, and including the supportive testimony of others who were told of it shortly afterwards.) In this account a nurse, Mary Wilson (the narrator), was sitting up at night attending a dying Mrs. Rogers. The patient had spoken of her eagerness to see her (deceased) husband Mr. Rogers and her children again, which made Nurse Wilson rather nervous. At about 2:30 A.M. Mrs. Wilson happened to glance toward the door of the room, and she saw standing there a red-bearded, florid-faced man who looked first at her, then at the unconscious Mrs. Rogers. Mrs. Wilson must have been startled, because she thought he was a living man, and the house was locked. However, his motionlessness soon made him seem uncanny. When the nurse looked away momentarily, then looked back, the apparition had disappeared. A search turned up no such person in the house, or any signs of entry. Inquiries the next morning from Mrs. Rogers' niece produced

3. Myers, *Human Personality*, II, 333-34.

the information that the apparition did not at all resemble Mr. Rogers, but looked exactly like the patient's first husband, Mr. Tisdale, thirty-five years deceased. Mr. Tisdale was completely unknown to the nurse and to any other persons in the area. Mrs. Rogers was apparently in a coma and did not awaken, so we do not have her testimony. Mrs. Wilson's narrative was published in 1908.[4]

4. Apparition of Dog

The case of an apparition of a dog to his chiropractor, written by his guardian Barbara Meyers, is as follows: Meyers had the practice of taking the dog, a white toy poodle named Skila, with her everywhere, including to appointments with her chiropractor. At a time Skila was suffering from partial dislocations in her spine, and Meyers persuaded her chiropractor to give Skila an adjustment. This happened on several occasions, and the adjustments were very successful Thus the chiropractor knew Skila very well; she had more than once come down the hallway of his office to greet him, and had enthusiastically jumped into his arms after the adjustment, evidently to thank him for relieving her back pain.

But not only was the chiropractor (like the nurse Mary Wilson) not hoping for such an apparition, he had been firmly convinced that all such claims were nonsense, fantasies generated by grieving guardians. After seeing the apparition he called Meyers in great agitation, very fearful that he was hallucinating and losing his mind. They discussed the matter several times, and she was able to reassure him that seeing apparitions happened to people who were psychologically healthy, so that when he saw Skila's apparition a second time several days later, he was able to cope. The experience led to a major change in his life in regard to his attitude toward animals, with the result that the man who had been uninterested in keeping an animal companion adopted a dog, and became very fond of him.[5] The case is strongly suggestive of animal survival.

---

4. Hyslop, *Psychical Research and the Resurrection*, 102-04.
5. Sheridan, *Animals and the Afterlife*, 169-71.

Appendix B to Chapter 24

5. Welcomer for Deceased Cat?

In 1987, while I was participating in the Nuremberg Actions peace vigil in Concord, California, I heard an account from another vigil participant, a widower whom I will call Burton Williams, of an experience he had had. A cat beloved by both Burton and his late wife had died, and as he was burying the cat's remains in his garden, he saw an apparition of his wife nearby, walking away with the cat in her arms.

6. Audrey Harris's NDE

Audrey Harris's NDE took place during childbirth in 1948. She was having problems, and as the attending physician was trying to sooth her, she lost consciousness. She found herself in a beautiful wooded area, with a wonderful fresh scent of earth, dampness, and flowers, both earth and grass in wonderful colors, some unknown on earth. Lions and lambs rested peacefully; animals gathered around the child Jesus, and cherubs above him. He was older than in traditional depictions of the Peaceable Kingdom, perhaps twelve. She felt deep peace. An angel flew overhead trumpeting good news which she could not make out; she thought perhaps it was the birth of her baby. I suggested that the happy news was that Audrey was back for a visit, an idea that appealed to her.

When she returned to consciousness after the birth of her baby son, she forgot the experience entirely. However, some days later, when the baby made a bleating cry like that of the visionary lamb, it all came flooding back.[6] Ms. Harris reported that when she retells the story, she can also still feel the peace.

---

6. Harris, Audrey G. Personal communication, mid-1990s. Harris, B. & Bascom, *Full Circle*, 135-36. *Theosopedia*.

Appendix C to Chapter 25

1. Heim Case

Nineteenth-century Swiss geologist Albert von St. Gallen Heim had a Near-Death experience while leading a mountain-climbing expedition in the Alps, which led to his collecting and studying other such cases. He recounts his experience in his essay "Notizen über den Tod durch Absturz" (Remarks on Fatal Falls). He lost his footing and plunged more than sixty feet. During the ten seconds or so that he was falling, his mind, quite serene and without fear, produced a torrent of clear and coherent thought, which he afterwards remembered in detail. Besides planning actions he would take if he survived, he saw, "as though on a stage," his "whole past life . . . in many images," united in "elevated and harmonious thoughts," despite the originally painful nature of some experiences involved.[7] He landed on snow, and thus survived.

2. Starr Daily Case

In another empathic case, a career criminal who had swallowed strong soap to make himself sick in order to get admitted to the prison hospital, became dangerously ill as a result. (This apparently took place in the 1920s.) He reported:

> I sank into a swoon-like condition. From physical pain I passed into a state of . . . terror. I dreamed while I seemed wide awake. It was like a scroll or motion picture film . . . And the only pictures on it were the . . . people I had injured. The minute history of my long criminal career was thus relived by me, plus all the small

---

7. Heim, "Reflections," Noyes & Kletti, "The Experience of Dying," *Omega* 3, 50.

injuries I had inflicted unconsciously . . . every pang of suffering I had caused others was now felt by me . . . .[8]

This was only the first of a number of visions he had as a result of his illness and harsh prison conditions; in one of them he had an encounter with a loving Jesus. He was profoundly transformed, and wrote an influential book entitled *Release* about his experiences, under the pseudonym "Starr Daily."

3. Tom Sawyer Case

Perhaps the most vivid description of an empathic life review is that of Tom Sawyer (his real name), late of Rochester, New York, whose NDE took place in 1978 while he was stretched out underneath a car doing repairs. It fell on him and began to suffocate him. Out of his all-encompassing reliving of his prior life (beginning in infancy) and its effects on others, he describes a few scenes in detail. For example, once during his teen years when he was stopped at a traffic light, a pedestrian almost walked right into his much-cherished pickup truck. Through his opened window Tom insulted this man, who responded by slapping his face. Feeling justified, Tom stepped out and punched him, not once or twice but thirty-two times. Later, during his life review, Tom not only re-lived his own feelings of indignation at the imagined affront to his pickup, he also in effect *became* the other, looked at Tom Sawyer's flushed face out of the man's eyes, and felt the pain and humiliation of every one of those blows. More, Tom knew the man's age, knew the house where he lived, and knew he was drunk because he was in grief at the death of his wife. He knew the barstool where the man had sat drinking, and the path he had taken to that street corner. He knew the man's home; he experienced intimate personal details of his life.

Tom also felt the effects of good things he had done, some seemingly trivial; for example, in his childhood he had once felt love for a beautiful tree, and he now felt the tree's responding well-being. This empathy applies also to animals, he reports, even to insects. All things affect all other things.[9]

One would expect that, reflecting on the implications of this powerful experience, especially its inclusion of animals, Tom would have become a vegetarian. He did change enormously in many ways—including ceasing to

---

8. Daily, *Release*, 35-36.
9. Farr, *What Tom Sawyer Learned*, 33-34.

Appendix C to Chapter 25

be a wife-batterer and instead becoming a counselor to wife-batterers who wanted to change their actions—but at the time I met and spoke with him in the 1990s, Tom had regrettably not stopped eating animals.

Appendix D to Chapter 30

1. Apparitions of Ramakrishna

MOST OF THE APPARITIONS of Ramakrishna were seen by his wife, Sarada Devi, and were instrumental in her transformation from a shy Indian woman to a strong figure of maternal leadership among the disciples. The first took place the evening of the day he died. Sarada was removing the gold bracelets that symbolized her status as a married woman, when the figure of Ramakrishna appeared to her. He took hold of her wrists to stop her, saying that he was still present, and she was to continue wearing them. (This is one of the rare instances of touching in apparition cases, almost always initiated by the apparition.) Sarada kept them on; she also continued to wear a modified version of the red-bordered sari of a married woman rather than the all-white sari of a widow. Besides this impressive initial experience, she saw apparitions of her husband several times during 1887. The first took place when she was on a train; he told her she was to take responsibility for the initiation of another of his disciples, Jogindra. But the diffident Sarada hesitated to do so until after the apparition appeared three more times, reiterating the message. When she learned that Jogindra had also seen a vision of Ramakrishna confirming her own, she finally complied.

One other of the disciples, Surindra Nath Mitra, saw his master's apparition within three weeks of his death, after the group's house had been given up; the figure told him to find another house where the scattered followers could live together (as monastics). Besides these clear encounters, about a week after Ramakrishna's death, at eight in the evening, two of his followers, Naren (later Vivekananda) and Harish, simultaneously saw a luminous figure approaching them in the garden of the group's currently rented house where various of the followers were staying. The two men interpreted the figure as Ramakrishna, but they did not see a face or hear a message.[10]

2. Crisis Apparition Case with Two Perceivers

An account that has the first, third, and fifth characteristics that make for a strong apparition case is that of an English couple, a Mr. and Mrs. William P. Because they were planning to leave betimes the next morning to visit relatives, they had gone early to bed on Christmas Eve in 1869. The only light in the room was from a dim lamp on a chest of drawers against the opposite wall; the bedroom door was locked. The wife was on top of the blankets, waiting for her baby girl to awaken for her evening snack; the husband lay with his back turned. Mrs. P. was just moving to sit up when she saw a man in a naval officer's uniform standing, resting his arms on the bedboard at the foot of the bed, his face in shadow to her. Astonished, she touched her husband's shoulder, asking "Willie, who is this?" Mr. P. turned, gazed in equal astonishment at the figure, then shouted "What in the world are you doing here, sir?" The figure said reproachfully "Willie! Willie!" As Mr. P. leaped out of bed, then stood irresolute, the figure turned toward its/his right and moved slowly away, casting a deep shadow as it or he came between the lamp and the bed, and disappeared into the wall. Mr. P., very agitated, took the lamp, unlocked the door, and searched the (locked) house, but found no one. When he returned, Mrs. P. told him she thought the figure might mean bad news about her brother Arthur in the navy. But Mr. P. said "Oh! no, it was my father!" His father, a onetime naval officer, had died fourteen years earlier, and Mrs. P. had never met him. Some weeks later, Mr. P. told his wife that he had been in serious financial trouble, and about to take some bad advice that would have led to "ruin or worse." The apparition's reproach caused him to decide against the planned action. Mrs. P.'s very detailed account, though not written down for fifteen years, was confirmed as accurate by Mr. P. and two friends of the family, Dr. and Mrs. C, who had heard it from her "some years" earlier.[11]

It is particularly significant in that the apparition, whose message was unmistakably for Mr. P., was seen by Mrs. P., who had never known her father-in-law and was not bonded to him, *before* her husband also saw it/him. This feature makes it less likely that the apparition was generated

10. Isherwood, Christopher. *Ramakrishna and his Disciples*, 306, 308, 314–15.
11 Myers, *Human Personality*, II, 328-29.

Appendix D to Chapter 30

(or generated wholly) by the unconscious mind of the anxious Mr. P., and strengthens the interpretation that it came from the surviving consciousness of the father. That Mr. P. took action as a result of seeing the apparition also strengthens the case.

3. Evidential Crisis Apparition Case

A case with the fourth characteristic, that the perceiver learn something he could not have known normally, is exemplified by the experience of Bible translator J.B. Phillips. While watching TV in his living room a few days after C. S. Lewis' death in November 1963, Phillips saw an apparition of C.S. Lewis, looking ruddy and vital, sitting in a chair near him. The apparition spoke a few words very helpful to Phillips, who was going through a very difficult time. The figure of Lewis appeared to him again a few weeks later with the same message.

Phillips had only seen Lewis on one occasion during the latter's lifetime, on a Sunday when Lewis was preaching, and at that time was wearing an academic gown. But the apparition was dressed in comfortable, worn tweeds, which Phillips later found Lewis liked to wear. Phillips recounted the experiences in his 1967 book *Ring of Truth*.[12]

4. Lapse of Memory Cases

One of the cases of an unaccountable lapse of memory took place in the Trianon gardens of Versailles, an area in which a number of persons have reported visions (in the years 1901, 1902, 1908, 1909, 1910, 1928, 1938, 1949, and 1955) of apparitions wearing eighteenth-century clothing, several of the cases involving two perceivers at once, and several occurring to persons who had never heard of visions taking place there. In nearly all the experiences the perceivers felt unaccountably depressed, and had a sense that the area was strangely deserted, still, and oppressive.

The forgetfulness case involved an English couple on holiday on May 21, 1955. Walking through the park, in an area where no other persons could be seen, they saw two men and a woman approaching them on a side path that intersected with their own. The men were dressed in black, with hats, long coats, breeches, stockings, and silver-buckled shoes; the woman

---

12. Phillips, *Ring of Truth*, 117. Roland, *Ghosts*, 163-65.

Appendix D to Chapter 30

wore a brilliant yellow floor-length gown, very full-skirted. The English wife noticed the lovely color of the gown and planned to get a better look at it when the trio came up, but was oblivious to the fact that its style was 200 years in the past. Her husband noticed the details of the men's garb, but also failed to see anything out of the ordinary about them. Then, abruptly, the trio was erased from their minds; the couple ceased to see them and forgot their existence altogether. A little further on, the husband suddenly remembered and asked his wife what had become of the three persons, thus awakening her memory also. Neither had any idea what had become of the figures, because there was no place into which they could normally have gone; one side of their own path was bounded by a wall and a muddy ditch, the area on the other side was quite open, and there were no other people in sight. (The husband was familiar with the 1901 and 1902 experiences, but the wife had not heard of any of them.)[13]

A second case involving inexplicable forgetfulness falls into a larger category referred to as "phantom phone calls." By way of preface, the idea of phone calls from the (apparent) dead seems so far-fetched to many people, even some parapsychologists, that they reject it out of hand; they've never heard of such an event, combining modern technology with seemingly far-fetched psychic experiences, so it can't be happening! In fact, a little investigation will uncover quite a number of cases, as two parapsychologists, Raymond Bayless and D. Scott Rogo, discovered in the 1970s. At the outset, they had shared the common prejudice; when a case first came to their attention, they had simply dismissed it. But when they made an effort to open their minds and made some inquiries, they found a quite a number of such cases.

Unsurprisingly, many of the experiencers were wary of telling their stories lest they be ridiculed, and only did so after being promised pseudonymity. One can hardly blame them; for, unfortunately, ignorance perpetuates prejudice perpetuates ignorance. Also unfortunate is the title Bayless and Rogo chose for their book, *Phone Calls from the Dead*, which sounds sensationalistic, though in fact the authors are careful and cautious, and consider several possible explanations for the calls other than communication with the deceased.

Bayless and Rogo found that their collection of cases fell into two main categories, the very short calls (the norm) and the lengthy calls, the latter few in number and (usually) involving the odd lapses of memory.

---

13. MacKenzie, *Adventures in Time*, 51.

Appendix D to Chapter 30

What follows is one of the lengthy calls. The original investigator in the case was psychiatrist and parapsychologist Berthold Eric Schwartz (1924-); the perceiver was a Mrs. Sherrin, one of the minority who had no anxiety about how her story would be received, and allowed her name to be used.

Mrs. Sherrin's experience involved her close friendship with her Aunt Lorraine; "we were like sisters." A year and a half before Mrs. Sherrin told her story to Schwartz, her beloved aunt had been killed in an auto accident. One afternoon about six months after her death, when Mrs. Sherrin was home alone, she received a call from Aunt Lorraine; but the sound of her voice caused no shock, because Mrs. Sherrin was quite amnesic about her death. They talked for about half an hour, "about different things we had done in the past, places we had been together, just sort of reminiscing." The call lasted about half an hour (the longest in Bayless and Rogo's collection). The moment she replaced the phone, Mrs. Sherrin thought "It was Lorraine! But she's dead. She was killed instantly in an automobile accident six or seven months ago!" Mrs. Sherrin added that she got chills just talking about it.

This case is not evidential; no one else was present in the house to overhear it, or take the phone for part of the time; the perceiver did not learn any facts she couldn't have known normally. It becomes significant only as part of a larger pattern of such calls.

The authors theorize that perhaps this odd selective amnesia, found in all but one of the lengthy calls (and only in the lengthy ones), may be what makes a prolonged conversation possible. In fact, it may be the shock a non-forgetting perceiver gets upon hearing the voice of a beloved deceased person that disturbs delicately balanced factors in her or his psyche, and ends the call quickly.

Although the forgetfulness in the Emmaus story pertains to the apparition's identity rather than to the fact that he was dead, as in the Sherrin case, this may be what made his appearance (assuming the story has a historical core) last long enough to include part of the walk and a short time in the house.

Bibliography

A. E. (George W. Russell). *The Candle of Vision*. London: Macmillan, 1919.
Ackley, A.H. "O list to the story that never grows old." In Rodeheaver, Homer A., ed. *Triumphant Service Songs*. Winona Lake, IND: Rodeheaver Co., 1934, 171.
Adams, Carol J. *Living Among Meat Eaters*. NY: Three Rivers, 2001.
———. *The Sexual Politics of Meat*. NY: Continuum International, 2010.
Akers, Keith. *Disciples: How Jewish Christianity Shaped Jesus and Shattered the Church*. Berkeley: Apocryphile, 2013.
———. *The Lost Religion of Jesus: Simple Living and Nonviolence in Early Christianity*. NY: Lantern, 2000.
Alford, Henry. "Come, Ye Thankful People, Come." In *The Methodist Hymnal*. NY: Methodist Publishing House, 1932.
Allen, Gracie. In Panagore, Peter P. *Two Minutes for God: Quick Fixes for the Spirit*. New York, NY: Touchstone, 2007. *Wikiquotes*. Online: http://en.wikiquote.org/wiki/Gracie_Allen.
Appiah, Kwame Anthony. *The Honor Code: How Moral Revolutions Happen*. NY: Norton, 2010.
Atwater, P.M.H. *Coming Back to Life*. NY: Dodd, Mead, 1988.
Aurobindo (Ghose). *The Life Divine*, 1, 2. Calcutta: Arya Publishing, 1939.
Austen, Jane. *Mansfield Park*. Oxford: Oxford University Press, 1923.
———. *Persuasion*. Oxford: Oxford University Press, 1923.
Barnard, Neal D., MD. *Power Foods for the Brain*. NY: Grand Central Life & Style, 2013.
Bekoff, Marc, and Jessica Pierce. *Wild Justice: The Moral Lives of Animals*. Chicago: University of Chicago Press, 2009.
Berger, Peter L. *The Sacred Canopy: Elements of a Sociological Theory of Religion*. NY: Doubleday, 1967.
———. *A Rumor of Angels: Modern Society and the Rediscovery of the Supernatural*. NY: Doubleday, 1969.
Berry, Rynn. *Hitler: Neither Vegetarian Nor Animal Lover*. NY: Pythagorean, 2004.
Blake, William. "Night." In *Poems That Live Forever*, edited by Hazel Felleman. Garden City: Doubleday, 1965, 404-05.
Bodo, Murray. *Francis: The Journey and the Dream*. Cincinnati: Franciscan Media, 2011.
Borg, Marcus J. *Jesus: Uncovering the Life, Teachings, and Relevance of a Religious Revolutionary*. New York, NY: HarperCollins, 2006.

Bibliography

Bowman, Faith L. "Be Known to Us." *Faith Poems*. No pages. Online: http://www.faithpoems.net/oldwine/beknown/.

———. "God is There." *Faith Poems*. No pages. Online: http://www.faithpoems.net/spiritualsongs/godisthere/.

———. "Kyria Sophia." *Faith Poems*. No pages. Online: http://www.faithpoems.net/spiritualpoems/kyria/.

———. "Splendor." *Faith Poems*. No pages. Online: http://www.faithpoems.net/spiritualsongs/splendor/.

Brueggemann, Walter. *The Prophetic Imagination*. Minneapolis: Augsburg Fortress, 2001.

Buck, Pearl S. *East Wind: West Wind*. NY: John Day, 1930.

Calvin, John. "The Word Our Only Rule." *Theology Network*. Online: http://www.the-highway.com/The_Word.html.

Campbell, Joseph. *The Hero With a Thousand Faces*. Novato, CA: New World Library, 2008.

Campbell, T. Colin, with Thomas M. Campbell II. *The China Study*. Dallas: Benbella, 2005

Cassel, E.T. "The King's Business." In *Psalter Hymnal*. Grand Rapids: Publication Committee of the Christian Reformed Church, 1934.

Castelli, William. Quoted in "Preventing and Reversing Heart Disease." The Physicians' Committee for Responsible Medicine. Online: http://pcrm.org/about/volunteer/preventing-and-reversing-heart-disease.

Chesterton, Gilbert K. "The House of Christmas." In *Poems*. NY: John Lane, 1915, 63.

Cobbe, Frances Power. *The Peak in Darien: The Riddle of Death*. London. No publisher,1882.

Cowper, William. *The Task and Other Poems*. No city: Dodo Press. No date.

Crossan, John Dominic. *Jesus: A Revolutionary Biography*. San Francisco: HarperSanFrancisco, 1994.

Daily, Starr. *Release*. NY: Harper, 1942.

Dante (Alighieri). *La Vita Nuova*. Translated by Mark Musa. Bloomington: Indiana University Press, 1954.

de Chardin, Pierre Teilhard. *The Phenomenon of Man*. NY: Harper, 1959.

Dickens, Charles. *A Christmas Carol*. New York: Simon & Schuster, 1939.

Dombrowski, Daniel A. *Hartshorne and the Metaphysics of Animal Rights*. Albany: SUNY Press, 1988.

Eadie, Betty. *Embraced by the Light*. Placerville, CA: Gold Leaf Press, 1992.

Eliade, Mircea. *The Sacred and the Profane: The Nature of Religion*. New York, NY: Harcourt, 1959.

Eliot, George. *Silas Marner: The Weaver of Raveloe*. New York, NY: New American Library, 1960.

Ellwood, Gracia Fay. "Batter My Heart." Matrix: Pendle Hill Pamphlets 282. Wallingford, PA: Pendle Hill, 1988.

———. *Psychic Visits to the Past*. New York, NY: New American Library, 1971.

———. *The Uttermost Deep: The Challenge of Near-Death Experiences*. New York, NY: Lantern Books, 2001.

Esselstyn, Caldwell B. *Prevent and Reverse Heart Disease*. New York, NY: Penguin Group, 2007.

Farr, Sidney Saylor. *What Tom Sawyer Learned From Dying*. Norfolk, VA: Hampton Roads, 1993.

Fox, George. *The Journal of George Fox*. Edited by John L. Nickalls. Philadelphia: Religious Society of Friends, 1997.

———. *No more but my love: Letters of George Fox, Quaker.* Edited by Cecil W. Sharman. London: Quaker Home Service, 1980.

Franck, Johann. "Jesus, Priceless Treasure." Translated by Catherine Winkworth. *The Cyber Hymnal.* Online: http://cyberhymnal.org/htm/j/p/jpricelt.htm.

Gillman, Harvey. "Meeting at Glenthorne." *The Peaceable Table* 86 (April 2012.) Online: http://www.vegetarianfriends.net/issue86.

Greene. Roger Lancelyn. *King Arthur and His Knights of the Round Table.* London: Puffin, 1953.

Griffin, David Ray. "9/11 and Nationalist Faith." DVD. Produced by Ken Jenkins. www.911TV.org.

———. *God and Religion in the Postmodern World.* NY: SUNY Press, 1989.

———. *Parapsychology, Philosophy, and Spirituality.* Albany: SUNY Press, 1997.

Hagen, Kristin. "Emotional Reactions to Learning in Cattle."*Applied Animal Behavior Science* 85, 3,4 (2003) 203-213. *Applied Animal Behavior Science.* Online: http://www.appliedanimalbehaviour.com/article/S0168-1591(03)00294-6/abstract.

Hardy, Thomas. "The Darkling Thrush." In *Immortal Poems of the English Language,* edited by Oscar Williams. New York, NY: Pocket Books, 1952, 451-52.

Harris, Barbara and Lionel C. Bascom. *Full Circle: The Near-Death Experience and Beyond.* NY: Pocket Books, 1990.

Heim, Albert von St. Gallen. "Remarks on Fatal Falls." Translated by Roy Kletti. In Russell Noyes Jr. and Roy Kletti, "The Experience of Dying From Falls." *Omega* 3 (1972) 50.

Hopkins, Gerard Manley. *Poems and Prose of Gerard Manley Hopkins.* Edited by W. H. Gardner. Baltimore: Penguin, 1953.

Hulme, Kathryn. *Look a Lion in the Eye: On Safari Through Africa.* Boston: Little, Brown, 1974.

Huxley, Aldous. *The Doors of Perception and Heaven and Hell.* NY: Harper, 1956.

Hyslop, J. H. *Psychical Research and the Resurrection.* Boston: Small, Maynard, 1908.

Isherwood, Christopher. *Ramakrishna and his Disciples.* NY: Simon & Schuster, 1965.

Iversen, Kristen. *Molly Brown: Unraveling the Myth.* Boulder: Johnson Books, 1999.

James, William. *The Varieties of Religious Experience: A Study in Human Nature.* NY: Modern Library, 1902

Jefferson, Thomas. Letter to Henri Gregoire, February 25, 1809. *TeachingAmericanHistory. org.* No pages. Online: http://teachingamericanhistory.org/library/document/letter-to-henri-gregoire/.

Julian, Anchoress of Norwich. *Revelations of Divine Love.* Grace Warwick, ed. London: Methuen, 1949.

Kalechofsky, Roberta. "Pontius Pilate: Lost in Translation: A Study of the Crucifixion as Roman Irony." Marblehead, MA: Micah Publications, 2014.

———, and Roberta Schiff. *Vegetarian Shabbat Cookbook.* Marblehead, MA: Micah, 2010

Kaufman, Stephen R. & Nathan Braun. *Good News for All Creation.* Vegetarian Advocates Press, 2004.

Kierkegaard, Søren. *Purity of Heart is to Will One Thing.* NY: Harper & Row, 1938.

King, Martin Luther Jr. *Strength to Love.* Minneapolis: Fortress, 2010.

Korb, Scott. *Life in Year One: What the World Was Like in First-Century Palestine.* NY: Riverhead, 2010.

Leake, Jonathan. "Cows Hold Grudges, Say Scientists," In *The Australian* (February 28, 2005). *Open Source.* No Pages. Online: http://zhivago08.blogspot.com/2005/02/cows-hold-grudges-say-scientists.html.

Bibliography

Lehane, Brendan et al. *The Book of Christmas*. Matrix: The Enchanted World. Chicago: Time-Life, 1986.

Lewis, C. S. *The Horse and His Boy*. NY: Macmillan, 1954.

———. *The Magician's Nephew*. NY: Macmillan, 1955.

Lieberman, Joe. *The Gift of Rest: Rediscovering the Beauty of the Sabbath*. NY: Howard, 2011.

Lorimer, David. *Whole in One*. London: Arkana, 1990.

Lucretius. *On the Nature of Things*. Translated by Martin Ferguson Smith. Indianapolis: Hackett, 2001.

MacKenzie, Andrew. *Adventures in Time: Encounters with the Past*. London: Athlone, 1997.

Malory, Thomas. *Le Morte D'Arthur*. Gutenberg Project. Le Morte D'Arthur, 2, 9. Online: http://www.gutenberg.org/files/1252/1252-h/1252-h.htm#link2HCH0201.

McDaniel, Jay. *Living From the Center*. St. Louis: Chalice Press, 2000.

McFague, Sallie. *Metaphysical Theology: Models of God in Religious Language*. Philadelphia: Fortress, 1982.

Miller, Peter. "Crusading for Chimps and Humans," In *National Geographic* 88, 6 (December 1995) 101–29. *National Geographic Today*. No pages. Online: http://ngm.nationalgeographic.com/1995/12/jane-goodall/goodall-text.

Mills, Milton R. "The Comparative Anatomy of Eating. *VegSource*. Online: http://www.vegsource.com/news/2009/11/the-comparative-anatomy-of-eating.html

Mitchell, Kurt. *Jonah*. Wheaton, IL: Crossway, 1983.

Moody, Raymond A. Jr. *Life After Life*. NY: HarperCollins, 2001.

Myers, Frederic W. H. *Human Personality and its Survival of Bodily Death*, Vol. II. NY: Longmans, Green, 1902.

Palmer, Horatio. "Yield Not to Temptation." *Hymnary*. Online: http://hymnary.org/media/fetch/128234

Phillips, J. B. *Ring of Truth: A Translator's Testimony*. New York, NY: Macmillan, 1967.

———. *Your God is Too Small*. New York, NY: Simon & Schuster, 1952.

Plutarch. "On the Eating of Animal Flesh." In *Ethical Vegetarianism*. Edited by Kerry S. Walters and Lisa Portmess. Albany: SUNY Press, 1999.

Pugh, Gillian. *London's Forgotten Children: Thomas Coram and The Foundling Hospital*. Stroud, Gloucestershire: History Press, 2007.

Rank, Otto. *The Myth of the Birth of the Hero and Other Writings*. Edited by Philip Freund. Knopf, 1932.

Rees, W. Dewi. "The Hallucinations of Widowhood." In *BMJ* 4 (1971) 37–41. Online: http://www.ncbi.nlm.nih.gov/pmc/articles/PMC1799198/pdf/brmedj02669-0049.pdf.

Rembrandt (van Rijn). *Supper At Emmaus*. Art and the Bible. Online: http://www.artbible.info/images/rembrandt_emmaus-open_grt.jpg.

Ring, Kenneth. *Heading Toward Omega*. NY: William Morrow, 1985.

Rogo, D. Scott, and Raymond Bayless. *Phone Calls From the Dead*. Englewood Cliffs, NJ: Prentice-Hall, 1979.

Roland, Paul. *Ghosts: An Exploration of the Spirit World*. London: Arcturus, 2012.

Ruether, Rosemary Radford. *Sexism and God-Talk*. Boston: Beacon, 1983.

Russell, Bertrand. "A Free Man's Worship." The Bertrand Russell Society. Online: http://www.users.drew.edu/~jlenz/br-fmw.html.

Schiller, Johann Christophe Friedrich. "Ode an die Freude." Translated by Faith Bowman. *Faith Poems.* Online: http://usuaris.tinet.cat/mrr/assignatures/textos/Schiller/an_die_freude.html.

Sears, Edmund H. "It Came Upon the Midnight Clear." *The Cyber Hymnal.* No pages. Online: http://cyberhymnal.org/htm/i/t/itcameup.htm.

Shakespeare, William. *Hamlet.* In *William Shakespeare: The Complete Works.* Edited by Linda Alchin. No pages. Online: http://www.william-shakespeare.info/script-text-hamlet.htm.

———. *Measure for Measure.* In *William Shakespeare: The Complete Works.* Edited by Linda Alchin. No pages. Online: http://www.william-shakespeare.info/script-text-measure-for-measure.htm.

Sheridan, Kim. *Animals and the Afterlife.* Escondido, CA: EnLighthouse Publishing, 2003.

Smith, E. Lester, et al. *Intelligence Came First.* Wheaton, IL: Quest Books, 1975.

Spiegel, Marjorie. *The Dreaded Comparison: Human and Animal Slavery.* New York, NY: Mirror Books/IDEA, 1997.

The Interpreter's Bible. 4. Edited by James D. Smart et al. Nashville: Abingdon, 1952.

Thompson, Francis, "The Kingdom of God." In *Poetry of the Victorian Period,* edited by Jerome Hamilton Buckley and George Benjamin Woods. Chicago: Scott, Foresman, 1953.

Tolkien, J. R. R. *The Annotated Hobbit.* Boston: Houghton Mifflin, 1937.

———. *The Fellowship of the Ring.* Boston: Houghton Mifflin, 1954.

———. *The Monsters and the Critics and Other Essays.* London: HarperCollins, 2006.

———. *The Two Towers.* Boston: Houghton Mifflin, 1955.

Traherne, Thomas. *Centuries of Meditation.* New York, NY: Harper, 1960.

Trivedi, Bjal P. "Sheep Adept at Recognizing Faces." *National Geographic News.* Online: http://news.nationalgeographic.com/news/2001/11/1107_TVsheep.html.

Tuttle, Will. *The World Peace Diet.* NY: Lantern, 2005.

Underhill, Evelyn. *Mysticism: A Study in the Nature and Development of Spiritual Consciousness.* NY: Dutton, 1930.

Wesley, John. "The General Deliverance." *Wesley Center Online.* No pages. Online: http://wesley.nnu.edu/john-wesley/the-sermons-of-john-wesley-1872-edition/sermon-60-the-general-deliverance/.

Wheelock, John Hall. "The Wood-Thrush." In *This Blessed Earth.* NY: Scribner's, 1978.

Wordsworth, William. "Lines Composed a Few Miles Above Tintern Abbey, On Revisiting the Banks of the Wye During a Tour. July 13, 1798." In *Immortal Poems of the English Language,* edited by Oscar Williams. New York, NY: Pocket Books, 1952, 255–59.

www.ingramcontent.com/pod-product-compliance
Lightning Source LLC
Chambersburg PA
CBHW070250230426
43664CB00014B/2472